SEDGEMOOR
1685

SEDGEMOOR
1685

From
Monmouth's Invasion
to
The Bloody Assizes

by

David G. Chandler

When thy star is in trine,
Between darkness and shine,
Duke Monmouth, Duke Monmouth,
Beware of the Rhine!

Soothsayer's attributed warning to Monmouth,
c. 1672

SPELLMOUNT
Staplehurst

This book is respectfully
dedicated to my uncle,
FRANCIS (FRITZ) PEABODY COLES
who first showed Sedgemoor
to a 12-year-old boy in 1946 –
and unbeknowingly inspired
a life-long interest

British Library Cataloguing in Publication Data:
A catalogue record for this book is available
from the British Library

ISBN 1-873376-42-1

First published in the UK in 1985 by
Anthony Mott Limited
This edition published in the UK in 1995 by
Spellmount Limited
The Old Rectory
Staplehurst
Kent TN12 0AZ

1 3 5 7 9 8 6 4 2

Printed in Great Britain by
St Edmundsbury Press Limited, Bury St Edmunds, Suffolk

Contents

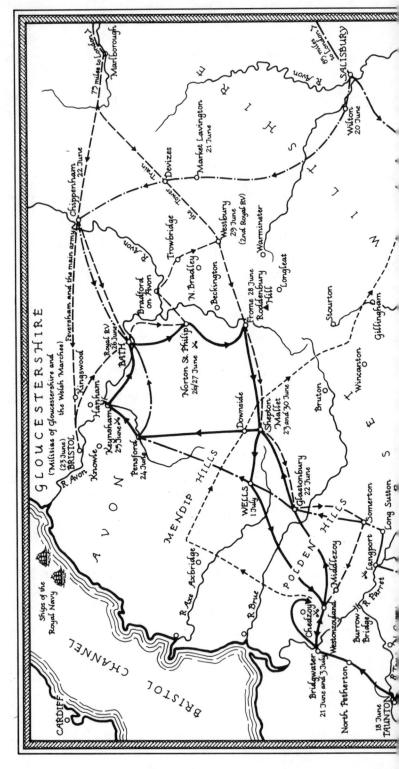

GLOUCESTERSHIRE
(Militias of Gloucestershire and the Welsh Marches)

72 miles to London?

Marlborough

R. Kennet

Chippenham 22 June

Devizes

Market Lavington 21 June

SALISBURY

R. Avon

Trowbridge 69 miles to London?

Wilton 20 June

Westbury 29 June (2nd Royal Rgt.)

Warminster

Longleat

Trowbridge

N. Bradley

Beckington

Frome 28 June
Roddenbury Hill

Feversham and the main army

Kingswood

BATH

Royal Rgt. 26 June

Bradford on Avon

Norton St. Philip 26/27 June

R. Avon

Hanham

BRISTOL (23 June)

Knowle

R. Avon

Keynsham 25 June

Pensford 24 June

Stourton

Gillingham

Wincanton

Bruton

Shepton Mallet 23 and 30 June

Downside

MENDIP HILLS

WELLS 1 July

Glastonbury 22 June

Somerton

Long Sutton

POLDEN HILLS

Ships of the Royal Navy

R. Axe Axbridge

R. Brue

R. Parret

Langport

Middlezoy

Burrow Bridge

Bridgwater 21 June and 3 July

Chedzoy

Westonzoyland

North Petherton

18 June TAUNTON

CARDIFF

BRISTOL CHANNEL

W I L T S H I R E

S O M E R S E T

A V O N

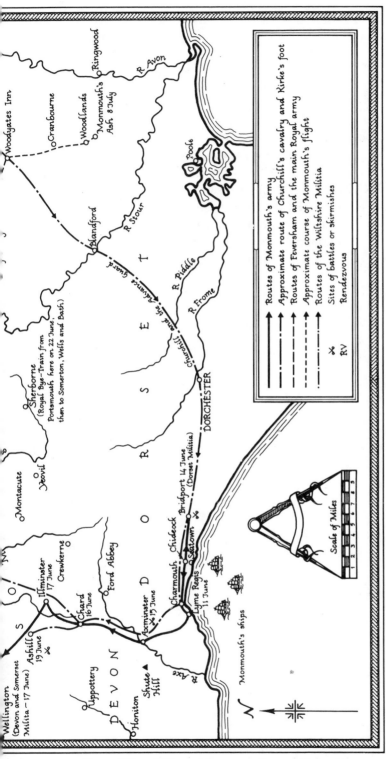

Legend:

Routes of Monmouth's army

Approximate route of Churchill's cavalry and Kirke's foot

Routes of Feversham and the main Royal army

Approximate course of Monmouth's flight

Routes of the Wiltshire Militia

Sites of battles or skirmishes

Rendezvous

✕   RV

Scale of Miles
1 2 3 4 5 6 7 8

N

Woodyates Inn

Cranbourne

Woodlands

Ringwood

Monmouth's
Ash 8 July

R. Avon

Poole

Blandford

R. Stour

the Adverse Guard

R. Piddle

R. Frome

S   E   T

Sherborne
(Royal Bye-Train from
Portsmouth here on 22 June;
then to Somerton, Wells and Bath)

Yeovil

Montacute

Illminster
17 June

Crewkerne

Ford Abbey

Chard
16 June

Axminster
15 June

R   O

D   O

Churchill and

DORCHESTER

Bridport 14 June
(Dorset Militia)

Charmouth, Chideock

Sea town

Lyme Regis
11 June

Monmouth's ships

Wellington
(Devon and Somerset
Militia – 17 June)

Ashill
19 June ✕

Uppottery

Shute ▲
Hill

Honiton

R. Axe

D   E   V   O   N

S   O   M

General Map: Military Movements June and July 1685

This book is respectfully
dedicated to my uncle,
FRANCIS (FRITZ) PEABODY COLES
who first showed Sedgemoor
to a 12-year-old boy in 1946 –
and unbeknowingly inspired
a life-long interest

Maps and Illustrations

ILLUSTRATIONS – HALF TONE INSET

Acknowledgements

1, 4, 14, 15, 17, 20, *The Mansell Collection*; 2, 4, 5, 6, 7, 16, 18, *The National Portrait Gallery*; 3, *The National Army Museum*; 8, 9, 10, 19, *The British Museum*; 13 *Hoare's Bank*; 12, The Duke of Roxburghe

Introduction

'Happy is the country that has no history,' runs an old saying. Rather more to the point is the comment of Santayana, 'The country that forgets its past is often doomed to relive it.' Certainly the West Country has undergone an eventful and historical past; equally certainly, there is no chance of any generation of its inhabitants wholly forgetting certain events in that history – prominent amongst them in fact and fiction, truth and myth, being those of the period between June and October 1685. And yet the first quotation contains a vital and happy national and regional truth in one respect. The year 1985 sees the commemoration of the 300th anniversary of the *last* pitched battle to be fought on English soil. There was a skirmish at Wincanton on 20 November 1688 during the Glorious Revolution, and another at Clifton near Shap Fell in Cumbria on 18 December 1745 as Bonnie Prince Charlie's Highland Army headed back towards Scotland; in the present century there was a German naval bombardment of West Hartlepool, Scarborough and Whitby on 16 December 1914, and the great Battle of Britain was fought *over* our soil that hot, anxious summer and autumn of 1940, to be followed by air engagements innumerable during the various stages of the Blitz, but the fact remains that no formal, stand-up fight between formed armies resulting in over two dozen casualties has taken place on English soil for three centuries. Scotland, Wales and Ireland – the 'Celtic Fringe' – have not been so fortunate (as memories of Falkirk and Culloden, Fishguard – tiny though that action was – Vinegar Hill, Ballinamuck or Cork (twice) and Kinsale, or the never-to-be-forgotten Londonderry, and above all the Boyne, all testify too tragically). But England's history has been singularly violence-free on any notable scale, and no country in the developed world can claim to have avoided the direct attentions of contending armies for so long a period of time. England is, when all is said and done, truly a blessed land, in many ways, and in none more so than this unique respect. May it for ever remain the case.

Sedgemoor and its preceding campaign and bitter aftermath, holds a special place in both our national and local heritage. Not only was it England's last battle, but it was also the first serious engagement of the post-1660 reconstituted English Army – the first truly regular or 'standing' Royal Army in our history. Many of its component regiments had seen active service on the Continent or in Tangier – fighting for or against Louis XIV and in the latter case in a protracted struggle against the Moors of North Africa – but the Campaign in the West of 1685 was the first time the red-coated Royal Army had been wholly mobilised to deal with a full-scale national emergency involving Scotland, Cheshire and above all the West Country. It was indeed vastly increased in size as a result: 1985 sees the tercentenaries of the raising of no less than ten regiments still to be found on the diminished and much-amalgamated British Army List. It is particularly tragic, therefore, that our Army's famous past should have its operational début in an event which saw brother shedding the blood of brother amidst today's tranquil and beautiful fields of Somerset; the acknowledgment of this is borne out by the fact that no battle-honour (to be carried proudly on colours, guidons, banners and mess-silver) was ever issued to commemorate Sedgemoor amongst the regiments that took part. Until recently, moreover, the Queen's Regiment (linear and titular descendants of 'Kirke's Lambs' of 1685 notoriety) was forbidden to recruit in the West Country. Constitutionally, politically and socially, too, 1685 holds a special place in the nation's history. There are clear indications that James Scott, Duke of Monmouth, was the true son born in wedlock of Charles II and thus his rightful heir. This fact, but for the hard but decisive 'trial by battle' (for many centuries 'might' – the ability physically to take and then hold the crown – has been as important as any technical 'rights' to its possession by birth or descent), might have held distinctly awkward repercussions for the Royal House of Windsor and simply dazzling prospects for the Dukes of Buccleuch, the direct descendants of the children of 'King Monmouth'. Politically, the events of the Western Rebellion have proved the last large-scale popular rebellion south of the River Tweed. Socially, and legally, the implications of the aftermath of that revolt and the severity and callousness with which its last traces were extirpated (although often over-stressed by unscrupulous politicians), have entered the consciousness of the Anglo-Saxon conscience – and not only in the British Isles.

My own interest was first drawn to the romantic story of Sedgemoor and the Western Rebellion in 1946, when, as a twelve-year-old schoolboy on his first holiday truly away from his Yorkshire home since 1939, I was taken by my revered uncle to visit Chedzoy and Westonzoyland. The passage of almost forty years has blurred my memory of the event – just as the passage of seven-and-a-half times as many more have softened and often distorted the folk-memories of 1685 – but I do recall, as a lad already fascinated by military history after the vicarious excitements of the Second World War, feeling a definite sense of envy that a relation of mine had the sheer (and possibly undeserved) good fortune to practically live *on* a historical site of such interest and importance. Unbeknowingly there was sown that summer's day a lasting and growing fascination in the events of 1685 in the West, which has led me to lead many a battlefield tour and give many a lecture; to run (or help plan) two large-scale historical re-enactments for the Sealed Knot Society with the aid of numerous local organisations which have brought me in touch with many individual facets of West Country personality and life; and now to write a book on the subject of Somerset's most important 'haunted acres'. There have been many more learned works on this subject, but I feel justified in adding to their number one more, on the grounds of a personal sense of involvement and empathy. Perhaps, I may now cease to be haunted by these particularly engrossing ghosts and shadows of long-gone yesteryear. Somehow I rather doubt it – and secretly that thought pleases me, for this particular story, with its many levels of significance and interest, has become a part of my very being.

What is true for me must be even more so for the estimated one million people of West Country antecedents – whose ancestors lived in Devon, Dorset, Cornwall and, above all, Somerset, and who took an active part in the dramatic events of 1685, all too often with tragic and catastrophic personal consequences to themselves and their families. The West Country is one of the most historical parts of the United Kingdom, and has more than its share of traditions and legends which, whether strictly-speaking true or not, go a long way to form local traits, feelings and aspirations. The region around Sedgemoor has its Bronze Age trackways, its Iron Age lake villages of Glastonbury and Meare, and its even older legends of water-sprites, hobgoblins and fairies. It has its deeply Christian traditions – not least linking Joseph of Arimathaea and the Holy Grail with Glastonbury Tor and its famous winter-flowering thornbush – whilst the area's profusion of fine per-pendicular church towers (such as the St Marys – three: at Bridgwater, Taunton and Westonzoyland) are for all to see – and there is small wonder that the religious issue featured so prominently locally in both the Civil Wars and 1685. The area has its Roman association – *Aquae Sulis* was famous throughout the later Roman world, whilst the tin-mines of Cornwall were as strategically important to the Roman legions throughout the Empire as, alas, the sources of titanium are to the superpower nuclear-weapon manufacturers of today (*not* that the West Country has any closer contact with such potentially devastating resources today than that represented by Hinkley Point 'A' and 'B' nuclear power stations). The Legions gone, it was left to the legendary Arthur and his 'court' at Camelot or possibly Cadbury to defend the last vestiges of Roman and Ancient British civilisation against the Anglo-Saxon hordes, just as a few centuries later it was the sacred task of Alfred and his Kingdom of Wessex to protect the eventually merged Roman and Anglo-Saxon ways-of-life against the atavistic perils represented by the ferocious Northmen. No schoolchild in the English-speaking and reading world, one feels, has not grown up on tales of Alfred and the cakes; few have not thrilled to see the reputed 'Alfred's Jewel' in the Ashmolean Museum at Oxford – found near his sanctuary amidst the marshes of Athelney. But Alfred is only one amongst a plethora of famous Anglo-Saxon and Danish names associated with the region – one has only to mention Ine, St Dunstan, Turstin, Nerlewin and the Danish King Guthrum. He not only induced the Danes to sign a famous peace at Wedmore which guaranteed the survival of Anglo-Saxon values and rule south of Watling Street but also, by being converted to Christianity, began the processes that permitted the eventual assimilation of the better features of the Danelaw into the national life. This process was brought to fullest fruition in the fullness of time after the painful Norman Conquest and the final development too, of the English racial characteristics – for better or for worse – that was to last (with a certain addition of Scottish blood) down to 1945. In the seventeenth century, the cloth industry of the south-west took over as the most important economic aspect of regional and indeed national life as the mines of Mendip and elsewhere slipped into deep recession, their wealth-earning seams of ore at last exhausted.

It is interesting to note that nowhere in Monmouth's most extreme proclamations did he demand or promise the keeping open of uneconomic pits – but let that comment pass! The name of 'King Arthur' means one person, and one person only, in the West, and although according to legend he is only – like Monmouth in some accounts – 'sleeping', and awaits the moment to return again to his people, it will definitely *not* be by courtesy of the National Union of Mineworkers, those new 'big, bad barons' of modern Britain who are in the traditions of the over-powerful so-called subjects of our weaker Mediaeval Kings – although they met their match in Henry II and Henry VII, and maybe the modern equivalents may have met their's in 'Queen' Margaret. But this is to digress. Today, problems still abound around Sedgemoor – not least the contention surrounding the issue of drainage versus natural conservation on West Sedgemoor – but that, at least, is a 'war without an enemy', using angry words rather than bullets.

Legends and folklore are part of the very fabric of the West, and those linked to Sedgemoor are numerous and varied. Stories of miraculous escapes are not hard to find – it has been suggested that the tale of Jan Swayne's 'leap' in Croxley Woods atop the Polden Hills is far more probably derived from a ninth or tenth century brush with

Danes and Norsemen than a seventeenth century happening. Certainly it has something of a Nordic touch of grim humour associated with it, although a John Swain, as will be seen below, was hauled before the courts in 1686 after, seemingly, escaping from the rough justice being handed out the previous Autumn. Similarly, dark legends are associated with the names of Col. Piercy Kirke and his 'Lambs', and above all with that of Baron Jeffreys of Wem, 'The Devil in Wig and Gown', the terrible tale of whose administration of the notorious Western Assize of late 1685 has lost nothing in the telling over three centuries. In fact, James II – incredibly – marvelled at his moderation in permitting the 'normal' (as understood at the time) processes of the Law to be implemented in the West Country. Many another monarch would have – and did – simply unleash the soldiery to do their worst with free licence. We are horrified by the Bloody Assize, and rightly so, but who now remembers – far less protests about – William the Conqueror's 'harrying of the north', or the terrible vengeance 'Good King Hal', Henry VIII, unleashed on the supporters of Rome in the North Country after the 'Pilgrimage of Grace' in the early sixteenth century? It is all a matter of perceptions and, it must be admitted, of propaganda. Only the 'Pacification of the Highlands' by 'Butcher' Cumberland after Culloden in the late 1740s and Oliver Cromwell's 'acts of Grace' such as the massacre of Drogheda in Ireland in the early 1650s have earned an equivalent place in our Nation's story. But for every hard fact there are at least two distortions or legendary applications.

To this day, legends are in the making. A member of a long-established Norton St Philip family is quoted in a recent prestigious travel book as having found evidence in local records that nine captured and convicted rebels were 'bound to stakes and burned alive' in 1686 in or near the town. The 'evidence' relates to sums expended on large amounts of wooden faggots purchased near the dread date. But this is not what happened at all. The grim sentence of death for high treason entailed 'hanging, drawing and quartering' – not 'burning at the stake' except for women (one of whom, in London, did pay that penalty, see Appendix D). The execution involved first hanging the victim – but cutting him down before he was dead; he was then revived, before being disembowelled, and was forced to witness the burning of his intestines and often his private parts in a fire – that is where the 'burning' came into this appalling saga. He was finally allowed to expire before, or while, having his head struck off his body and his arms and legs – the 'quarters' – hacked or torn away (strong shirehorse teams were sometimes used for the purpose) for subsequent display on gibbets at cross-roads as grim warnings and deterrents throughout the area. All very unpleasant to be sure, but male rebels were not, *pace* the new legend, burnt at the stake. So there we have a case of myth in the making.

Two last examples demand attention. Many in the West believe that since 1685 no member of the British ruling house has visited the 'disaffected area'. Queen Victoria, the legend goes, even used to have the blinds drawn in her Royal Train as she passed along the G.W.R. to the far West whilst passing the Taunton area! Once again, this is not the truth, however good the story. Indeed, as early as 1686, the year after the battle, King James II deliberately visited Bridgwater and the site of the battle at Westonzoyland – so that particular story must be given short shrift, for that was an 'official' visit if ever there was one. Furthermore Monmouth is supposed to have been warned by a sooth-sayer in Germany years before '. . . to beware the Rhine'. And, of course, it was the Langmoor and Bussex Rhines that led to his catastrophic failure early on the morning of 6 July 1685 – but the story is almost certainly apocryphal.

So much for the romance of legend. To conclude, a few – hopefully supportable – historical observations. Monmouth's chief failings were two: over-reliance on selfish and misguided advisers, and a poor sense of timing. His attempt to drive his uncle from the throne was paradoxically both too late and too early: too late in that he proved unable to mount his blow before the new King had time to consolidate his succession immediately after Charles II's death, and then failed to co-ordinate the various Scottish, Cheshire and West Country aspects of his challenge; too early in that James II had not been given enough time to show his true colours – and still in June and July 1685 enjoyed the loyalty of the mass of his subjects. The final irony of Sedgemoor and the 'Bloody Assize' was that it would take only three short years for James to forfeit the trust of his people, both high and lowly, and the support of his army (which certainly had served him proud in 1685), through a combination of stubborn pride, an ill-considered religious policy and a preference for tyrannical, personal rule. The harshness displayed after Sedgemoor indubitably hastened the processes of popular alienation against the King that ultimately led to the Glorious Revolution of 1688, but the point should not be laboured.

The passage of three hundred years has to a degree softened the bitterness and agony undergone by so many in 1685 – but the events of that year are far from forgotten in the West Country. The purposes of this book – and, indeed, of all the commemorations, re-enactments and ceremonies of June and July 1985 – are not, however, for one moment an attempt to re-open old wounds or revive ancient controversies – stirring up 'old, unhappy, far-off things, and battles long ago.' Few would deny that all wars and battles are regrettable acts of human folly causing unjustifiable agony and distress to combatants and non-combatants, the guilty and the innocent alike – but these considerations should not preclude the serious study of these aspects of our national heritage, however red in tooth and claw parts of that story indubitably are, if only in the hope of helping us and our descendants to avoid the mistakes of the past which caused such dire events as Sedgemoor. This book, then, sets out to retell a well-known and much analysed story, to provide the reader with some of the raw materials used by the historian, and in the process to salute the gallantry of the ordinary men – whether soldiers or peasants – who fought the campaign through to its grim conclusion.

The wording of the inscription, composed by the late Major M. F. Cely-Trevilian, on the memorial adjacent to the Grave Field at Westonzoyland, forms an apt summary:

To the Glory of God
and in memory of all who,
doing the right as they saw it,
fell in the Battle of Sedgemoor
6th July 1685,
and lie buried in this field
or who for their share in the fight
suffered Death
Punishment or Transportation.
Pro Patria.

Acknowledgments

'No man is an island', as John Donne reminds us; nor is an author anything but dependent on a whole host of people who have aided him in one way or another, great or small, in the completion of his self-appointed task. I would like to thank the following for their assistance: first of all Anthony Mott, for the vision and practical encouragement that led to this book seeing the light of day. Next Stephen Maison, the cartographer, who transformed my rough drafts of maps into accurate and wonderfully clear examples of his art; and Stephen Beck, whose imaginative drawings have provided a taste of the late-seventeenth century's flavour. I owe a debt of gratitude to Ann Nason and Sue Dring for typing a very messy manuscript with such accuracy and forbearance; to Jim Reynolds of the Dianne Coles Literary Agency, for professional service; and, as always, another to Gill, my wife, for tackling the index. People who have advised and aided me over the years that I have studied the Sedgemoor episode are too numerous to mention here, but a few I feel bound to mention – from the Mattravers, whose hospitality I have often enjoyed at their hostelry in Westonzoyland during a number of visits to the site, to 'Gaffer' in their public bar who has often given me the benefit of his local wisdom; from my colleagues at Sandhurst (including John Hunt, Librarian); to my good friends and boon-companions of the Sealed Knot Society, headed by Brigadier Peter Young, Tony and Iris Tallents, Arthur Starkie and Dr Alistair Bantock; from the noted local historian Mr W. MacDonald Wigfield and the former Vicar of St Mary's Church, Westonzoyland, Rev. Charles Meredith, to the local farmers who have allowed me access to their land either to study the original site or to prepare the 1985 re-enactment, and in this connection I must mention the useful advice of local schoolmasters Terry McCretton (secretary of the *Sedgemoor 300, Westonzoyland Tercentenary Committee*) and Stuart Taverner; and last but not least, that fine actor and playwright, my good friend Eric Jones-Evans of Fawley, whose knowledge of, and enthusiasm for, the sad yet stirring tale of 1685, has several times imparted extra life and direction to my efforts. To everyone I say a heartfelt 'thank you'.

Together with the Publisher, I also wish to acknowledge the following for granting permissions as requested:

For the reproduction of manuscript sources and letters, in whole or in part – the Trustees of *The British Library*; the Directors of C. Hoare & Co., bankers; John Murray, Publisher; Harrap Ltd; Lionel Leventhal of *Arms and Armour Press*; and B. T. Batsford Ltd publishers; the Editor, *Somerset & Dorset Notes and Queries*; and the County Archivist, Somerset County Council, and Dr. R. W. Dunning for permission to reproduce Map 10 which first appeared in *Somerset Archaeology of Natural History, 1980*.

Sandhurst and Yateley   DAVID CHANDLER
20 October, 1984

Explanatory Key
to symbols used on maps

⬛▷ ..... Royal horsed cavalry or dragoons

▨ ..... Royal foot or infantry

◼▷ ..... Rebel horsed cavalry

◼ ..... Rebel foot or infantry

▭ ..... Main position of a regiment

⬚ ..... Secondary position of a regiment

▭⟵ ..... The protrusion indicates direction the unit is facing

ᕲ ..... Cavalry piquet

ᕱ ..... Foot piquet

🛒 ..... Waggon

✦ ..... Artillery

Λ ..... Camp

✺ ..... Windmill

⬩ ..... Church with tower

⬩ ..... Church with spire

PART ONE

I

Plotting and Preparation

On 11 June 1685 in the late evening, a handsome figure stood in the centre of the cliff-clinging seaside town of Lyme Regis surrounded by eighty-two armed followers and a large crowd of excited townsfolk. This was the Protestant James Scott, Duke of Monmouth, illegitimate son of the late King Charles II, come to challenge the accession of his Roman Catholic uncle, the former James, Duke of York, to the throne of the three kingdoms.

He had not landed in Lyme Regis by chance. During the Great Civil War, the town had been noted for its Puritanism, and had defied King Charles I's nephew, Prince Maurice, in a formal siege, the defence being inspired by two colonels – Robert Blake (later the famous Admiral) and John Weare. Its protracted resistance – until relieved by the Earl of Essex – became a symbol of Parliamentary support in the predominantly Royalist (Plymouth excepted) West Country. Since those exciting days in 1644, Lyme had time and again been the scene of controversy over religious issues, and as recently as 1682 had been described as being 'overrun with fanaticks'.[1]

At Monmouth's side Joseph Tyler read out a seemingly interminable Declaration, the work of the Rev. Robert Ferguson, already notorious as 'the Plotter'. This document did not claim the crown for the Protestant duke, but in the most extreme and often fantastic terms it did denounce the right of the recently-anointed King James II to wear it. The newcomers had arrived, the reader proclaimed, to vindicate 'the laws, rights and privileges of England from the invasion made upon them, and for delivery of the Nation from the usurpation and tyranny of James, Duke of York'.[2] It went on to assert that 'the ingratitude of the bloody and wicked man, the Duke of York, is manifest to the whole world in murthering a Brother who had ruined himself and his people to preserve and protect him from punishment'. Not only did the document thus denounce James generally, but later it specifically claimed that he had poisoned King Charles II. Further, James, Duke of York, was blamed for starting the Great Fire of London, for instigating alliances with Catholic France and wars against the Protestant United Provinces, for inspiring the Popish Plot of 1678, and for hiring villains to murder the lawyer, Sir Edmund Bury Godfrey, and the Earl of Essex (who died in the Tower after the

Rye House Plot): in fact practically every notorious *affaire célèbre* since 1660 was laid at King James's door. 'Wee therefore do declare that James Duke of York as a traytor to the Nation, a Tyrant Popish Usurper, a Murtherer and an utter enemy to all things that are good.' Once success had been visited upon the just arms of the Duke of Monmouth, his Declaration went on to promise, no practitioners of the Protestant religion would be persecuted; Parliaments – properly elected – would be held annually; city corporations would also be freely elected, the ancient borough charters restored, all judges appointed by Parliament, and all proper resolutions would be advertised by the Privy Council. It might be thought, with some reason, that Ferguson, Monmouth's self-appointed propagandist and ideological adviser, did 'protest too much'. But such was the gist of the Proclamation that formally launched the Western Rising of 1685, to many historians 'the last popular rebellion'.[3]

Older historians have usually supported the pervasive romantic legend. Thus George Macaulay Trevelyan in 1904 could not ignore the strong Whig image of his great relation and predecessor, Thomas Babington Macaulay, writing a half century before.[4]

'The readiness of the rural population to turn out and die for their faith was a new thing in Somerset, and in England. For the peasant followers of Monmouth, the dark Puritan faith glowed in all the colours of personal romance. They loved the young man more than they loved their lives . . . The record of this brief campaign was the lifting of a curtain: behind it we can see for a moment into the old peasant life, since passed away into the streets and factories, suffering city change. In that one glance we see, not rustic torpors but faith, idealism, vigour, love of liberty and scorn of death.'[5]

Such sentiments do not wholly commend themselves to all contemporary historians who tend to treat idealism and patriotism with scepticism, and look hard beneath the surface for the harsher realities. For one thing, they assert, by the lights of the late seventeenth century the 'rural' west was in fact England's major industrial region. It was the hard facts of economic recession in the Mendip mines[6] and economic problems in the vital clothing towns – Axminster, Taunton, Shepton Mallet, and Frome in particular – that ensured that Monmouth's rebel army contained miners and a very high proportion of textile workers and associated tradesfolk. It was the local agrarian problems that struck the freehold yeomen farmers (who were far from being peasants) who accounted for another significant proportion of the host. Nonconformity certainly was a major issue, and the personal popularity of James Scott in the region another, but as G. N. Clarke has written, 'poverty and unemployment were Monmouth's recruiting agents'.[7] But there is no denying that the rising *was* unusual: as

Robin Clifton has most recently demonstrated, Monmouth's revolt was very different from the Glorious Revolution just three years later, or the abortive Jacobite risings of 1715 and 1745–6, in that the rank and file rallied to his standard without any aristocratic leadership or any trace of foreign support or subsidy. West Country folk then, as now (typified by the modern disputes over the future of West Sedgemoor), were truly independent in their attitudes. The land of England was not then owned by the few, nor are large parts of Somerset today, as the profusion of small farm-holdings attests.

What then lay at the roots of this extraordinary manifestation, with its tragic consequences for so many families? As so often the case in history, it was politics. The death of King Charles II on 6 February 1685 was the immediate cause of the crisis that led a few months later to the Revolt in the West and the threat of a renewed civil war. Charles had no immediate, legitimate successor (although there was a large progeny of royal bastards born to a succession of royal mistresses), and therefore his constitutional heir was his brother James, Duke of York. James had an impressive reputation as a fighting admiral during the Second and Third Dutch Wars, and had proved a good naval administrator, and therefore was at the outset quite a popular figure – but he had one serious disadvantage from the point of view of the vast majority of his subjects in that he was an openly-professing and practising Roman Catholic; and from the outset of his reign he made no secret of his intention to reduce the constitutional and legal penalties imposed on his co-religionists. This appeared a threat to the constitutional settlement which had emerged from the hard-fought Civil Wars of the 1640s and the subsequent restoration of Charles II in 1660, as well as to ancient legal instruments against foreign influence going back to the reigns of Henry VIII and the first Elizabeth. For such a policy might well encourage a greater disruptive role in English politics and life for Louis XIV, *le Roi Soleil*, who in October of this same year of 1685 was to revoke the Edict of Nantes, driving out the French Huguenots.

The problem of the succession had in large measure dominated Charles II's later years – calling for all his great tact and political flair to prevent a critical outburst of discontent. The late 1670s had seen the notorious Popish Plot, when one Titus Oates had played the part a certain Senator Macarthy would adopt in the United States in the 1950s; Charles became so disillusioned with his schism-rent and religiously intolerant Parliaments that from 1681 he managed to rule without either Lords or Commons, preferring to become a pensioner of Louis XIV. To defuse the succession issue he had at various times made sure to send abroad both the Catholic James and the widely preferred Protestant rival, the handsome and popular royal bastard James, Duke of Monmouth.

James Scott (born in 1649 at The Hague in the United Provinces) was the natural son of Charles Stuart and Lucy Walters. After his mother's death, he was brought up as a Protestant by Lord Crofts. In 1663 King Charles acknowledged his paternity, and created the young man Duke of Monmouth.[8] The same year Monmouth married Anne Scott, Countess of Buccleuch, and adopted her surname. A series of military appointments followed, including service against the Dutch in 1672 and against the French five years later, so Monmouth was a popular and experienced soldier long before 1685. Indeed, he commanded the 1st Troop of Horse Guards (1668–79), and in 1678 became Lord General. Young John Churchill – a former page to the Duke of York and an up-and-coming courtier-soldier – once saved his life and shared a celebrated exploit with him at the siege of Maastricht in June 1673 when Monmouth led a 'forlorn hope' of volunteers, and captured – and then held – two important fortifications. Years later Monmouth hoped, albeit in vain, that this friendship would stand him in good stead. Soon the personable, athletic young Duke, revelling in the popular acclaim that seemed to await him everywhere, became embroiled ever deeper in Stuart court politics. In 1679 his father banished him abroad, but he impudently returned without leave and was promptly required to forfeit all his posts and preferments. This notwithstanding, he made a triumphal progress through the West of England attended by a retinue of several hundred gentlemen and acclaimed by the local Protestant population, which led him to believe he had strong support in that part of the country. Charles II accordingly forgave him and restored him to favour in his easy-going way. The year 1682 saw another triumphal progress through Cheshire – but Monmouth later became implicated in the Rye House and other plots against his father and uncle. After confessing his complicity he was again banned from the Court, and in 1684 he retired abroad to Zealand with his mistress, Lady Henrietta Wentworth. He at once became the focal point of much Protestant-based intrigue inspired by Archibald Campbell, Earl of Argyle, and a number of adventurers, including Lord Grey of Warke. William of Orange, Stadtholder of the United Provinces (the future King William III), permitted these intrigues to continue, and when news arrived of Charles II's death – his last words being to apologise for being so long a time dying and a plea 'let not poor Nellie starve' – the rather impressionable and weak-willed Monmouth allowed himself to be talked into mounting a challenge for the throne. Once again William stood by, but revealed the plot to James II and even offered to land a force in England to crush the revolt.

The plotters promised Monmouth much. Argyle would sail for

Scotland and raise a major revolt, as a distraction. Cheshire, he was advised, waited but the word. London, he was assured by Colonel Danvers and Major Wildman, would provide 10,000 adherents to his cause once the signal was given. Old army friends would flock to his side, and in the West Country – scene of the much-remembered triumph of 1679 – gentry and populace would rush to his standard, and with them he could soon take possession of Bristol with its merchant wealth, arsenals of weaponry and shipping (which would permit him, after a fashion, to link together Scotland, Cheshire and the West). A triple advance on London amidst public adulation and all would be over for 'the usurper', James II. The blandishments were tempting – and Monmouth succumbed to temptation.

In fact Monmouth was being made the dupe of scheming men. He was surrounded by a group of malcontents and selfish plotters. Several were Cromwellian ex-soldiers in exile and convinced republicans, and there was little talk of taking the crown at this stage from Wildman or Danvers. Others were criminals, ne'er-do-wells and bankrupts. Most trusted of all, Ford Grey, Lord Grey of Warke – the sole English nobleman about him – was a grandson of the Cromwellian General Ireton and had barely escaped with his life after being implicated in the Rye House Plot. This scheming Whig politician pressed his services as second-in-command. Eventually a mixed group of eighty-two supporters gathered around Monmouth at Amsterdam. On 2 May Argyle sailed for Scotland on what was to prove from the start a hopeless venture. Bad weather and official obstruction delayed Monmouth for twenty-eight critical days – and only on 1 June was he able to sail into the Channel after bidding a lingering farewell to Lady Henrietta. The expedition sailed in three small vessels, carrying his handful of supporters, four light field guns, 1,500 muskets and as many breastplates. Thus began what Winston Churchill would describe as 'the most irresponsible and audacious enterprise in English history'.[9]

There is no doubt, however, that there were reasons for Monmouth to hope for a good response in the West Country. As mentioned, the area had recently been in the grip of a serious economic recession affecting the Cornish tin miners and the weavers and clothiers of Somerset, Devon and Dorset. Many in the area were of Low Church persuasions, including Quakers, who looked aghast towards 'Babylon', as they chose to regard London, and regarded a Catholic monarch as little preferable to the Devil himself. Modern opinion is that the religious motive was probably the most important one of all: the Nonconformists were strong in the three counties most concerned, and had suffered almost as much persecution at the hands of the authorites as had the Roman Catholics until the accession of James II. Charles II's attempt to introduce true toleration, as in 1672, had foundered in an intransigent and suspicious Parliament. The majority of those who would take up arms were Presbyterians, a few Baptists and Independents – in other words Dissenters – justifying their actions on the grounds of their fear of the re-establishment of Popery, full of memories of the Popish Plot, the aftermath of which had seen a clamp-down on all Dissenters.

Although some modern historians have tried to represent Monmouth's supporters as men of strong political motivation, and even as precursors of a 'People's Army', there seems to be little evidence of this. Some leaders apart, the rank-and-file were not republicans at heart, nor did they wish to overturn the social hierarchy. They were sober, pious and earnest. They came from the skilled artisan and middle-classes rather than the peasantry (the legend notwithstanding), and were mostly aged between twenty-five and forty, and thus in middle-life by seventeenth-century standards.[10] If at one end of the scale there were very few of the gentry or officers (to Monmouth's great disappointment), there were equally few rural labourers and even fewer unemployable vagrants or 'sturdy vagabonds'. They were weavers, wool-combers, tailors and cobblers; coachmen, tanners, blacksmiths and goldsmiths; brewers and sailors as well as yeoman landowners – as we know from examination of many of the records of the 'Bloody Assize' that have survived. The men who rallied to Monmouth's green and gold standard were not risking life and limb on a mere whim. Driven into revolt by economic problems, they were fighting for the rights of democracy and the Protestant religion as they understood those terms, with some retrospective feeling for the principles of the period of the Civil War, which had been much fought in the West.

It is more difficult to understand the inner motivation of Monmouth. To embark on such a desperate venture so ill-prepared was to court disaster. One gets the impression from the scanty available evidence that his heart was not in it. Many at his side in the West Country noted his deep lethargy and despondency from almost the start of the active revolt. On his person when he was captured near Blandford was a small notebook which is still preserved in the British Library.[11] In it are few codes, lists of supporters or military and political intelligence, as one might have expected. Instead there is a potpourri of love ditties, remedies for common ailments – the stone, loose teeth ('a recipie to keep the goms [gums] well'), 'for the bloody fluxe' – and, perhaps revealingly, numerous beauty hints. 'To make the face fair'; 'how to make hair grow'; 'for heat in the face, redresse and shining of the nose'; 'to take away a corne'. There are long lists of boys' and girls' Christian names, a few monetary conversion tables, a number of addresses in Rotterdam, and lists of 'casulties' (or disasters) that befell English monarchs from William the Conqueror to Elizabeth. Only a very few items have any direct relevance to matters in hand that desperate summer of 1685, although there is a recipe for invisible ink. 'To write letters of secrets – take fine allum, beat it small, and put into water. Then write. To read – steep the page in running water.'[12] There is also a complex 'rule for knowing a person's fidelity, and if he will keep his word' based upon numerical calculations taken from baptismal names 'in Latin', the date of the month and similar mumbo-jumbo. One gains the impression of a cultivated but none too bright young man, who would far prefer a life of dalliance, sport and social intercourse to one of dark plots of state and intrigues surrounding the throne of the Three Kingdoms. Here was a victim of circumstances – a well-connected puppet being manipulated by unscrupulous men who wished to use him for their own ends. His weakness was to cost him dear. The two 'charms against enemies' and his morning and evening prayers all faithfully jotted down in his pocket-book were to avail him little.

The preceding months had provided the English Government with clear indications that something was in the wind. Supposedly secret messages were being passed in London, the West and Cheshire. 'May all be prepared' ran part of one intercepted letter.[13] 'Monmouth will be here by end of month',[14] declared one William Way to a County Coroner – who duly passed on the information to higher authorities in London. There was talk of men arming and drilling, of mysterious movements by bodies of horsemen at dead of night. There are also strong indications that the Dutch Stadtholder, William of Orange, was sending some information to his father-in-law, James II. Dutch William appears to have been playing a devious, double game. On the one hand he made no serious attempt to obstruct Monmouth's departure from his shores apart from one or two half-hearted and, one suspects, deliberately belated delaying orders on his shipping. On the other, once the revolt was under way, he lost no time in offering to come over to England to lead a force to help his father-in-law suppress it. Whatever happened, William felt that he would come out on the winning side. If Monmouth succeeded – then a Protestant monarch in England would be no disadvantage. If his expedition misfired, then at least England would most probably be plunged back into civil war, and that would effectively neutralise the country in terms of European politics, preventing any effective alliance between the Catholic James II and his powerful Catholic neighbour over the Channel, William's sworn enemy, Louis XIV of France.

What then, can we make of James II himself, in these, the first months of his reign? Born in 1633 the second son of Charles I, he had been created Duke of York. Sixteen years older than his nephew, the

36-year-old Duke of Monmouth, James had in 1685 succeeded to the thrones of the kingdoms of England, Scotland and Ireland. His youth had been dominated by the Great Civil War and its aftermath. From 1646 he had been a prisoner in the hands of Parliament for two years before escaping to the United Provinces, and this experience, together with the execution of his father, Charles I, cannot have imbued him with any great love for the institution. During the Interregnum he served as a volunteer in both the French and Spanish armies. He saw service under the great Marshal Turenne during the Fronde revolts against the youthful Louis XIV and his minister, Cardinal Mazarin, and was present at the Battle of the Dunes (1651), where his instincts as an Englishman overcame his repugnance for Cromwell's red-coated New Model Army, although he was serving on the Spanish side. He also gained some not-inconsiderable experience at sea in a quasi-piratical role. At the Restoration of his brother as King, he was created Lord High Admiral and thus began a close association with the development of the Royal Navy that proved one of his most useful and long-lasting contributions; in 1665 and 1672 he commanded the fleet in two victories over the Dutch, at Solebay and Southwold Bay respectively. Although he professed his new religion relatively incon-spicuously (he had been converted to the Roman Catholic faith in 1669) at this time, he nevertheless fell a victim to the Test Act in 1673, and was forced to relinquish his naval post.

As it became clear that Charles II was unlikely to have an heir, the succession issue – closely linked to religion – began to dominate national politics. James's first marriage to Anne Hyde, daughter of the great statesman, the Earl of Clarendon, produced two daughters – Mary, who married William, Stadtholder of the United Provinces and Prince of Orange (joint-rulers as William III and Mary II from 1688) and Anne, married to Prince George of Denmark, who subsequently became Queen in 1702. On his first wife's death James married a second time, choosing the Catholic Mary of Modena (1673). This marriage caused a protest in the House of Commons, and anxiety rapidly grew in case a male heir from this union might result in a Catholic monarchy being permanently restored. The Duke became ever more criticised after private correspondence of a compromising religious nature was discovered, and Charles II several times required him to move overseas – to The Hague and then to Brussels – so as to ease the mounting tension. Behind much of the intrigue was the unscrupulous Earl of Shaftesbury who, as leader of the Country Party (or 'Whigs') from 1672, was striving to secure toleration for Noncon-formists, and increasingly championed the popular and youthful Duke of Monmouth as a possible Protestant successor to the throne. He manipulated the furore surrounding the notorious Popish Plot to compel Charles II to recall Parliament, and once this had been achieved he persuaded the Commons to pass the first Exclusion Bill in 1680, the King's serious illness of the previous year adding weight to the urgency of his arguments that owing to his faith the Duke of York must be denied the succession to the thrones of the Three Kingdoms. The bill had been introduced in Parliament while James was abroad (he had been recalled when it appeared that Charles II might die) but Charles dissolved the Parliament before it could become law.

Charles now sent his brother to Scotland with special powers to enforce the Nonconformist legislation in that kingdom as High Commissioner, and once there, after a brief period of moderation, his severity towards the Scottish sectarians earned him still more criticism, which contrasted markedly with the good reputation young Monmouth had earned by his leniency after defeating a Covenanter insurrection at Bothwell Brig in June 1679. His uncle, however, harrassed the Scottish Lowlanders without mercy, enforcing the oath of allegiance. The Ninth Earl of Argyle took the oath but made certain minor reservations, which James and his advisers seized upon to have him tried and convicted for high treason on grounds, another English statesman of the time asserted, for which 'we should not hang a dog here'. Argyle managed to escape to the United Provinces, where he became a focal point for Protestant dissidents and general intrigue against the Duke of York. The King meantime, alarmed by Monmouth's popularity, sent him abroad in his turn for a time also. By now the rivalry between the two Jameses was quite clear.

Once the King had called the bluff of the Whigs and decided to dispense with the services of Parliament in 1681, thereafter relying on subsidies from Louis XIV, and using the recalled garrison from Tangier and his regiments of Guards to back his authority, James was able to re-emerge at the centre of affairs. Shaftesbury, after trying to force through a second and then a third Exclusion Bill during the short-lived Parliaments of 1680 and 1681, had at last been outmanoeuvred by the King and Court Party (the 'Tories'), and was compelled to flee into exile, where 'the false Achitophel . . . a name to all succeeding ages Cursed', according to Dryden,[15] died two years later. With Monmouth in 1683 implicated in the Rye House Plot[16] and consequently again banished overseas, James seemed to have won the power struggle. In 1682 he had been readmitted to the Privy Council, and in 1684 was reappointed Lord High Admiral. The fortunes of the Whigs appeared at their nadir as the legislation against Nonconformists was strongly enforced, and the borough charters of pro-Whig towns were confiscated and redrawn to ensure Tory electoral majorities, and all seemed set for an easy – and accepted – transfer of the crown to the Duke of York. James was present when Charles secretly became a Roman Catholic on his deathbed, and following his brother's protracted demise, on 6 February 1685 James was duly proclaimed King.

At the outset of his reign, therefore, James II appeared to be in an impregnable position. He was very nearly an absolute monarch, thanks to his brother's latter-day actions. He could choose his own ministers, and thanks to the changes in borough charters – including those of the great Whig stronghold of the City of London and adjacent boroughs – he could strongly influence the choice of MPs – as he proceeded to demonstrate when he summoned the first Parliament of his reign, which was dominated by compliant Tories. He could select his magistrates in both town and country. The opposition – Whigs and Dissenters – appeared very much cowed, and had removed their activities underground. Their most redoubtable leaders were dead, and the remainder were abroad in exile. The members of the judiciary were very much aware of their positions as 'lions under the throne', and Lord Chief Justice Jeffreys and other luminaries of the King's Bench and Common Pleas were strong supporters of James personally, as they were to demonstrate in no uncertain manner before the year was out. He was also supported by a small but tough regular army, several of whose regiments had until 1683 seen considerable active service in Tangier before being withdrawn to England.[17]

The reign began, indeed, on a note of rejoicing and even loyal anticipation. The Tories – believing that the Protestant Mary would be James's heir – rallied strongly behind the new King, with the mass of the nobility and gentry associated with their embryonic party. The established Anglican church of the realm accepted James's Catholicism with resignation, and seemed to support the concepts of Divine Right and Passive Obedience, or at least the doctrine of Non-resistance. The bishops thoroughly approved the continuing – even stepped-up – persecution of Dissenters and Nonconformists, as the callous treatment of the notorious Titus Oates by Judge Jeffreys indicated. James's accession address to the Privy Council – widely reported – struck just the right note. 'I have often heretofore ventured my life in defence of this nation,' the King declared, 'and I shall go as far as any man in preserving it in all its just rights and liberties.'[18] The most loyal Parliament the Stuarts had encountered since 1661 hastened to approve the King's request for a vote securing him for life the revenues his brother had occasionally enjoyed – some £2,000,000 per annum. They baulked, however, at a further suggestion that the Test Acts might be relaxed in favour of Roman Catholics, and James was wise enough not to press the issue at this stage. Less sensibly, he began to demonstrate his religion more openly, to the anxiety of some of his subjects, and secured the release from prison of a number of Catholics jailed on religious grounds. Parliament, however, would prove totally loyal in the crisis to follow in 1685: not only would they pass an immediate Act of Attainder on Monmouth's head, but in their second session they would approve James's proposals for the raising of new forces to replace the old shire militias, which were not going to show themselves in a particularly favourable light during the events of mid-summer. This, however, is to anticipate.

There was, however, a reverse to the coin. In many ways James was to reap the whirlwind that his brother had sown over the religious and succession issues, but had been adroit enough to sidestep. The Anglican churchmen, in particular, now relied on 'Parliament and the Protestant squires' for their support, no longer just the throne, as in earlier reigns.[19] This represented a significant shift, albeit an as yet largely undetected one, and once James's catholicising ambitions became manifest from 1686 onwards, a new opposition would arise in the country far more powerful, ultimately, than that encountered in parts of Scotland and Cheshire and above all in the West Country at the outset of the reign. By his own lights, James was well-intentioned towards his subjects, but believed he knew what was best for them. His firmness was fast to deteriorate into inflexibility and obstinacy, and the inherently unstable equilibrium of the constitutional position – which Charles II had managed to maintain with such skill – would lead to his downfall just three short years after his acclaimed accession and, it must be admitted, his successful suppression of the Revolt in the West. However, in 1685 the great mass of his subjects were indubitably behind their new King – and only his mistaken severity in the post-Rebellion phase (much played up by his new critics, as we shall see) and subsequent errors concerning his attitude towards Church, Parliament, the Universities and the Army, would throw away and destroy the popular support which was still his to enjoy in July 1685. James II could have been a great monarch instead of the greatest disaster since 'bad King John'.

There were those, however, who from the outset thought otherwise on this matter of the popularity of the new King, namely the groups of exiles living abroad. In the event, they were completely to misread the omens and reap disaster as a result. We must next turn, therefore, to examine in rather more detail the intentions, plans and preparations of the plotters in the United Provinces. James and his two Secretaries of State – Lord Sunderland and the Earl of Middleton – were well served on the whole by their spies and agents, particularly in Scotland (the source of their chief initial concentration) and the United Provinces, where the English envoy, Bevil Skelton, kept a sensitive finger on every pulse. The first sign of true danger came in early April when Monmouth and the Earl of Argyle were reported to have met in

Rotterdam. Skelton reported: 'It is whisperd about that Monmouth intends speedily to passe over into England and land in the west part of the Kingdome and that Mathews and those whoe are gone before are sent to prepare for his reception.'[20] Other information arrived that Argyle was soon likely to sail for either Scotland or Ireland. This was all remarkably accurate as far as it went, but like all intelligence the issues were fogged by other impressions and reports leading to other possible conclusions. But from mid-April at the latest the English Government had firm indications of what was in the wind, and were thus in no way taken by surprise by events during the following months. The Government's attempts to induce the Dutch Government to put obstacles in the ways of the potential rebels were patently less successful, however. In early May Argyle sailed without let or hindrance, and some reports claimed that Monmouth had left with the body of Scottish malcontents and mercenaries. Reliable information had to be separated from mere rumour and sheer, deliberate misinformation. It soon became clear that Monmouth and the English plotters were still in the Netherlands, at Amsterdam, but for how long, and whither and exactly when they would travel – those matters were not yet clear. As a general precaution, the English and Scottish authorities began to round up known malcontents in the two kingdoms – but there was as yet little sense of urgency.

Monmouth's preparations, such as they were, now approached completion. Of course in some respects the plotting went back some considerable time. In 1683, prior to his exile following implication in plots against his father and uncle, there had been a series of meetings in London which he had attended. The earlier part of Nathaniel Wade's confessions – which constitute by far the most revealing rebel source for the whole Monmouth episode, although he wrote them with some skill to avoid implicating fellow-rebels who had not been brought to book by late 1685 – gives many apparently convincing details, *post-facto*. How far Monmouth took a direct part in these treasonable discussions we do not know, but he was not wholly an innocent – perhaps he should be described as an ineffectual ditherer incapable of making up his mind. The really serious debates were those held with Argyle in Rotterdam in April 1685. Monmouth was no match for the tough and determined Scottish nobleman who, according to another interesting informant, Lord Ailesbury, extracted from him an oath that he 'would take no other title than 'Protector of England', were his cause to prosper'.[21] For the rest Monmouth allowed himself to be persuaded on insufficient evidence that his landing would be greeted not only in the West but also in London and Cheshire. The Royal Army – which naturally had to be taken into account – would have been surely sent north to meet Argyle's challenge in Scotland, or at least split in two, and in any case influential desertions were confidently predicted. James II's remaining supporters would drop away as the Duke's bandwagon began to roll, and all would be over in a month or two, if not just a few weeks, and a just Government would be installed to the heartfelt relief and applause of the lords, clergy and commons of England. These were heady arguments, and Monmouth succumbed to a combination of pressures and temptations.

The key men around him were the following: Ford Grey, Lord Grey of Warke, a close friend of Shaftesbury, had been implicated in the Rye House Plot but escaped abroad. He was also an old friend of Monmouth's, a boon companion of earlier, happier years, and now a malign influence upon him. Nathaniel Wade, a lawyer of some ability, was the son of a Cromwellian major-general, a convinced republican and Nonconformist. He, too, had been forced to flee in 1683, in his case to Switzerland. A man of fair military skill, as he was soon to show, he was particularly trusted by Monmouth and Grey, who used him as their main agent for the purchase of arms, cannon and gunpowder and the hiring and fitting-out of shipping. A third was the Rev. Robert Ferguson, a shadowy cleric called by Aylesbury 'the noted plotter in two reigns'[22] – an unscrupulous Whig ideologist who had aspirations to become Archbishop of Canterbury. In the end, when it was too late, Monmouth would see through him. Then there was Fletcher of Saltoun, a Scottish laird, a distant relation of our informant Ailesbury, who described him as 'a brave and ingenious man, but of a head never to be quiet . . . always a malcontent'.[23] Then there were two groups of military men. Samuel Venner was a former Cromwellian captain, who was to prove something of a disappointment in the months to follow. Maj. Abraham Holmes was a firm Baptist and a republican, with known complicity in plots against Charles II going back to before 1660. Other officers, such as John Foulkes and James Fox, were dissidents from the English regiments presently in Dutch pay. Others too numerous to mention were London merchants and lawyers, and Thomas Dare, short-lived paymaster to the expedition, was a sometime distinguished member of Taunton corporation and a goldsmith, not famous for tact but considered very reliable. Anton Buys, 'the Brandenburger', and an unknown Dutch gunner, were mercenaries recruited to serve the rebel guns. Other soldiers of experience included Maj. John Manley, Mr Rose, an English gunner, and Captain Robert Bruce, with recent service in the army of the Elector of Brandenburg. Such is a selection of the adventurers,[24] idealists, criminals, unfortunates who, with a group of six of Monmouth's personal servants and his domestic chaplain, the Rev. Nathaniel Hook, were to make up the party about to risk their necks, 'embarked for that temerarious and foolish expedition', which was 'agreeable to his (Monmouth's) weak head'.[25]

Money, all of which according to Wade 'for both expeditions came out of the purses of the people beyond the seas',[26] presented problems. To hire, fit out, provision and arm the frigate *Helderenburgh* alone cost all of £5,000, the largest single item of expenditure. The two remaining vessels of his small fleet, a pink and a dogger – little more than fishing boats – were cheaper, the former carrying the expedition's gunpowder. A ship such as the fifth-rate frigate was needed as there was danger of a brush with Royal Navy warships – although only about a dozen were actually in commission when Monmouth sailed. Somehow a bare minimum of money was procured: Dare proved especially able at acquiring substantial sums from well-wishers in Amsterdam, but Monmouth's mistress, Lady Henrietta Wentworth, had to sell her jewels, and Monmouth himself pawned one of his 'Georges' of the Order of the Garter, and sold plate and jewels. Between them, another group of supporters raised £1,000. But they were less well provided for than Argyle, who with large estates in Friesland was able to raise £9,000 from his own resources for the Scottish expedition, obtaining three ships, 500 barrels of gunpowder and a reputed 8,000 stand of arms. Monmouth had to operate on a smaller scale, and Wade obtained 'two small ships, and about 1500 foot arms, 1500 curasses, 4 pieces of Artillery monted on feild carriages, 200 as I take it barrels of gunpowder, with some small quantity of Granado shells (grenades), match and other things necessary for the undertaking . . . all which cost £3000.' Small wonder, that when Monmouth put to sea he had barely '£100 in gold and silver'[27] remaining in his military chest. Great reliance was therefore also placed on monetary support in England.

Financial problems, last-minute hitches, some Dutch half-hearted obstruction, and above all contrary winds delayed the sailing of the expedition until at last, on 1 June, the three ships slipped out of the mouth of the River Texel and set off down the Channel. The departure did not go unobserved or uninterpreted. 'The Duke purposeth to land and set up his standard at Lyme a small sea port in Dorsetshire . . .' reported a spy in Utrecht on 6 June.[28] He went on, however, to suggest erroneously, that the Mayor of Lyme, Gregory Alford, was in the conspiracy '. . . and shall befriend his landing'. News could travel fast, even in the late-seventeenth century. The very day of Monmouth's landing, the same maligned Gregory Alford received an official intelligence sheet from London. In it the British envoy in the United Provinces reported and described the sailing of three suspicious armed ships from Holland, speculating that this squadron might well be carrying the Duke of Monmouth to either England or Scotland.

Mayor Alford was informed, about 10 a.m. on Thursday, 11 June, that three ships, one large and two small, were coming over the horizon towards Lyme. By 1 p.m. the squadron, showing no flags, firing no signal guns, had hove to in Lyme Bay. Strangely, no boats put off to land cargo or passengers, or to warp the vessels towards the Cobb. The long afternoon wore on. Thomas Tye, Surveyor of the Port, put off in the customs boat. Even more strangely, he did not return. Then, at 5 p.m. the mail arrived with the London Newsheet. As the sun began to set, seven boats filled with men set out for the shore. No longer in any doubt, Alford sent for his horse and rode inland to raise the alarm. The enigmatic newcomers could only be Monmouth's expedition.

Chapter One
NOTES AND SOURCES

1   The Tanner MSS. No. 129, folio 87 (Bodleian Library, Oxford).
2   Included in the Axe Papers, Harleian MSS. 6845, ff.256–9 (British Library).
3   Most recently, for example, Robin Clifton, *The Last Popular Rebellion: the Western Rising of 1685* (London, 1984).
4   See below, pp. 149–155 for Lord Macaulay's view.
5   G. M. Trevelyan, *England under the Stuarts* (London, 1930), 21st edition (1951), pp. 357–8.
6   See J. W. Gough, *Mines of Mendip* (London, 1930), pp. 164–8.
7   G. N. Clarke, *The Later Stuarts* (Oxford, 5th printing 1949), p. 115.
8   Perhaps the most useful modern biography is J. N. P. Watson, *Captain-General and Rebel Chief* (London, 1979).
9   Winston S. Churchill, *History of the English-speaking Peoples* (London, 1956), Vol. II.
10 See particularly the valuable studies of Peter Earle, *Monmouth's Rebels*, W. MacDonald Wigfield, *The Monmouth Rebellion* and R. Clifton, *op.cit.* W. MacDonald Wigfield is shortly to publish a new study on the victims of the Revolt in the West.
11 The Egerton MSS. 1527 (British Library).
12 *ibid.*, p. 56.
13 Letter from 'F.R.' (conjectured to be Robert Ferguson's initials reversed) to James Carryer, a blacksmith of Ilminster in Somerset. Included in the Axe Papers f.286.
14 *ibid.*
15 Dryden's famous poem, *Absalom and Achitophel*, treats in allegorical form the rivalry between James, Duke of York and James, Duke of Monmouth.
16 This conspiracy, masterminded by Col. Richard Rumbold, was an attempt to seize and kill Charles II and the Duke of York near Hoddesdon in Hertfordshire, as they were returning from the races at Newmarket. The plot misfired, and ten weeks later an informer betrayed details to the authorities. In the witch-hunt that followed the Earl of Essex, Lord Russell and Algernon Sidney all died, the first by his own hand. Lord Grey, Nathaniel Wade and many others implicated on the fringes of the conspiracy fled abroad, and Monmouth was forced into exile.

17   See Appendix B, Special Note p. 181 below for information on the English Army
      of 1685.
18   Cited by G. N. Clarke, *op.cit.*, p. 111.
19   Trevelyan, *op.cit.*, p. 356.
20   Add. MSS. 41,812, f.17 (British Library).
21   *Memoirs of Thomas Bruce, 3rd Earl of Ailesbury* (Edinburgh, 1840), Vol. 1, p. 113.
22   *ibid.*, p. 116.
23   *ibid.*, p. 117–18.
24   For a full, excellent account of the conspirators see W. MacDonald Wigfield,
      op.cit. Ch. 2, 'The Men who came with Him', passim.
25   Ailesbury, *op.cit.*, Vol. 1, p. 114.
26   N. Wade, *Narrative*, and *Mr. Wade's Further Information, October 4, 1685*, are in
      Harleian MSS. 6845, ff.264–282. These key documents are also reproduced in
      full (but unannotated in detail) as an Appendix in W. MacDonald Wigfield,
      op.cit., p. 149–171. I have used the Harleian MSS, throughout. The present
      quotation is to be found at f.271.
27   *ibid.*, f.264.
28   Add MSS. 41,817, f.142 (British Library).

Note: References and Notes for Chapters 5 to 7 in Part Two, are placed for the
convenience of readers at the foot of the pages to which they belong or refer.

2

Invasion and Rebellion

Although the voyage down the Channel had been unopposed, contrary winds made it slow, and all of ten days elapsed before the 400-mile journey was accomplished. Early on Thursday, 11 June the flotilla – frigate, pink and fishing-vessel – was off the Dorset coast, showing no flags. A boat was dropped to put ashore at Chideock Thomas Dare and a companion, whose mission was to warn influential supporters inland that the Duke was at last at hand, and to gather horses and riders. The vessels sailed slowly west, and hove to off Lyme Regis. When a port officer was rowed out to investigate the enigmatic newcomers he found himself arrested and his boat impounded. Then, in the late afternoon, the seven boats put out for the shore, and beached west of the Cobb. Monmouth – in purple coat resplendent with the star of the Garter – knelt to pray; then, accompanied by his followers bearing arms, he set off for the town amidst the cheers of the spectators, who were soon chanting 'A Monmouth! A Monmouth!' By the time the town hall was reached quite a procession had formed behind the green, gold-fringed standard on which were emblazoned the words 'Fear Nothing but God'.[1]

Not quite everybody joined in the welcome. Shortly before the landing Gregory Alford was observed to ride off inland in great haste; reaching Honiton, the mayor proceeded to warn the Lord Lieutenant of Devon, Lord Albemarle, and sent off an urgent letter to London. Meanwhile Samuel Dassel, a customs officer, had tried to find gunpowder to fire the warning gun in the town, but his intention was frustrated. After discreetly questioning some of the newcomers, he slipped quietly out of Lyme, and with a comrade, Anthony Thorold, rode to Crewkerne, and then post-haste towards London. There they presented themselves at the door of Sir Winston Churchill, M.P. for Lyme, who at once took them with his son John, Lord Churchill, to the royal apartments. Thus it was at about 4 a.m. on the 13th – less than thirty-six hours since Monmouth's landing, that James II was awakened to learn the news. Rewarding the two exhausted messengers with £20 apiece, the King lost no time in issuing orders.[2] Thus the reaction of authority was very prompt.

At Lyme meanwhile, Monmouth was landing most of his war-like stores and setting about enlisting the eager supporters who came

1. Monmouth Landing at Lyme

flocking in. Ninety-five local men were allowed to form an independent company; others from Dorset and Devon were assigned to what became the Red and Green Regiments as they arrived. By early on the 12th he had over 800 supporters, and more were appearing hourly. A mounted group rode over to Bridport to seek further recruits, and brushed with the Dorset Militia, which was collecting in its vicinity, killing two – the first blood spilt in the rebellion. Reports came in from Exeter that the Devon Militia was also slowly mustering. The same day saw Dare return with some forty horses collected from Ford Abbey and elsewhere, whilst the latest supporters were being enlisted into the White and Yellow Regiments. By nightfall there were possibly 1,500 rebels under arms, and simple training was taking place all around Lyme.

Monmouth, however, had his anxieties. There were singularly few of the local gentry to be found in his ranks and apart from a few dozen supporters arriving from London there were scant signs of his arrival being widely welcomed, the capital remaining calm. On the other hand the mobilisation against him of the shire militias – however variable as a threat – seemed to be progressing at Bridport, Exeter and Salisbury. He must make his move soon, although his army, however enthusiastic, was still very unprepared, or he might be faced by converging royal forces – and there were disconcerting reports that regular troops were preparing to leave London for the West. There was no news from Scotland, and an ominous silence from Cheshire. An unanticipated blow fell on the 13th when the paymaster, Thomas Dare, was shot by Andrew Fletcher, commander of cavalry, in a brawl over possession of a fine mount. Dare was a sad loss, and the experienced Fletcher had to be disgraced and sent back aboard the frigate. The Duke could afford neither man – particularly as he had decided to launch 450 men against the Militia at Bridport, who constituted the nearest threat to Lyme.

Led by Lord Grey and Colonel Venner, the detachments drawn from the Red and White Regiments marched overnight through thick mist towards Bridport. Although the Dorset Militia was not wholly taken by surprise, the rebels stormed the western bridge and occupied the greater part of the town early on Sunday, the 14th. Venner was preparing to attack the main force beyond the eastern bridge when he was wounded in the belly. As Grey came up with his forty horsemen the exchange of volleys caused the horses to bolt, taking their commander with them; and although Major Wade was at hand, to support and rally the 'forlorn hope', the stricken Venner ordered a retreat.[3] The Militia made no attempt to counter-attack, and so for the loss of perhaps half a dozen men killed a side the affair of Bridport petered out. Monmouth met his retiring column two miles east of Lyme, and was pleased to discover that their rumoured rout was exaggerated; indeed his force had a number of prisoners and a few captured horses to display as proof of their martial prowess, whilst a fair number of red-coated militiamen also deserted to join the cause. The Duke therefore claimed a victory – but was secretly not impressed with the performance of Lord Grey (whom he had been forced to appoint in overall command of his cavalry *vice* the disgraced Fletcher). The wounding of Venner was another setback, the veteran having to be relegated to an appointment on the Duke's staff. Wade was appointed to acting command of the Red Regiment in his place.

Monmouth had now been almost four days ashore, and it was high time to leave the coast. Intelligence arrived indicating that Lord Albemarle, at the head of the Devon Militia, was in full march for Axminster, no doubt planning to hem in the rebels to the south and east of the River Axe, whilst the Somerset Militia approached from the east. Accordingly Monmouth's army set out from Lyme Regis at 3 a.m. on the 15th, and by dint of hard marching narrowly won the race for possession of Axminster. There was a brief confrontation around the town – it hardly merits the description of a fight – but there is no doubt that part of the Somerset Militia turned and ran, abandoning amounts of its weapons and equipment. This event was not unnaturally a cheering sight to the foot-sore rebel army – now perhaps 3,000 strong – but Monmouth refused to follow it up, probably wisely given his men's untrained state. His objective was to reach Taunton with an intact force. There, he hoped, the gentry would at last reveal their hands and join his cause.

By this time the Government in London – now fully aware of Monmouth's arrival – was caught in a flurry of activity. On James II's behalf the two Secretaries-of-State, Lord Sunderland and the Earl of Middleton, issued orders. On the 13th the militias in the West Country were mobilised – and to stiffen them the King ordered four troops of the Blues (the Earl of Oxford's Regiment of Horse), two companies of the Royal Dragoons and five companies of Kirke's Regiment of Foot, recently returned from Tangier, to march west as the advance guard of the Royal Army. On the 14th command of this force was given to Lord Churchill. As further regular units were placed on stand-by to march west, the Board of Ordnance at the Tower of London prepared a train of artillery, sixteen guns strong, and orders were sent to the arsenals of Portsmouth to form a bye-train of eight cannon. A compliant Parliament declared Monmouth an outlaw, and voted the King a large grant to finance the suppression of the rebellion. Even more reassuring, royal agents reported that London was quiet, and that the population of the country as a whole – the West Country, apart – was evincing little sign of excitement about Monmouth's arrival. As for Scotland, countermeasures against Argyle were already well in hand. The Ninth Earl's small convoy of three vessels – the *Anna*, *David* and *Sophia* – had conveyed 100 men and several thousand stands of arms, and reached the West Highlands in late May. The King had reacted by mobilising the 22,000 men of the Scottish militias and 4,000 troops of the Scottish kingdom's regular forces,[4] and sent the trusted Catholic, George, Earl of Dumbarton, to take command. First reports from the north were that few had joined Argyle, and that the countermeasures were taking effect. Indeed, by 18 June all would be almost over in Scotland.

King James was not one to underestimate the possible dangers of the situation in the West, however. Further orders brought regular troops marching towards the capital, and instructions for the raising of new regiments were issued. The Scots brigade serving in the United Provinces under the Prince of Orange was recalled, and troops from Ireland transferred. On 17 June further instructions would be despatched, ordering the Duke of Beaufort to lead the militias of Gloucestershire, Herefordshire and Monmouthshire towards Bristol – which by then would have become Monmouth's likely first major objective – whilst further county militias received orders to stand by as a precaution. On the 19th, as all around London remained quiet, the

King ordered two battalions of the First Guards, the Coldstream, and more cavalry from the Blues and the Royal Dragoons to move down the Great Bath Road to reinforce Churchill's advance guard, whilst part of the Royal Scots escorted the Tower train, and several companies of Trelawney's Regiment – a unit (like Kirke's) with Tangier experience – performed the same function for the Portsmouth bye-train. Thus the establishment mobilised its resources with commendable speed and decision. Churchill, riding ahead of his hard-marching infantry by way of Salisbury, Blandford and Dorchester, reached Bridport with 300 horsemen on the 17th. There he rallied the shaken Dorset Militia before pressing on the next day to Axminster. His role was to observe Monmouth's every move and to shadow the rebel army. The 18th saw the first brush between the regular troops and the rebels near Chard when patrols briefly clashed.

Following their arrival at Axminster ahead of the Somerset Militia on the 15th, the rebels had marched on and occupied Chard the following day. Men were still joining Monmouth in large numbers – although there were reports that the militia units in the surrounding counties were now intercepting groups of travellers and turning them back or making arrests if they could not justify their journeys. That did not prevent 80 men enlisting at Axminster, 187 more at Chard, and 54 at Ilminster – whence the rebels moved on the 17th.[5] Still, however, there was no sign of the 'quality' joining Monmouth's cause – and this was a cause of mounting anxiety. The marchers proceeded through Hatch Green, Stoke St Mary and Shoreditch – and at length reached Taunton – the intermediate objective. News that Albemarle and his militia were presently at the village of Wellington caused Monmouth to place the Red Regiment and two guns across the main road on Thursday, the 18th. Thoughtful for his rear, he also sent off Cornet Legg and some seventeen horsemen to the south on the 19th, with orders to discover the precise whereabouts of Churchill's cavalry.

That same day Lord Churchill ordered a Lieutenant Philip Monoux, a Quartermaster and twenty troopers of the Blues to patrol forward from Chard. The two parties encountered each other on 'Fight Field' near the village of Ashill. A brisk fight took place and four rebels – including their commander – were killed and a number more wounded. These – and their comrades – fled for Taunton: once again the unreliability of Monmouth's cavalry had been demonstrated. Lt. Monoux was also killed and two more royal cavalrymen wounded – and the Quartermaster assumed command of the party and returned to Chard to report. Churchill remained at Chard for two more days, attending a church service with his men, collecting what intelligence he could, and awaiting the arrival of Kirke's five companies of foot,

2. John Churchill attending Divine Service at Chard

who duly appeared on the 21st after their long march. Less welcome was the news that the King had appointed Louis Duras, Earl of Feversham, the overall commander-in-chief over his forces in the West, with the rank of Lieutenant-General, on 19 June. Feversham was a nephew of the great French marshal Turenne, and James probably felt he was more reliable than Churchill, who had been a friend of Monmouth in the past and shared some feats of arms with him on the Continent. Indeed, Monmouth had sent a clandestine letter to remind Churchill of their comradeship on the 19th – which that officer prudently sent on straight to the King in London. The latter was also in communication with the Duke of Somerset but was privately informing the Government that not much was to be hoped of from the militia regiments. He also busied himself collecting country carts for the transportation of his military stores.[6]

Taunton was an important turning-point in the history of the Revolt in the West. Monmouth had arrived there to a great popular welcome at the head of some 4,000 followers, and the scale of the response in terms of recruits was sufficient to persuade him to form the Blue Regiment from men of Taunton, centre of the trade in serge, under Col. Richard Bovet or Bassett. But more important than this was a critical political decision. Up to this point, despite the urgings of some of his advisers, including Lord Grey, he had not had himself proclaimed as king. For one thing, he had promised Argyle that he would not do so until the crown was offered to him by newly-elected Parliaments in both England and Scotland. For another, a strong party amongst his original followers were firm republicans, including Wade and Venner. Therefore on landing at Lyme his initial proclamation[7] had, as we have seen, duly denounced James II's sins – real and imagined – but had stopped short of claiming the crown. This proclamation was again read out on the 19th in Taunton. Then a procession of schoolgirls – shepherded by a Miss Blake bearing a sword in one hand and a Bible in the other, and by a Miss Musgrave – appeared outside Monmouth's lodgings in Capt. Hucker's house. Each of the twenty-seven girls was carrying a banner to present to the Duke, who rewarded each damsel, to the delight of the crowd, with a chaste kiss. Miss Blake had also presented him with the Bible, which caused him to vow to give his life to defend the truths therein. The last standard was presented by Mary Mead, the senior girl, and this was embroidered with the initials 'JR' topped by a crown to indicate the wishes of the people of Taunton.

Monmouth now faced a hard decision. It would annoy some of his supporters if he declared any monarchical ambitions; on the other hand, Ferguson was always at his side insinuating that such a declaration would be the only means to win over the gentry who, to date, had been so conspicuous by their absence. The decision could no longer be put off. The Duke forthwith called a Council of War. He sought its advice as to whether they should retrace their steps and fight Albemarle – or press ahead towards London or Bristol. They settled for the last course. Monmouth then drew Wade and other republicans aside, and urged upon them that he should be proclaimed king. Only thus, he argued, could the gentry's fear of a new Commonwealth be allayed, and their active support attracted. He made his point, although not without difficulty. 'We submitted to it', was Wade's comment.[8] Next day, the ultimate act of rebellion was committed. Before the unwilling magistrates of Taunton, Capt. Tily duly read that 'We . . . do recognise, publish and proclaim the said high and mighty Prince, James Duke of Monmouth, our lawful and rightful sovereign and king, by the name of James the Second . . .' To prevent any confusions, the rebels settled for the title of 'King Monmouth' for their leader.

Despite all the euphoria surrounding him, Monmouth was not a happy man. He knew the risks he was taking; he was aware that his army – now almost 5,000 strong – was untried and unlikely to show well before his uncle's regular troops unless some of the latter could be suborned, with their leaders, into joining him. Ever since the murder

P.S.W.B.

3. The Maids of Taunton presenting colours to Monmouth

of Dare he had been low in spirits. A Quaker who had seen him during his triumphal progress through the countryside just five years before noted a change in him. 'I thought he looked very thoughtful and dejected in his countenance, and thinner than when I saw him four [in fact five – the year was 1680] years before as he passed through Ivelchester . . . so that I hardly knew him again, and was sorry for him as I looked at him.'[9]

Monmouth had now tarried at Taunton for the better part of three days – and every hour was allowing the forces of retribution to draw closer. Next morning, therefore – Sunday, 21 June – the army was ordered to march out of Taunton and take the Bridgwater road. This departure disappointed Robert Ferguson, who was all keyed up to preach the sermon of his life from the pulpit of the county church. But that was not to be.

The day that Monmouth was proclaimed king at Taunton, James II's newly-appointed general-in-chief in the West left London. Feversham was a commander of some experience and besides his utter loyalty – Protestant though he was – to James II, he was at least as well-known a soldier as John Churchill at this period. Born in France in 1640, Louis Duras was Marquis de Blanquefort in the French peerage, but in 1665 he had become naturalised in England.[10] By 1667 he was commanding the Duke of York's Guards; in due course he was given command of a troop of the Blues, and later was made Master of the Horse and an English peer. In 1675 he had led the English embassy at Nymegen, and two years later became Earl of Feversham and continued to serve in court and diplomatic capacities. In 1685, as a Lord of the Bedchamber, he had been present when the dying Charles II was received into the Roman Catholic church, and the newly-crowned James II had hastened to make him a Privy Councillor. Although James II's motives for making Feversham his senior military man in the West were clearly political and personal, at heart, as already mentioned, there is no reason to doubt his overall qualification as a soldier for the post. True, the effects of a serious head injury sustained during a house-fire years before would have a bearing on his showing at Sedgemoor, but there is no reason for doubting that Feversham was a competent soldier. Naturally, his appointment was not to Churchill's liking – he would have preferred the command himself. As the future Marlborough was to write on 22 June, 'My Lord Feversham has sole command here so that I know nothing but what it is his pleasure to tell me . . . I see plainly that the trouble is mine, and that the honour will be another's.'[11] He soon overcame this touch of pique, however, and co-operated with his chief both loyally and effectively.

In strategic terms, much depended on the fate of the great city and port of Bristol. There is no doubt that Monmouth had many potential supporters there, and his agents were ahead of him planning his reception. The capture of the second port in England would confer great benefits on his cause. There were large arsenals of stored arms, and the wealth of the merchants – once tapped – would place his impecunious rebellion on a stable financial footing. Access to the shipping and command of the River Severn would permit contact to be opened with Lord Delamere and Monmouth's other supporters in Cheshire. Above all, the prestige of such an occupation would rally many men throughout the country to his Protestant cause – and hopefully trigger off the awaited (but still unstarted) rising of the strong Protestant groups in distant London. His army swollen to perhaps double or treble its present size, well-armed and better trained, Monmouth might hope that his old friends in the regular army might after all desert to join him, and then a triumphal march towards the capital (assisted by a second advance by his Cheshire supporters and a third from Scotland – at this time he had no tidings of Argyle's fate) would assuredly settle the fate of his uncle, and the throne (or at least power in the realm) would be his. At the very least, and even if everything did not run smoothly, Bristol should provide him with a refuge and a means of seeking sanctuary abroad again should this become necessary. For these reasons the final decision –

confirmed at Shepton Mallet on 23 June – is quite understandable.

The importance of Bristol was not lost on James II and his advisers. Although the Duke of Beaufort was already present there with militia from three counties, it was clearly desirable that this key post should receive regular troops to over-awe the citizens of the city, and that was now Lord Feversham's prime concern. Escorted by 150 Blues and 60 Horse Grenadiers, he rode westwards fast by way of Maidenhead, Newbury and Marlborough. Reaching Chippenham early on the 23rd, he detached Col. Theophilus Oglethorpe to obtain the latest news of the rebels, whom Churchill was presently shadowing from near Langport. A clash between two parties of twenty horse a side on the 22nd ended in another distinct repulse for the rebels, and the frequency of incidents was to rise considerably over the following days.

Meanwhile, behind the royal cavalry and their commanders the main body of Feversham's army pressed on westwards at the best speed they could muster. The 29th had seen leave London three half-strength[12] formations of Guards – 12 companies (including 2 of grenadiers) of the Royal Regiment of Guards (or First Guards), subdivided into two small battalions, and 7 more (including one of grenadiers) of the King's Footguards (the Coldstream) – or about 1,150 soldiers in all, commanded by Henry Fitzroy, Duke of Grafton, the bastard son of Charles II and Barbara Villiers, Duchess of Cleveland. Grafton's orders were to reach Bath to link up with the Wiltshire Militia and the commander-in-chief. Further behind came the ponderous guns of the Tower Train comprising 16 brass cannon (two 12-pounders, four demi-culverins,[13] as many 6-pounders, four sakers and two minions) with their waggons of munitions and equipment, escorted by 5 companies (one being grenadiers) of Dumbarton's Regiment (the Royal Scots) under command of Lt.-Col. Douglas. From Portsmouth, a bye-train of four iron 3-pounders and four brass falcons, under Controller Henry Sheres, with Capt. Edward Dummer[14] as his Quartermaster. Sheres, who was to assume overall command of the artillery once the two convoys met, had for escort 5 companies (one being grenadiers) of Trelawney's Regiment (later the King's Own or 4th of Foot) commanded by Lt.-Col. Charles Churchill, younger brother of Brig.-Gen. John, currently commanding the cavalry screen. In all this amounted to some 1,800 infantry and 26 cannon, preceded by some 250 cavalry. John Churchill, of course, had some 400 cavalry and dragoons and 300 infantry of Kirke's Regiment (5 companies including one of grenadiers) already in contact with the rebels.

After leaving Taunton, Monmouth's array – perhaps 6,000 strong at this juncture – marched on through Westonzoyland to Bridgwater, where another enthusiastic welcome awaited them, and Monmouth was proclaimed king again by the mayor, Alexander Popham. More recruits swelled the regiments. The problem was presently one of finding arms and equipment for the volunteers. Monmouth had issued a warrant on the 20th to all neighbouring villages 'to will and require you, on sight hereof, to search for, seize and take all such scythes, as can be found in your tything, paying a reasonable price for the same'.[15] Old muskets, pikes and sickles were all pressed into service, and in due course each of the five rebel regiments had a company of some 200 scythemen apiece. On the 22nd (Monday), Monmouth marched to Glastonbury through heavy rain – and his spirits were further dampened by news of the skirmish at Langport already mentioned. On the Tuesday he reached Shepton Mallet, where another Council of War was held. The outcome was a confirmed decision to make Bristol the immediate objective, but on Wade's advice (he was a citizen of the city) the Duke was dissuaded from advancing upon its southern side as this could be easily defended. Instead, it was agreed that the rebels should head for Keynsham, capture the bridge over the Avon outside the town, and then sweep round to advance on Bristol from its Gloucestershire side, which appeared open to attack.

Lord Feversham and his escort reached Bristol at midday on Tuesday, 23 June, entering the city by way of Kingswood. He found an uneasy atmosphere amongst the citizenry, but the presence of the Duke of Beaufort and the Earl of Pembroke at the head of substantial militia forces had kept the situation under control. He at once set about improving the dispositions of the troops. His own men, and Pembroke's militiamen, drew out south of the city to watch the most obvious approach. Bristol itself was entrusted for the present to Beaufort. Royal orders had already been given two days earlier for the destruction of the bridge at Keynsham. 'Being informed there is a bridge at a place called Keinesham,' James II had written to Beaufort from Whitehall, 'I would have you by all means to endeavour to breake the same immediately upon the receipt hereof.'[16] The Lord Lieutenant had taken appropriate action, and one arch of the crossing was destroyed during the 23rd. This was hardly to prove sufficient action, as events were to demonstrate. The next day Feversham, still awaiting the arrival of his main force, visited Bath, checking that all crossings over the Avon were broken or guarded, for there was talk of Monmouth heading east for London. He then returned to Bristol for the night.

Monmouth also knew about the damage to Keynsham bridge, and on the 24th he sent Capt. Tily and a strong party of horsemen to take possession of the town and do what was possible to restore the crossing. At the rebels' approach, a troop of horse from the Glouces-

4. Rebels repairing the damaged bridge at Keynsham

tershire Militia lost no time in abandoning the town, leaving a prisoner
in Tily's hands. Using sturdy planks, Tily bridged the gap, wasting
no time in informing Monmouth (who had reached Pensford, harassed by Churchill's cavalry) that he had carried out his orders. The
rebel army poured into Keynsham early on the 25th, and by ten
o'clock were over the bridge and drawn up on Sydenham Meadow in
Gloucestershire just across the Avon. Such a sight drew spectators,
and a Lady Hart sent a message offering 'some hundreds of cheeses'
should the army pass Filgrove farm en route for Gloucester.[17] An
observer, Francis Creswicke, noted that the rebels had ploughs included amongst their baggage waggons, four teams of draught horses
(doubtless harnessed to the four cannon) and large numbers of oxen
for the transport. The rebels' arms were of variable standard, he
observed,[18] but their strength he overestimated at 9,000. The martial
displays on Sydenham Mead were abruptly interrupted by a violent
storm of rain in the afternoon, and the rebels were ordered back over
the Avon to seek shelter in Keynsham. There was much talk of a night
attack on Bristol, but confidence was low.

Worse was to follow. Hardly had the men scattered amongst the
houses than the alarm was sounded. The town was under attack from

two directions at once. From the south came Col. Oglethorpe with 100 troopers of the Blues. He had been on a detached reconnoitring mission on Feversham's orders since the 22nd. He was in Pensford just ninety minutes after the last rebels had left for Keynsham the previous day, and now, in the late afternoon of the 25th, his troopers were cutting their way through Keynsham's streets. Simultaneously but with no deliberate co-ordination, Capt. Parker and another party of horse – 250 strong – who had swum the Avon below the town, came trotting in from the Bristol side, trumpets blaring. Confusion reigned as the rebels rushed to arms; Monmouth sent Venner up the church-tower to see if a general attack was taking place.[19] In due course Oglethorpe and Parker extracted their men, leaving perhaps six troopers dead and a prisoner or two to be sure, but having inflicted fourteen dead and many more wounded on the rebels. Worse, this relatively trifling affair had a bad effect on Monmouth's and his men's morale.

All talk of attacking Bristol was now abruptly abandoned. At a Council of War Monmouth spoke of his repugnance at unleashing heavy fighting on a densely-populated area. 'God forbid that I should bring such calamities as fire and sword on so noble a city.'[20] Wade, with his inside knowledge of Bristol's sympathies, was astounded at this argument. But after toying with the idea of a march on Glouces-ter, the Duke had an alternative course to offer. A Mr Adlam had ridden in during the day to say that some 500 armed horsemen were but awaiting the word to rise in Wiltshire. Could these be the long-awaited gentry? Perhaps a direct advance through Wiltshire and Hampshire towards London would be the correct course to pursue after all. Monmouth accordingly changed his mind again, and ordered that the army should slip away from Keynsham at dead of night along the south bank of the Avon towards Bath. Although no one present fully suspected it at the time, the Revolt in the West had reached its high-water mark. By turning away from Bristol, Monmouth was effectively surrendering the initiative to Feversham and the Royal Army. The tide was turning.

The Government in London was now bringing psychological pressures to bear. The King had been pleased to offer a free pardon to any rebel-in-arms who forthwith surrendered his arms within eight days. Whispers of this act of grace went through the ranks even before actual copies of the offer were seen a few days later at Frome. Sodden by days of rain, hungry, and now very much aware (thanks to the four prisoners of the Blues who had fallen into their hands) that the main Royal Army was close at hand, many a man of Somerset, Devon and Dorset began to think even more longingly of home. Passing Bath in the early hours of the 26th, Monmouth sent a messenger to demand

the surrender of the town. The only reply was the death of the
messenger, shot on his horse outside the gates. The rebels passed on,
and came to camp at Norton St Philip. The gesture before Bath was,
claimed Wade, 'only in bravado, for we had no expectation of its
surrendry'[21] but the event had not rallied morale. Despondency was
becoming marked on every side.

Whilst the miserable rebels crouched around their smoking fires in
saturated bivouacs at Norton St Philip, and Monmouth made a show
of setting up a few rudimentary defence posts to guard the approaches
to the village from a possible repeat of the surprise at Keynsham, Lord
Feversham – newly returned to near Bath at the head of his cavalry –
was at last at the head of almost a full army. Grafton and the Guards
had arrived at Bath, the guns were approaching from Westbury under
Sheres, and last but by no means least, Brig.-Gen. Lord Churchill and
Col. Kirke finally made their appearance to join the main force. It was
the end of his independent command for John Churchill, but he
concealed his innermost thoughts under his customary bland exterior,
and gracefully assumed the role of second-in-command. Perhaps
2,500 royal troops were now present – about half Monmouth's
number. Having learnt that the rebels had passed by Bath, Feversham
desired confirmation of their present whereabouts. Dissatisfied by a
patrol's report that Monmouth was preparing to march from Norton
St Philip, the Earl directed that a 'forlorn hope' of 45 grenadiers under
Capt. Hawley, supported by 500 more infantry from the Guards
under Grafton and Col. Kirke, not to forget a strong force of the Royal
Horse and Dragoons, was to press forward to the village.[22] Hawley
did not think too seriously of the rebels' fighting power, and blundered straight into an ambush in the early hours of Saturday, 27 June.

Monmouth, planning to slip away south to Frome, and thence to
swing into Wiltshire towards Warminster, had already left Norton St
Philip after snatching a few hour's sleep at the George, when he heard
his rearguard, watching the Bath road under Capt. Vincent, open a
brisk fire. He promptly counter-manded the army's march, and
returned to the village atop its steep hill. In his dispatch, Feversham
claimed that Hawley's party, as he had intended, 'drew the enemy's
fire. But . . . the place was on my line of march, and (I was) indeed so
near that the vanguard, which was confident of beating the enemy, if it
should encounter them, had advanced so fast and in such close order
that it was at the entrance of the place within the very hedges, where
there was a barrier.'[23] The first serious engagement of the rebellion
was in the making.

Monmouth threw off his lethargy and played a prominent role in
the fight that followed. Summoning Wade's Red Regiment to take
post on Vincent's right, and Col. Holmes's Green Regiment to

5. The Duke of Grafton unhorsed at Norton St Philip

prepare a concealed move on the left, he soon had the royal advance guard in a tricky situation. Feversham's report, though biased, gives the gist of what took place, as rebel musketeers poured close-range shot into the highly exposed royal advance guard. 'I halted the party,' writes the commander-in-chief, 'which I had sent to draw the enemy's fire, and . . . I ordered my Lord Churchill to advance a company of grenadiers . . . The Duke of Grafton commanded the detachment, and showed great courage . . . for he marched at the head of the grenadier's company of his regiment of footguards, of which Hawley is captain, and which advanced to the entrance of the village, where they encountered a very heavy fire. When I saw the affair to be serious, and those ahead were certainly in great danger, I ordered the horse grenadiers to pass the barrier and cover their retreat . . . and at the same time commanded the musketeers to line the hedges. I was at the barrier when they told me of the Duke of Grafton's danger. I hurried on the horse grenadiers, who had already passed the barrier, and they arrived just in time. For there was a considerable body of Monmouth's cavalry, who were approaching by another way to cut off their retreat.'[24]

After recalling his men and guns, Monmouth had sent Wade and the Red Regiment by way of a gentleman's house to take the Guards in the flank. 'The regiment being much superior in number,' recalled Wade, 'wee fell with a good part of them into theyr reare so that they were surrounded on all hands save the left flank by which way through the

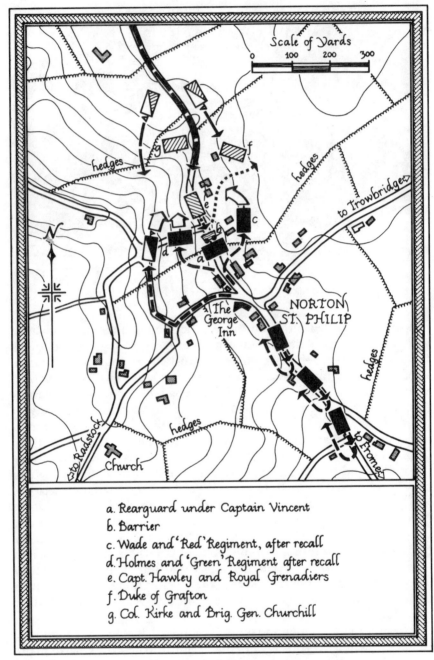

Scale of Yards
0   100   200   300

to Trowbridge

hedges

hedges

hedges

f

g

e

c

d

a

b

g

NORTON
ST. PHILIP

The
George
Inn

to Radstock

hedges

Church

to Frome

a. Rearguard under Captain Vincent
b. Barrier
c. Wade and 'Red' Regiment, after recall
d. Holmes and 'Green' Regiment after recall
e. Capt. Hawley and Royal Grenadiers
f. Duke of Grafton
g. Col. Kirke and Brig. Gen. Churchill

1. The Action of Norton St Philip: The Initial Contact

hedge many of them escaped.'[25] Monmouth now sent the Green
Regiment forward to drive the redcoats from a hedge that was
threatening the Red Regiment's flank as it pinned down the royal
vanguard. Col. Holmes made great progress over the next hour,
driving the royal troops from hedge to hedge until he came to the edge
of a large area of ploughed land, on the further, higher side of which
was drawn up the greater part of Feversham's army, 'about 500 paces
from the hedge' according to Wade. 'Wee . . . drew up all our foot
ranging in one line all along the hedges, our horse behind them, and
drew up 2 pieces of canon into the mouth of the lane and guarded them
with a company of sithmen. Our remaining two [guns] were planted
on a little eminence on the right side of the lane.'

Prior to these moves, part of Monmouth's horsemen had also
passed along Wade's route and were soon threatening the royal
advance guard's line of retreat up the lane. Feversham was only too
glad to extricate his men, and above all the Duke of Grafton, who had
lost his horse but managed to mount another wounded one, arriving
'much out of breath'. Feversham asked him not to expose himself
again in so rash a manner, 'for it was too much of a good thing, though
all very well once in a way'. Stage by stage he pulled back his horse
grenadiers, the battered footguards, and supporting cavalry, to the
ridge. Fortunately the rebel horse did not attempt to come to grips –
had they done so, as Feversham admitted, 'the dragoons and the
cavalry were so huddled together, that I do not know what would
have happened if they had fallen upon us from any other direction.'
Accordingly the royal cavalry was pulled back first to the ridge in rear,
whilst Churchill remained with the foot supported by three squadrons
of the Blues.

On the ridge Feversham awaited the arrival of his remaining
infantry from the direction of Bath and above all of Mr Sheres' guns,
much delayed by the poor roads, which had not been improved by the
recent bad weather. Meanwhile Monmouth deployed his array along
the last lines of hedges facing the Royal Army, some 500 yards to their
front. Two rebel cannon, guarded by a company of scythemen, were
sited at the entry to the land which had been the scene of the previous
fighting. The remaining two were placed on a low knoll to the right of
the lane about an hour later. Monmouth was now facing a decision:
whether to follow up his advantage and attack over open ground, or to
hold his present position amidst the covering hedgerows. At one time
it seemed as if the bolder – if rash – alternative would be adopted. Gaps
were carved through the hedges to permit a general advance when the
word was given. But others – including Venner – argued strongly
against it, and by the evening had persuaded the Duke to resume his
march under cover of darkness. Throughout the long afternoon the

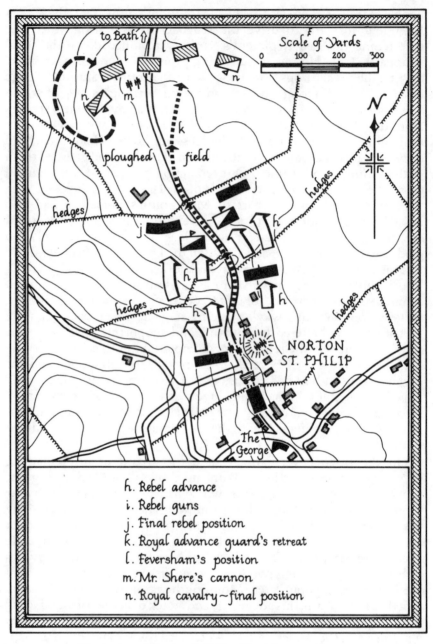

to Bath

Scale of Yards
0   100   200   300

ploughed   field

hedges

hedges

hedges

hedges

NORTON
ST. PHILIP

The
George

h. Rebel advance
i. Rebel guns
j. Final rebel position
k. Royal advance guard's retreat
l. Feversham's position
m. Mr. Shere's cannon
n. Royal cavalry~final position

2. The Action of Norton St Philip: The Afternoon Engagement

two armies remained 'in presence'. The arrival of the royal artillery (about 10 a.m.) had signalled the beginning of a desultory cannonade by both sides that lasted, on and off, for six hours. It does not appear to have been very effective – Wade claims that only a single rebel was killed during this phase – but the rebels were not comfortable under their first experience of cannon fire.

Feversham was no more eager to come to grips with the rebels behind the hedges than Monmouth was to sally forth. The Earl debated whether to hold his position 'all the night, but we had very heavy rain, which would have caused much inconvenience, as we had no tents; so I decided, with the concurrence of the colonels[26] that the very best thing we could do was to march, which we did.' Leaving Col. Oglethorpe with eighty horse dragoons to watch the rebels, Feversham led his army off to Hinton Charterhouse and thence to Bradford-on-Avon. The Royal Army required time to recover from the distinct rebuff sustained during the morning's fighting, and its commander needed time to reconsider his strategy: at all costs the rebels must be headed off from any possible route towards London. The royalist Capt. Parker noted Monmouth ride forward with five companions to watch the Royal Army's withdrawal.

The Duke could claim a small victory, and doubtless this served to rally the morale of his army. It appears that the rebels had lost eighteen men killed, including several officers. Several dozen more had been wounded, some of whom subsequently died; Col. Holmes lost an arm, which reputedly he amputated himself with a cook's cleaver in the kitchen of The George. As he fought at Sedgemoor a little over one week later, he must have recovered amazingly quickly. Feversham's apologetic dispatch admitted to only seven or eight royal troops killed and twenty wounded, but other accounts claim up to eighty royal casualties.

That night, as the Royal Army fell back towards Bradford, Monmouth resumed his march. Leaving large bonfires burning in the hope of deluding royal patrols that he was still at Norton St Philip, the Duke quitted the village at 11 p.m. amidst driving rain and set out for Frome, just six miles distant. Under the prevailing conditions it took nine hours to reach the town, and the exhausted rebels were at last allowed to find quarters and rest.

Monmouth spent two days in Frome. As the army's funds were now all expended, free rations and quartering were exacted. The town had already received two brief visitations – one from each side. On the 24th, a rebel party of horse had arrived, and induced the Constable to read Monmouth's Royal Proclamation. The 25th had seen a visit from Col. Wyndham's regiment of Wiltshire Militia; the proclamation had been torn down, the town searched for arms, and the Constable arrested. Now the townsfolk had several thousand dispirited rebels wished upon them.

Monmouth spent several anxious hours in council with his senior officers. The mood was dark and depressed, for news had just arrived of the collapse of Argyle's revolt in Scotland. The plan on their arrival at Frome had been to swing east towards Westbury and Warminster, and quartermasters had been sent to the former town to mark out quarters. Copies of James II's offer of indulgence were circulating clandestinely amongst the rank and file – and from this time forward desertions would begin to mount as the euphoric mood caused by the events of the 27th soon wore off.

It was against this unpromising background that Monmouth's colonels met their leader around the council table. They found him as demoralised as most of themselves. The bad tidings from Scotland, the failure of the Cheshire rising to materialise, the non-appearance of the 500 Wiltshire horsemen, or any deserters from the Royal Army, the lack of any backing from supporters in London – all these arguments were mentioned by the Duke to support his view that he should forthwith leave the army, ride for Poole, and return overseas. This view was 'mightily applauded by Coll. Venner, but my Ld. Grey and others opposed it as a thing so base that it could never be forgiven by the people, to be so deserted, and that the Duke must never expect more to be trusted.'[27] The argument continued – but the vacillating Monmouth eventually dropped his own suggestion, although he probably now felt that the rebellion was, unless a miracle occurred, doomed and that his supporters – their leaders apart – might have been wise to avail themselves of James II's offer of pardon. But before any decision was announced, Venner, accompanied by Maj. Parsons of the Green Regiment, slipped away and headed for the coast, being of the opinion that Monmouth had agreed to leave the army. Lest their example should prove infectious amongst the officers, it was announced that they were travelling to Holland to seek further supplies of arms.

Orders issued on the Monday night still spoke of marching towards Westbury, but then two pieces of news arrived that caused a radical change of plan. First, it was confirmed that Feversham had marched to Westbury himself, and was clearly determined to block the rebel route into Wiltshire. Second, an unidentified Quaker arrived, announcing that 'a great Club army that were in the marshes in Somersetshire about Axbridge', all of 10,000 men strong, were only awaiting his arrival there to join his ranks. In the event fewer than 160 were ever to materialise – but this imprecise promise of aid from Clubmen[28] was seized upon by the Duke – clutching at straws – to justify a change in the line of march. Abandoning all talk of a march towards London,

Monmouth ordered that the army should head westwards for Shepton Mallet. There was now little disguising from the discerning that the rebel army was on the run. Another turning point had been reached.

The royal force, after smoothing down its ruffled feathers at Bradford-on-Avon, had set out for Westbury on the 29th to rendez-vous with the Wiltshire and Hampshire militias – the former including Drummer Adam Wheeler[29] – and also with the heavier guns of the Tower artillery train, which arrived in the early hours of the 30th after their slow march from London. Once it became quite clear from the questing cavalry that Monmouth was heading westwards, Feversham ordered his army to move forward with some understandable caution to Frome, where they camped for two days above the town on the western side. Up to this point much of the army had been expected to bivouac in the open despite the heavy rain over the recent days, and the remainder to billet upon the local population, but now at last tentage had appeared amongst the artillery stores, and the troops were in consequence more comfortable than formerly. But the many horses drawing the artillery train required large quantities of hay, and this was only procured by requisition. There was also some looting of the houses of Frome despite warning edicts. Henry Shere, Controller of the train, wrote pessimistically to Lord Dartmouth, Master-General of the Ordnance, that 'what we every day practise among this poor people cannot be supported by any man of the least morality'.[30] From Frome, the army followed the rebels to Shepton Mallet, but then – in response to intelligence that Monmouth might try to break away towards the south coast – Feversham decided to swing away to place himself in an intercepting position, and therefore the column headed for Glastonbury on 3 July and thence to Somerton, where another camp was established on the 4th.

The rebels' march requires mention, as it was certainly more eventful. Leaving Frome on Tuesday, 30 June, the column marched towards Shepton Mallet much harrassed by Feversham's cavalry. They marched past Nunney castle and Doulting to camp outside the town, where they found a cooler reception than formerly. Without funds the rebels had resort to free quartering and pilfering of supplies. In an attempt to raise a better glow of martial ardour, Monmouth held an exercise in battle array – a secret purpose of which was probably to assess how many men were already slipping away to avail themselves of the King's proffered pardon. On Wednesday, 1 July the army moved on again towards its promised rendezvous in mid-Somerset with the Clubmen, and passing through Croscombe over the slopes of the Mendip Hills descended upon the cathedral town of Wells, arriving there in the morning. Wade ascribes this move to 'infor-mation that there were some carriages left there of the King's, guarded

6. Lord Grey defends the High Altar in Wells Cathedral

by a small party of Dragoons, which wee took'.[31] This proved to be a
wagon or two of equipment intended for Col. Kirke's Regiment, and
a sum of money was also captured. Unfortunately some of the rebels
got out of hand, and inflicted considerable damage on the cathedral,
seeking out 'idols' in their Protestant iconoclastic wrath, firing their
muskets into the west front, and tearing lead from the roof to melt and
pour into their musket-shot moulds. Some attempted to desecrate the
altar, but this Lord Grey, sword in hand, would not allow. Eventually
the tumult died down, and the men settled down for the night in the
cathedral amongst their stabled horses and in the clergy's houses
around the Close.

Thursday found the rebels marching towards Bridgwater – and the
promised Clubmen host, 'which proved to be about 160 instead of
10,000', as Wade laconically chronicled in his 'Confession'. Yet again,
wild promises of support had proved wholly illusory. The rebels
passed a disconsolate night on the moors.

Bridgwater's citizens were now in a quandary. Rumour of
Monmouth's impending return had preceded the event by some
considerable time. Andrew Paschall, Rector of Chedzoy, had been

determined to dissuade the hotheads amongst his parishioners from joining the Clubmen. On 27 June 'we heard by deserters of the difficulties which their companions in the rebel army laboured under in their motion eastwards' and the Rector made sure this news was spread amongst his flock. On Monday, 29 June, he visited Bridgwater, and found three companies of none-too-sure Somersetshire Militia in the town, almost as anxious about the Clubmen collecting on the moor as about Monmouth's still distant army. On Tuesday the Militia Captain formally required the Clubmen to disband, but they replied that Monmouth was expected to arrive the next day and in that case they would certainly join him. The same day a Quaker arrived in the town. 'He brought word that the Duke and his army was certainly returning, and would be speedily in Bridgwater. Upon that the town was in a hurry.'[32] It would seem that the militiamen decamped at this juncture, no doubt reflecting that discretion was the better part of valour. It was therefore an anxious township that awaited the entry of the rebels' army within its gates on the Friday of the same week.

That morning Monmouth – to make the most of the little aid the Clubmen in fact represented to his cause – placed himself at their head, and riding in front of their insignia (a simple white apron displayed upon a pole), led the column into Bridgwater to find a distinctly cool welcome. There was scant sign of the enthusiastic greetings of just twelve days before, and the mood of the hungry and despondent rebels did nothing to ease the situation. Soon there were numerous complaints being lodged with the town authorities of threats, extortion and open pillaging being resorted to as the ragged army sought food and fodder in growing desperation.

And so the scene was almost set for the culminating military phase of the Rebellion in the West.

Chapter Two
NOTES AND SOURCES

1 See B. Little, *The Monmouth Episode* (London, 1956), p. 95.
2 J. Y. Akerman (ed.), *Moneys Received and Paid for Secret Service of Charles II and James II* (London, 1851), the Camden Society, Vol. 52, p. 106.
3 Wade, *Confessions* . . . , Harleian MSS. 6845, f.277.
4 At this time the English and Scottish, like the Irish, military establishments were separate. See Childs, *The Army, James II and the Glorious Revolution* (Manchester University Press, 1980) p. 1.
5 See W. MacDonald Wigfield, *The Monmouth Rebellion*, p. 41.
6 *The Book of the Axe* (Axminster town records), p. 347.
7 Harleian MSS. 6845, f.256 et seq. And see p. 3.
8 Wade, *op.cit.* Lansdowne MSS. 1152, I, f.310 (British Library).
9 John Whiting, *Persecution Exposed* (London, 1715), p. 142.

10 See *Dictionary of National Biography*, Vol. XVI, p. 247.

11 Letter to the Earl of Clarendon, *Correspondence and Diary* (London, 1827), Vol. 1, p. 141.

12 A full regiment comprised on paper 780 men divided between 13 companies (including one of grenadiers). Between one-fifth and one-third carried pikes; the rest muskets and plug-bayonets. All carried swords in addition. Officers might total 40; they carried spontoons as an indication of rank as well as a weapon. Sergeants carried halberds. Body armour for infantry was fast disappearing by 1685.

13 'Demi-culverins' fired 8-pound cannonballs; 'sakers' were a type of 6-pdr. piece; 'Minions' were 3-pdrs., and 'falcons' were 2½-pdrs. See D. G. Chandler, *The Art of Warfare in the Age of Marlborough* (London, 1975), Part Three, Ch. 11 *passim*.

14 Dummer's account will be found on p. 124.

15 Printed in S. Heywood, *A Vindication of Mr. Fox's History of the Early Part of the Reign of James II* (London, 1811), Appendix 4, p. 45.

16 *Somerset and Dorset Notes and Queries*, cited by W. MacDonald Wigfield, *op.cit.*, p. 50.

17 *Historical Manuscripts Commission*, 5th Report, Appendix 1, p. 328.

18 *ibid.*, Note 437, pp. 327–8.

19 See p. 121 for Venner's attributed account.

20 See Note 17 above.

21 Wade, *op.cit.*, 'Further information . . .', f.278.

22 See Feversham's report, dated Bradford-on-Avon, 28 June (*Historical Manuscripts Commission*, 9th Report, Part 3, p. 3). It is also printed complete in *Proceedings of the Somerset Archaeological and Natural History Society* (1911), Vol. LVII (Third Series Vol. XVII), Part II, pp. 20–24, as an Apppendix, in French.

23 *Proceedings . . .*, *op.cit.*, p. 20 (this author's translation).

24 *ibid.*, p. 21.

25 Wade, *op.cit.*, f.279 (reverse).

26 As Feversham makes no mention of Lord Churchill here, it may perhaps be concluded that the decision was not approved by his second-in-command. *Proceedings . . . op.cit.*, p. 22.

27 Wade, *op.cit.*, f.280.

28 The Clubmen were farmers who had originally banded themselves together for self-defence against all-comers during the Civil War in the 1640s. They were armed for the most part with staves.

29 See p. 130.

30 The Dartmouth Papers, *Historical Manuscripts Commission*, Vol. 1, p. 126.

31 Wade, *op.cit..*, Harleian MSS. 6845, f.270.

32 See *A Vindication of Mr. Fox's History . . . etc.*, *op.cit.*, p. xxxiii. This source includes a 17-side enlarged version of the Paschall narrative as written to one Dr James. The original is in the Ayscough MSS. 4126.

3

Sedgemoor

Once again, arrived within the town of Bridgwater, Monmouth was having to make up his mind about future action. His first thought was to prepare the place for a siege, and orders were issued for the local villages to send in workmen and labourers to assist with the task, as well as large amounts of requisitioned supplies. The citizens of the town did not relish the prospect: Bridgwater had sustained a major siege in 1645, and a large part of the town had been destroyed in a disastrous fire. Memories of the Civil War died hard; it was one thing to cheer a handsome 'King Monmouth' and his supporters through the streets when his cause had appeared to be on the flood-tide; it was quite another to be expected to support him to the last now that his fortunes were so clearly on the ebb. A delegation of burghers accordingly waited upon the Duke and begged him to reconsider – in much the same way as only the previous day the mayor of Taunton had sent him a message requiring assurances that the rebel army would not return thither. The local peasantry relished even less the prospect of having both their labour and their remaining cattle and grain committed to what to many must already have been seen as a 'lost cause'. Paschall rode with his family to seek safety at Honiton.

According to Wade, who after all was privy to many of Monmouth's plans, the idea of the rebels sustaining a siege at Bridgwater was only a cover for a more ambitious scheme. 'Wee lay in the moore all night and marched next day being Friday to Bridgwater to refresh our men and fix our arms which were very much out of order, sending warrants before to summon in the country people with spades and pickaxes to worke, as if wee intended to fortifye. Something of that nature was done, but only to secure our quarters and amuse the world, intending nothing less than to stay there.'[1] Thus the work of fortifying was in fact restricted to throwing up rough earthworks to protect the approaches to the town, and to fool Feversham into believing that he had brought his opponents to a halt at last. Monmouth's real plan was to rest his army, and then march hard for Keynsham once more, cross the Avon, and head deep into Gloucestershire and thence to Cheshire, reputedly an area much committed to his cause. He still harboured hopes that the Protestants and Whigs of London would rise in his favour – and at this juncture he dispatched two more emissaries thither, a Maj. Manley and his son. As an experienced soldier, the last thing Monmouth wanted was to be bottled up within an under-fortified town by his uncle's regular army. His only hope of survival lay in mobility, thus retaining some freedom of action and forcing the Royal Army to seek him out. But the idea of a break-out to the north-west of the country was a pretty desperate scheme. By this time his belief in brave promises of massive support must have been wearing thin.

News that Monmouth appeared to be contemplating withstanding a siege reached the Earl of Feversham very quickly, and when the Royal Army moved forward from Somerton to Westonzoyland on the Sunday they were preceded by their commander-in-chief and his staff, who reconnoitred the old Cromwellian siege positions on the moor, which would seem to indicate that the possibility of a blockade of Bridgwater was very much in Lord Feversham's mind. But of course, competent soldier that he was, he doubtless had to prepare for all eventualities. As his army marched northwards towards Westonzoyland in the early hours of the 5th, cavalry patrols pressed to within sight of Bridgwater to observe the foe.

On Saturday, 4 July, Monmouth appears to have finally decided not to stand a siege within Bridgwater. The edicts summoning the local peasantry were revoked, and those few who had already appeared were sent home. Even had the local mood been favourable to a siege, the proximity of the Royal Army at Somerton (on that day) would have meant that at best the defences would have been in a very rudimentary state – if seriously started at all – when the enemy came to the gates. Furthermore, the possession of only four guns, all of them light pieces, would have made a fixed defence inconceivable. So Saturday was passed exercising the troops, although, incredibly – as Wade tells us – 'great numbers went from us to Taunton, to see their friends and returned for the most part againe on Sunday'.[2] It would be fascinating to have an idea of how many went off – and whether with permission or not – and what proportion returned at the end of their furlough to rejoin their regiments, but there is no information. However, the Blue (or Taunton) Regiment was going to be some 600 strong by Wade's estimate at Sedgemoor – so it would appear to have lost several hundred men, most by desertion, since its first raising just two weeks earlier. But if Monmouth and his officers consented to the leave-taking this could be seen to reinforce the view that the decision to undertake a long march to Gloucester and Cheshire had been firmly taken – and the chance offered the local rebels to say goodbye to their wives, sweethearts, families and friends. The remainder of the army spent the Saturday in refurbishing their arms (there must have been a great deal of rust to contend with after all the recent rain) and in exercising. Most of these activities took place on Castle Field on the northern side of the town, where the bivouacs were established, for the citizens of Bridgwater offered scant hospitality to the motley host so compromisingly and inconveniently wished upon them. It was certainly a time for a man to examine his loyalties carefully, and there is little wonder that intelligence of what the rebels were doing and planning was made available to Feversham's cavalry. The only military clash of the day was an inconsequential brush between two parties of rival cavalry near the approaches to the town, but Monmouth also sent out two troops of horse towards Minehead to secure some cannon that were said to be at that place.

On Sunday, 5 July, the Royal Army marched from Somerton to Westonzoyland on receipt of their commander's orders. Barely three miles now divided the two armies as the climax of the campaign approached. The 1,500 infantry received orders to pitch their tents in order of regiments behind a large drainage ditch, the Bussex Rhine, which ran from west of the village to the Black Ditch to its north-east. Space was left between the tent lines and the Rhine for a forming-up area. The cavalry and dragoons – perhaps 1,000 in all – were quartered in the houses of the village, and headquarters established in Weston Court near Westonzoyland church. The royal colonels took possession of the better houses – including the rectory and the inn

7. The Royal Army pitches camp at Westonzoyland

adjoining St Mary's. The three regiments of Wiltshire Militia (some 1,500 men) were stationed in Middlezoy and Othery respectively – a mile or so to the south. When the massive guns of the trains arrived they were all positioned near the bridge over the Bussex Rhine at the extreme south-west of the royal position, dominating the main road running from Bridgwater towards Taunton, which was the most obvious line of approach.

All this flurry of activity was being carefully noted through a spy-glass from Chedzoy church-tower by a devoted Monmouth supporter, a farmer by the name of William Sparke, who sent off his servant – a man named Benjamin Godfrey, or by some accounts, Newton[3] – to report what he had seen to the Duke in Bridgwater. Godfrey arrived about 3 p.m., and delivered his message. Up to this time Monmouth had everything nearly prepared for a march that night towards Keynsham, as already described. His forty-two wagons and four artillery pieces and their teams were already drawn up in a long line through the town. Up to this moment he had not the least wish to try conclusions with Feversham in a stand-up battle outside Bridgwater – for the regular troops would have had too great an advantage.

However, the latest intelligence brought by Godfrey caused him to reconsider. With a number of his senior officers Monmouth climbed up the tower staircase of St Mary's church, Bridgwater, and squeezed their way into the small turret at the base of the spire. As he scanned the moor towards Westonzoyland through his spy-glass, tradition has it that he was able to pick out the regimental colours of the Royal Army about four miles away, and to identify the formations he had once served with during happier times. This is extremely unlikely, as a visit to the vantage-point will establish. Although the moor has many more trees today than formerly, and Bridgwater is a far larger township, it is highly improbable that the Duke could have picked out much more than Westonzoyland church spire and perhaps an indication of the camp fires and tentage on the outskirts of the village. He needed to know more, so Godfrey was dispatched to spy out the lie of the royal camp in greater detail, and particularly whether the troops were throwing up fortifications. The council was then adjourned.

By 5 p.m. Godfrey had returned. He seems to have made his way very close to Westonzoyland, for he reported that the royal guns were all placed near the Bridgwater road some way apart from the main camp, that many of the troops were carousing on the local cider, and – most crucial point of all – he had found no signs of fortifications being prepared. Wade and other accounts – including that of King James II[4] – make much of the fact that Godfrey made no mention of the Bussex Rhine to the fore of the royal camp. It may well be that he did not do so

8. Monmouth surveys the Royal camp from St Mary's Church, Bridgwater

as it was a permanent feature of the terrain, and its existence hardly came into the category of a military earthwork. Although apologists explain Monmouth's failure to surprise the royal camp next morning to the 'sudden' meeting with the Bussex Rhine, there is little doubt that Monmouth was aware of its existence. He had, after all, travelled from Bridgwater to Glastonbury through Westonzoyland on 22 June and according to Paschall's maps returned by the same route on 2 July, and must therefore have passed over the Rhine *twice*; and he had sufficient professional officers around him who must have reconnoitred the area since their re-arrival at Bridgwater whilst the Royal Army was camped at Somerton. Perhaps he did not know the watercourse's depth or width accurately, but it is hard to believe that he had no knowledge of its existence.

Monmouth now faced the last major decision of the rebellion. Taking the advice of his field officers that it might be possible to launch a surprise attack against Feversham if there were no fortifications to contend with and providing the royal cannon could be avoided, he forthwith abandoned his intention to steal away towards Keynsham and the north-west. Assured by Godfrey that he knew in every detail of a route over the moor that would bring the rebels to the northern extremity of the royal camp – and thus to the point furthest

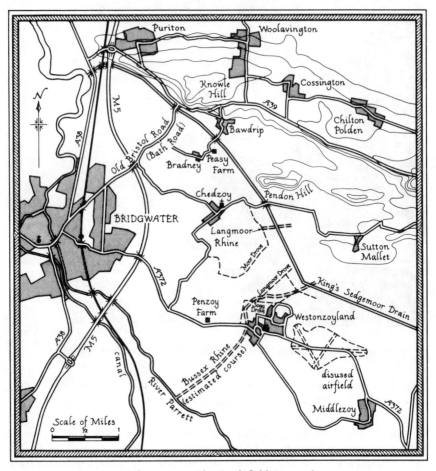

3. Sedgemoor 1: The Battlefield Area today

from the guns – he ordered that the army should leave Bridgwater at 11 p.m. that night.

Much depended on the state of the security precautions the Royal Army had undertaken for the protection of its camp. During the morning and afternoon these appeared to Monmouth's agents to be minimal – and there is some evidence that the Duke made a serious error in underestimating the professionalism of his opponents. True, they had blundered into a trap at Norton St Philip ten days earlier, but this had put their commanders very much upon their guard, and on the afternoon of Sunday, 5 July, Feversham and Churchill put into operation a comprehensive series of security measures which in the event – despite the dense mist the night would bring – proved efficacious in the hour of trial. They may not have been expecting a night attack on the part of the rebels, but it would be wrong to assert that they were not prepared for most unforeseen contingencies. As an experienced soldier himself, Monmouth knew this. During his second viewing of the royal camp from the turret of St Mary's, Bridgwater, he is supposed to have identified Dumbarton's Regiment – later the Royal Scots – with their distinctive white facings and cuffs, a unit he had known well on the Continent. 'I know these men will fight,' he commented, 'and if I had them I would not doubt the success.'[5]

Before detailing the guards and patrols established by the royal commanders, it is necessary to describe the twenty-five square miles of countryside that was about to become the scene of intensive military activity. The map drawn the next day by Andrew Paschall, Rector of Chedzoy, is of the greatest assistance,[6] and when its features are compared to those of the modern map, a larger number of similarities than of dissimilarities becomes apparent; for although the drainage system has been radically altered and many more fences and hedgerows now cross the area than existed 300 years ago, many of the basic components remain unchanged despite many assertions to the contrary. The main area of the action was delimited by two important watercourses. South of Bridgwater ran the western limit, the River Parrett, a major obstacle to movement making the crossings at Bridgwater and Burrow Ridge (five miles apart) of strategic importance. Travelling two miles north-east from Bridgwater, the Bristol road crosses the modern King's Sedgemoor Drain. This did not exist in 1685, but running from several marshy ponds around the village of Bawdrip a few hundred yards to the north-east of the modern watercourse there was the Black Ditch, of which barely a trace remains today. However, for the first mile of its course to the south-east it ran close and parallel to the modern King's Sedgemoor Drain in order to pass below the clearly recognisable feature of Pendon Hill, whence it curved past Sutton Hams, by-passing Sutton Mallet, after passing the junction with the Langmoor Rhine, another disappeared watercourse of great importance to our story. At Sutton Mill – another landmark no longer with us – there was a confluence with the Bussex Rhine flowing north-east from Westonzoyland, and then the Black Ditch itself swung away to the north-east towards Moorlinch. A line of ditches exists to this day from Sutton Hams ridge to Moorlinch which must closely represent the line of the original Black Ditch, and from these its divergence from the King's Sedgemoor Drain becomes evident.

Two more watercourses require description. To the south of Chedzoy on its slight eminence and to the north of Westonzoyland which stands some thirty feet above the moor, ran the Langmoor and

Bussex Rhines respectively. The former (long since filled in) encircled part of Chedzoy 'East field Corn' – a large fertile area south of the village and its church which has changed little in three hundred years – before running down through what Paschall calls 'Langmoor Lake', with a line of stepping-stones and the large Langmoor Stone lying parallel to its course to the junction with the Black Ditch already mentioned. The Bussex Rhine's exact course has long been the subject of debate, it having been filled in during the nineteenth century; but modern aerial survey techniques, based upon measuring heat traces in the soil, has established that it ran from a junction with the River Parrett between the modern Linden and Raymonds farms to a bridge over the Taunton road (today's A372) some eighty yards east of the entrance to today's Sogg Drove, and then described a broad curve before following a straighter course through 'Sedgemoor Lake' (or marsh) to its junction with the Black Ditch below Sutton Mill. Near the beginning of each end of the curve of the Bussex Rhine were two cattle crossing points – known as the 'upper' and 'lower plungeons' – where the banks of the ditch were cut away to permit herds to pass over. These, too, would play an important part in what was to follow.

Roads rarely keep their exact course over the centuries, but in broad terms the network of seventeenth-century highways and tracks can still be guessed at with some degree of confidence. Running north-east from Bridgwater was what Paschall's map calls 'Bridgwater Long Causey' (or causeway), which forks at Knowle Hill, the Bristol road bearing north-west towards Puriton whilst the Bath and London road climbed above Bawdrip to run along Poulden Hill, following the course of the old Roman road which is now the A39. During its earlier course several lanes – 'Chedsey short causey' and 'Bradney Lane' – strike out over the moor to Chedzoy and Bradney villages respectively. Off Bradney Lane another track – Marsh Lane – descends around Peasey Farm on its hilltop towards the large ponds around Bradney – from which ran the Black Ditch. Next, from Bridgwater to the south-east ran what is today the A372 to Westonzoyland, Middlezoy and Othery, whence it crosses the A361 from Taunton to Glastonbury before continuing towards distant Yeovil. This was the most obvious line of attack against the royal camp in 1685. Finally, to the west of the Parrett ran the main road from Bridgwater to Taunton (today the A39) which Paschall labels 'D. of Ms march from Bridgwater to Glastonbury, Munday Jun 22 1685 & back to Bridgwr. July 2 1685'.[7]

The actual security measures undertaken by the Royal Army to protect its position at, and near, Westonzoyland, were as follows: to watch its left rear, Capt. Coy and a force of dragoons were sent to occupy Burrowbridge on the River Parrett – with orders to keep a close eye on the main highway between Bridgwater and Taunton.

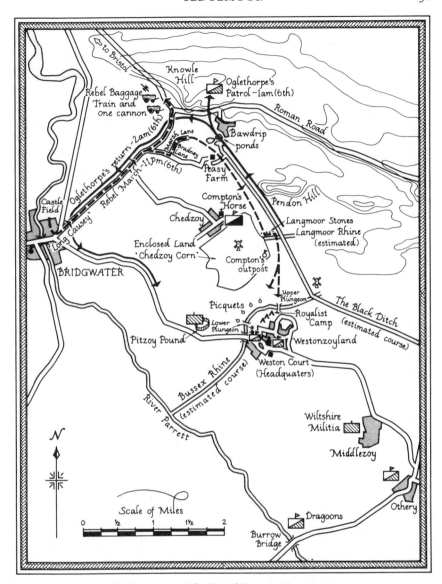

4. Sedgemoor 2: The Royal Security Precautions

Capt. Sir Francis Compton, with 100 Blues and half as many dragoons, was sent forward to the area of Chedzoy, to watch the moor
and the Langmoor Rhine. Fifty foot-soldiers were stationed as an
advanced post in a stone sheepfold called Pitzoy Pound, from where
they could both watch the Bridgwater-to-Westonzoyland road and, if

necessary, offer Compton some support. Col. Oglethorpe with possibly 200 Blues was ordered to conduct a night patrol towards Bradney
and the Bristol road and to keep a close watch on the rebels in
Bridgwater, in case they attempted to break away to the north-east.
Such was the outer line of the Royal Army's precautions, designed to
give an early warning of any major move by Monmouth.

For the immediate safety of the camp behind the Bussex Rhine the
following steps were taken. The guns – with a guard of forty cavalry –
were positioned south of the Lower Plungeon overlooking the road
from Bridgwater leading into the village. A mistake, as it was to
prove, was the decision to send all the horse teams and their civilian
drivers to take up quarters in the village itself. Each of the Regiments
of Guards and Foot in the main camp established a picquet to protect
its front, and sentries were posted. An interval was deliberately left
between the tent lines and the Bussex Rhine to provide a forming-up
place for the troops in the event of an alarm. The regiments were
placed as follows: nearest to the Upper Plungeon but some way to its
south were Dumbarton's, holding the right flank. Next to them came
the two battalions of the First Guards (commanded by Grafton), and
the Coldstream (under Col. Sackville), forming the centre of the line.
The left, stretching away towards the area of the Lower Plungeon and
the distant guns, comprised Trelawney's Regiment and, last of all,
Kirke's.

All in all these positions and precautions were sensible and comprehensive. Indeed, various rumours that Monmouth might attempt
some type of move that night had reached the royal camp, and
Feversham himself – *pace* certain accounts – was out with an escort on
the moor near Chedzoy until the early hours of the morning, waiting
for news from Oglethorpe and the outlying patrol. Some time after
midnight he returned to his quarters in Weston Court and retired,
leaving the immediate command to Lord Churchill, the general-
officer-of-the-day. A thick mist had appeared by this time which did
not ease the task of the sentries and outposts, but there seems to have
been little sense of impending crisis in the royal camp. However, as a
precaution, orders had been given that the horses stabled in the village
were to be left saddled, and at least one regimental officer of the foot
was alert to possibilities. This Capt. Macintosh of Dumbarton's had
the foresight to place tapes between his men's tents and the Bussex
Rhine to guide them, should the need arise, to their alarm posts in the
regimental line.

During the day a visitor to the royal camp had driven up in his coach
and four – Peter Mews, Bishop of Winchester. From 1672 to 1684
he had been Bishop of Bath and Wells before being translated to
Winchester, and he was therefore knowledgeable about local con-

ditions and personalities. Moreover, he owned property at Taunton Deane. Furthermore, he had fought in the Civil Wars as a member of King Charles I's Guards, been wounded in one eye and was consequently known as 'Old Patch'. Feversham dined with his guest before setting out to visit his outposts. The presence of Bishop Mews in the royal camp on this fateful night was to prove an important factor in regard to what took place.

Since the final decision on the night attack had been taken by Monmouth and his council, Bridgwater had been the scene of great activity. The line of wagons – already laden for the proposed march towards Keynsham – was having its tandem-teams of draught horses harnessed up. The same was being done to the four light cannon – but at this awkward juncture it was discovered that one had a defective wheel. The rebel regiments were paraded on Castle Field, and Ferguson and other preachers accompanying the army harangued the men on the justice of their cause, invoking the Lord's blessing upon their leader, and reminding one and all of the vital need for them to perform their duty. Liberal draughts of local cider were made available to the rebels as they sharpened their swords and scythe-blades, carefully measured out gun-powder into their bandoliers or 'Twelve Apostles',[8] and checked their powder horns and muskets (those that had them). Around Monmouth's quarters there was a buzz of activity as last-minute consultations were held. Col. Matthews arrived to suggest that the 600 cavalry should have the command divided so that they could operate in two bodies. This could also be deemed a reflection on Lord Grey's reliability – and Monmouth declared that he would not at this late stage affront his only noble supporter by re-allocating the command arrangements. While all this was afoot, and the news that they were to attempt a night attack spread through the regiments, it was inevitable that word would also spread to some of the townsfolk and thence to the neighbouring villages. It is amazing that full details did not reach the royal camp. According to Bishop Kennet, a captain of the Life Guards told him of a young girl – loyal to James II – who in fact made her way to Westonzoyland to tell what she had heard, but was so abused by the royal soldiery that she 'fled in agonies of rage and shame, leaving the wicked army to its doom',[9] her message undelivered. However, as we have seen, Feversham's security measures were soundly devised even if he and his staff had scant expectation of being subjected to that most difficult of military operations even for regular fully-trained troops – a night attack.

Although Paschall places the time the rebel army left Bridgwater at between 9 and 10 p.m. most accounts follow John Oldmixon's and Nathaniel Wade's assertions that it took place an hour later. 'About 11 a clock that night wee marched out of the towne'[10] recorded the latter.

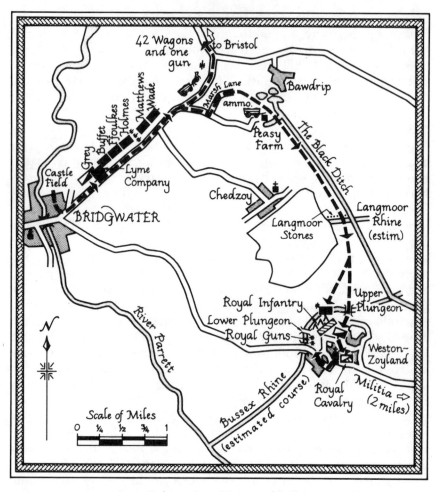

5. Sedgemoor 3: Monmouth's Plan

Probably both estimates were correct. A total of 600 horsemen, some 2,500 foot divided between five unequal regiments and an independent company, four guns and all the wagons and carts would have taken a little time to draw up, and it is highly probable that the leading elements would have set out from Bridgwater some time before the advance was formally ordered. Indeed some accounts speak of the column forming along the 'eastern causeway' or the old Bristol road prior to the march. Oldmixon's evidence is that he saw Monmouth and his escort moving off. 'About 11 o'clock at night I saw the Duke of Monmouth ride out, attended by his Life Guard of Horse, and tho' then but a boy, observed an alteration in his look, which I did not like.'[11] Monmouth would have surely ridden out last once his column was formed, to give him the chance to inspect his army by torchlight and to be seen by his followers.

It is time to describe Monmouth's precise plan. As we have seen, his decision to stake all on achieving a surprise attack on the royal camp represented a great risk – and was at best a calculated gamble. However, were it to succeed, his prestige would soar both locally and nationally – and he might expect a rapid growth of support for his cause; at the very least, it would offset the disappointments in Scotland, Cheshire and London and regain him the initiative, which since the rebels entered Frome after the fight at Norton St Philip had been seized by Feversham. In one sense, the timing of his intended blow was correct. Every day that passed inconclusively would afford the Government in London time to mobilise more troops to swell the numbers of the Royal Army in the West. Seasoned regiments had already been sent orders of recall from the United Provinces; the royal forces in Scotland could now be transferred south and further units had been summoned from Ireland. A large number of new formations – no less than nine Regiments of Foot and twelve more of horse and dragoons[12] – were in process of being raised throughout the country. The details of this would not have been known to Monmouth, but he was soldier enough to realise that the one thing he could not afford to squander was time. As Napoleon was to remark much later, 'Space I may recover, time never.'[13]

Monmouth's plan necessarily fell into three parts – the approach march, the attack and then (presuming it to have been successful) the exploitation. Basing everything on local reports that the royal camp was not fortified, and that wholesale indulgence in the heady local cider would have laid out cold many of his opponents, and hopefully reduced both their state of readiness and their precautions against an attack, Monmouth had first to reach his objective outside Westonzoyland undetected. His fastest route would have been to turn south soon after crossing the River Parrett on quitting Bridgwater and follow the Glastonbury and Yeovil road. This would mean marching barely three miles to the target. However, this was also the most obvious route – and spies and wayfarers had reported the long line of brass cannon drawn up to command this approach. If any part of his army was properly guarded, it would be Feversham's train of artillery. The close proximity of the village behind the guns would make it easy for the superior royal cavalry and dragoons – who time and again over the past two weeks had demonstrated their professional skills over the brave but less well trained and mounted rebel horsemen – to rally and protect the artillery before counter-attacking. For these reasons, Monmouth ruled out the most direct approach.

There was no way for the rebels to attack the royal camp from the rear. To follow the river southwards from Bridgwater would have been feasible, but as well as affording protection for such a move the Parrett also constituted a serious obstacle. It would have to be crossed at Burrow Bridge, which Monmouth guessed would be guarded. Even if he could have reached Othery and Middlezoy undetected to surprise the Wiltshire Militia – who might well have fled at the first threat or indeed been overwhelmed in their tents and quarters – the alarm would undoubtedly have been raised at this juncture; and as a mile and more separated these villages from Westonzoyland the royal main body would have been afforded time to react and form line of battle before even Lord Grey's horsemen could hope to reach the southern outskirts of the village.

There was, however, a third possibility – a circuitous march some six miles in length designed to fall on the further, or northern, flank of the royal camp. Such a march held certain advantages and perils. The first two miles would take the rebel column along the main road towards Wells, Bristol and Bath, and would constitute a clear route and good going underfoot. As Monmouth planned – the victory won – to head back towards Bristol for reasons already described, he would be able to leave his wagon-train – less the ammunition – together with his fourth, defective gun, moving towards Keynsham through the darkness, after escorting it on the first part of its journey. However, it would be necessary to avoid the notice of any royal patrols in the vicinity; and above all to bypass the village of Chedzoy, known for its loyalist sympathies (indeed Rector Paschall had set up a village guard of eight men to dissuade any of his flock from joining the rebel cause, and to protect the village from depredations by small parties of marauders of whatever persuasion.)[14] Monmouth, therefore, would have to pass by the road leading down to Chedzoy, and continue his march to the next turning, Bradney Lane. A quarter of a mile further, and the column would swing left into Marsh Lane, a narrow route leading down towards Bawdrip and the ponds from which led the Black Ditch (an early section of which would have to be crossed), and also skirting the small hill atop which was Peasey Farm. Here Monmouth decided to leave his ammunition wagons – a mistake as it was to prove. From Peasey Farm onwards the route lay at first through a rather narrow corridor to the (then) relatively open moorland beyond, with the Black Ditch providing the eastern boundary and the rather higher ground around Chedzoy and its cornfields a limit to the west of the restricted area. Silence would be vital throughout the march but nowhere more so than from this point on if Feversham's camp was not to be given warning of something being afoot. Leaving the farm on their right, therefore, the rebels would proceed south-eastwards, relying on the local knowledge of Godfrey (now to be guide) to bring them safely on towards the royal camp. One more major obstacle lay ahead – the Langmoor Rhine. This ran directly across the front of the army's route, and would have to be crossed. It was known to be full of water – so the regular crossing near the Langmoor Stone[15] would have to be negotiated. That would bring the army on to Langmoor itself, with about three-quarters of a mile to go to the Bussex Rhine over open moorland. The Upper Plungeon, if it could be secured by Grey's horsemen riding ahead of the guns and regiments of foot, would provide the rebels with a route into the royal camp from the least likely direction, and thence not only direct access to the royal tent lines but also a sure route to the village of Westonzoyland, where the senior officers' quarters and much of the cavalry were known to be situated. If Grey was able to surprise the village and isolate the royal commanders and their cavalry from their guns and infantry behind the Bussex Rhine several hundred yards away, the chances of bringing off a victory would be vastly enhanced. The numerical superiority of the five rebel regiments of foot and the effects of surprise would be strong factors in their favour as they pounced upon the royal tents near which the leaderless royal foot would be striving to form up in the darkness. A massacre might well ensue – or at least a notable victory – and the effects of this could be expected to be dramatic.

This was the plan for which Monmouth finally opted. To be sure it was a gamble. Much depended on Godfrey the guide, on the accuracy of reports concerning the laxity of Feversham's security arrangements and on the discipline in the rebel ranks. A night attack was one of the most difficult operations for even regular troops to undertake, but the chances of success by any other approach were slim indeed, and Monmouth – his army beginning to melt away – was a desperate man. It would be a case of 'risk all to gain – or lose – all', indeed.

The army – foot, horse, wagons and guns – was at last ready to move off. As the highway was broad, it was at first organised into two columns, the cavalry bringing up the rear. Strict orders were issued about maintaining silence. 'What man soever that made a noise should be knocked in the head by the next man.'[16] Such draconian instructions were no doubt necessary, as 'many came forth half drunk'.[17] As the last glimpse of summer twilight faded and the mists began to rise and to lie in dense banks over large areas of the surrounding countryside, the rebel army marched forth to submit its cause to trial by battle.

The route to Chedzoy was passed, and the columns swung down Bradney Lane, and then turned left into Marsh Lane as intended, whilst the forty-seven wagons and the defective gun – which had possibly developed a squeaking wheel – left the main body and continued down the main road towards Bath and distant Keynsham. It

9. Silently, the Rebels crept down Marsh Lane

is not known how long the column was, but the 2,600 foot soldiers, three cannon and 600 horsemen, and the pair or more of ammunition tumbrils, cannot have taken up less than a mile of road space, from Wade and the Red Regiment in the van (accompanied by the nervous Godfrey) to Foulkes's White Regiment now bringing up the rear. About midnight, as the head of the column passed Peasey Farm and moved towards Parchey, an urgent order to halt was whispered down the line. In the mist a few hundred yards away the sound of passing horsemen could be heard. This was Oglethorpe's patrol of the Blues as it approached Knowle Hill. Fear must have been in every rebel heart at this juncture – and doubtless the religious euphoria or effects of rough cider had by now worn off – but their luck continued to hold. Shrouded by both night and mist, the rebel army was not spotted by Oglethorpe's patrol, which jingled and clattered on its way. The rebels breathed again. The halt was used to position the ammunition wains and their handlers below the farm, and to pass Lord Grey and his cavalry to the head of the column. The word was then passed for the advance to be resumed. Safely crossing the Black Ditch and then keeping to their left, the column moved forward again, heading past Parchey for the Langmoor Rhine and the vital stone marking the crossing.

Although Oglethorpe's troopers knew nothing of the rebel move, and Monmouth was taking care to avoid Chedzoy, their passage was not going entirely unremarked. Two villagers had seen the army in Bradney Lane, and hastened full of excitement to inform the Chedzoy village watchmen before proceeding to the windmill in Eastfield Corn to secure a grandstand view of what was to follow.[18] Clearly, neither they, nor the 'loyal watch', informed Capt. Compton or his men of what had been seen. That officer, indeed, had been so convinced that all would be quiet that, after Lord Feversham had left to return to his quarters in Weston Court, he had withdrawn his outlying post on the Langmoor Rhine some time after midnight. This could have been a fatal decision.

However, the good fortune that so far had blessed the rebel march was about to run out. After encountering a denser patch of mist than hitherto, Godfrey suddenly found himself on the banks of the waterfilled Langmoor Rhine, perhaps eight foot across, but *not* at the Langmoor Stone. In panic he sought up and down the bank. Unwarned of the hitch, the horsemen crowded up in the darkness; horses stumbled and neighed; men ran into one another; horses whinnied and snorted; a weapon or two were dropped; men doubtless cursed. This time they were heard.

10. The unknown trooper of the Blues sounds the alarm

The time was shortly after one in the morning. Suddenly there was a flash in the darkness, followed by the sound of a shot. Separated by about a mile from his objective, Monmouth's plan to 'silently get behind the (royal) camp, seize the officers in their beds, as also the 18 guns and 160 wagons standing all together and, if occasion were, turn the guns, as they might have done easily, upon the King's Camp and thus give them a terrible alarm on that side'[19] was effectively doomed. But it was now too late to turn back – the die was cast. Grey's horsemen at last found the elusive crossing point over the Langmoor Rhine, passed over, and on Monmouth's order rode off at a fast trot into the mist, heading for – they hoped– the Upper Plungeon. We may wonder if the were-woman's warning of years before passed through the Duke's mind. 'The Rhine' had indeed proved his downfall, as events were about to demonstrate.

The question of who fired the fatal shot has occasioned some controversy. According to Daniel Defoe, the future author of Robinson Crusoe who in 1685 was a member of the rebel army, it was discharged 'either by accident or by treachery'.[20] In the confusion along the Langmoor Rhine as the column crowded up in the dark and men jostled one another it is indeed conceivable that a firearm went off by accident. Many accounts blame Capt. John Hucker for deliberately giving the alarm and thus betraying Monmouth's design. But Hucker had entertained Monmouth in his house in Taunton in June, and his daughter had been one of the maids who presented colours, so it is doubtful whether the charge levelled against this commander of a troop of rebel horse is anything more than malicious hearsay.[21] Most modern authorities accept Paschall's view, written down soon after the event, following his return from Honiton, that the pistol shot was fired by an unknown trooper in the Blues left as an outlying vedette by Compton in the cornfield adjacent to the Langmoor Rhine. Aware that the single shot might have been muffled by the mist or even been mistaken for a poacher in the marshes, Capt. Compton ordered one of his soldiers – possibly the same trooper – to ride at full speed over the moor to alert the camp. This regular cavalryman – the 'excellent trooper' as Col. Alfred Burne has dubbed him[22] – kept his head admirably and more than performed his duty. 'Immediately a trooper rides from that placeward full speed to the camp,' recalled Paschall, 'calls with all imaginable earnestness, 20 times at least, 'Beat your drums, the enemy is come. For the Lord's sake, beat your drums.' He then rode back with the like speed the same way he came,'[23] to rejoin his unit. 'It was this person, and not the pistol, which gave the alarm,' Paschall added, with justice, in his longer account.

At once the royal camp began to stir. Officers-of-the-day shouted for their sergeants, sergeants shouted for the drums, and the drummer-boys came tumbling out of their tents 'even barefoot for haste' to beat the alarm. Frantic but orderly activity ensued as the regular soldiers, hardly pausing to rub the sleep from their eyes or to shake their heads to dispel any lingering traces of their earlier dissipations, quitted their tents to seize muskets or pikes from the bells-of-arms or tent sides, and then began to run towards the open space between the tent lines and the Bussex Rhine to fall in around the young ensigns displaying the company colours marking their alarm posts. Many troops were only half-dressed, but all had their weapons and ammunition. Within minutes, the six battalions were formed in line of battle, whilst the musketeers of Dumbarton's Regiment – still equipped with the out-dated matchlocks (their colleagues in other regiments had the newer flintlock land-muskets) – began to light their lengths of slow-match and attach them to their pieces, causing a glow in the darkness. Brig.-Gen. Lord Churchill, officer-of-the-day, hastened up with his staff to take control. Of Lord Feversham, commander-in-chief, there was no sign – although his guest, Bishop Mews, was dressing rapidly and pulling on his breeches, hose and shoes as the alarm was repeated throughout the village. A mile away in Middlezoy Private Wheeler of the Wiltshire Militia was the first to beat the alarm in that village, according to his own account. From front to rear the royal encampments buzzed with life like a disturbed hornet's nest – but it was disciplined activity. However, there were exceptions: some civilian drivers of the artillery train seem to have absented themselves, with their draught-horses, or at least to have been thrown into confusion, as Lt. Dummer somewhat embarrassedly noted in his account.

Meanwhile there was considerable activity out on the moor. Compton, obeying his orders – in the event of an alarm to 'fire and retire' – rode off fast at the head of his 150 troopers and dragoons to reach the Upper Plungeon. En route they ran into part of Grey's advancing horsemen, and although details are uncertain, in the ensuing clash the Blues' captain was shot in the chest. In a second brush, his second-in-command, one Capt. Sandys, was also wounded. Nevertheless, the Blues reached the plungeon first, turned about, re-ordered their ranks and prepared to defend the crossing on whose early capture so much depended for Monmouth's plan. Grey's 600 horsemen rode on through the darkness until they reached the Bussex Rhine. Not realising that it was only muddy rather than waterlogged, and unable to see clearly how wide it was as an obstacle, they made no attempt to cross or jump it. Instead, the horsemen split into two bodies. One body, perhaps 200 strong under Capt. John Jones, a veteran of Cromwell's Ironsides in the Civil War, wheeled left, and were soon engaged in hard fighting with Compton's command. The royal horsemen soon gained the upper hand, but much admiration

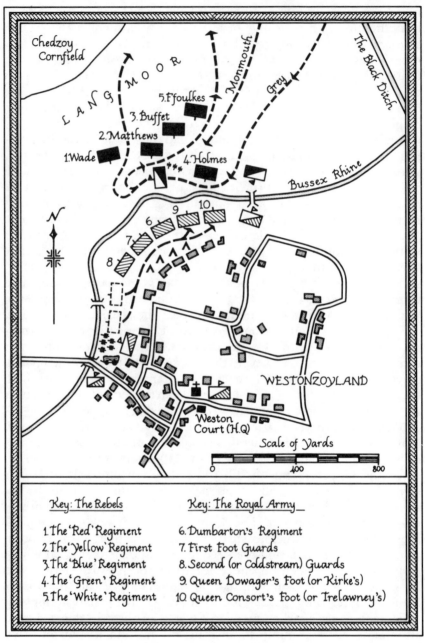

Key: The Rebels

1. The 'Red' Regiment
2. The 'Yellow' Regiment
3. The 'Blue' Regiment
4. The 'Green' Regiment
5. The 'White' Regiment

Key: The Royal Army

6. Dumbarton's Regiment
7. First Foot Guards
8. Second (or Coldstream) Guards
9. Queen Dowager's Foot (or Kirke's)
10. Queen Consort's Foot (or Trelawney's)

6. Sedgemoor 4: Monmouth's Attack at approximately 1.30 a.m.

was later expressed for Jones's valour and skill in this engagement (although it was not to save him from eventual execution). The larger body of 400 horsemen swung, with Grey, to the right, and rode along the bank of the Bussex towards the dimly-discerned glow of Dumbarton's matches. They were allowed to ride past unfired on, after Grey called out that they were mounted militia from the Duke of Albemarle. The officer commanding the sleeve of musketeers on the right of the Guards battalion next in line, one Capt. Berkeley, was not so easily deceived. To his challenge, the dimly-perceived horsemen replied they were 'For the King.' 'What King?' 'King Monmouth and God with us!'[24] came the response. 'Then take this with you!' shouted Berkeley, and the Guards opened fire. The firing spread down the battalion lines as each wing or sleeve of musketeers came into action in turn. This was too much for the untrained and terrified horses of Grey's main body. As the Earl of Aylesbury later recorded, 'The Duke's horse could not well be relied on, it consisting chiefly of mares and horses feeding in the moors and pastures, and no wonder that the great fire put them into confusion.'[25] Wheeling away out of control, the horses bolted the way they had come, 'and march off', as Paschall laconically remarked.

Unfortunately they did more and worse than simply quitting the field. At the moment when the warning shot was fired, Monmouth had ordered Grey to press on ahead whilst he remained with the long column of foot and guns, which he would bring up as fast as he could to engage the royal infantry. The leading regiments – the Red, the Yellow and the Green – practically doubled over the moor for a mile, and behind them the remaining regiments inevitably became strung out – indeed, the White, bringing up the rear, would hardly reach the field before the issue was all but settled. The leading regiments, however (with which the three guns kept up so they must indeed have been small), were perhaps two-thirds over the moor when they encountered the fleeing horsemen, whose steeds plunged round, or in some cases through, their ranks, disordering the formations, flooring many, and carrying a good many more away with them in their panic-stricken flight towards the rear. Still worse, the leading fugitives, on reaching Peasey Farm, called out to the ammunition handlers (whose task it was to carry forward ammunition to replenish their comrades' supply in the firing line) that all was lost and that they should save themselves without delay – which they promptly attempted to do. At one stroke, therefore, Monmouth lost most of his cavalry, had his infantry disordered before they had fired a shot, and effectively lost all his reserve of powder and shot. It was hardly an auspicious start to the battle. However, Lord Grey did not quit the field, but reined in and sought out his commander, and at last some horsemen (probably Captain Jones's command) rallied behind the foot.

All was not yet quite lost, and the main battle had still to be joined. Wade's account of what happened to his Red Regiment is the best that has survived from the rebel side. 'By that time our foot came up wee found our Horse all gonn and the K's foote in order. I advanced within 30 or 40 paces of the ditch being opposite to the Scotch batalion (i.e. Dumbarton's) of the K's. as I learnt since, and there was forced to make a full stop to put the Batalion in some order, the Duke having caused them to march so exceeding swift after he saw his Horse runn that they were all in confusion. By that time I had putt them in some order and was preparing to pass the ditch (not intending to fire till I had advanced these to our enemyes), Coll. Matthews was come up (on Wade's left) and began to fire at distance, upon wch. the battalion I commanded fired likewise, and after that I could not gett them to advance. Wee continued in that station firing for about an houre and an halfe, when it being pretty light, I perceived all the Batalions on the left running (who as I since understand were broken by the K's. horse of the left wing) and finding my own men not inclinable to stand, I caused them to face about and made a kind of disorderly retreat.'[26] This action was significant on several counts. First, Wade thought – in error – that he had brought the Red Regiment up against the Tangier regiments of the Royal Foot at the left of their line. In fact he was only opposite Dumbarton's Royal Scots on the extreme right. This formation, therefore, became the target for not only the fire of the rebel Red and Yellow Regiments, but also for that of the three cannon, which were brought into action by Buyse and the Dutch gunner immediately to Wade's left, and also of the Green Regiment beyond. The glowing matches gave the rebels an excellent aiming mark, and although their musketry probably did little harm (the King's account, however, does mention some troops to the rear being hit by indirect fire) the well-served cannon certainly wrought havoc, and it is estimated that most of the fifty royal troops that were slain and many of their wounded fell victims to the rebel canister shot fired at close range.

Even regular troops cannot withstand close fire indefinitely, and Dumbarton's (who lost five officers) began to recoil. There was still no sign of Lord Feversham on the field, but John, Lord Churchill had not been Marshal Turenne's pupil for nothing. Realising that the weight of the rebel attack was upon, and overlapping, the right wing of the royal line, he took the extremely sensible step of ordering the two left-hand units – Trelawney's and Kirke's, which of course were not yet engaged – to prepare to march behind the rest of the royal line to extend the right wing, thus bringing support to the Scots and a greater weight of fire against the three rebel regiments at present within range and in action, and against the three death-dealing enemy cannon. This was a sensible and relatively simple decision – but it was made in the midst of a surprise attack delivered at night, although the eastern horizon by this time was beginning to lighten. Churchill also placed his own regiment – the Royal Dragoons – in a line behind the battered Royal Scots; a very reasonable precaution to take under the circumstances.

The halting of Wade's intended attack at close quarters was fatal for any remaining chance of the rebels achieving a success. Had their troops managed to pour over the Bussex Rhine – and although there were muddy pools at some stretches of its course at others it was, apparently, almost dry, so this they might well have done – and engaged in the hurly-burly of close contact, the terrible scythes and pikes and clubbed muskets could have overwhelmed the wavering Dumbarton's Regiment, and then one thing might have led to another. As it was, however, it was Col. Matthews' Yellow Regiment opening a premature firefight that robbed Wade's Regiment of its forward impetus, and once this was lost there would be no means of regaining it. From that moment – about 2.30 a.m. – the outcome of the battle (bar totally unexpected upsets) was virtually a foregone conclusion. It was just a question of how long it would take for the superior fire power and discipline of the regular royal infantry to overwhelm the rebels.

Up to this point, however, the Royal Army lacked three vital components – artillery in action, a full complement of cavalry and its commander-in-chief in the field. All deficiencies were soon to be made good. Bishop Mews was the hero of the hour where the artillery was concerned. Although Dummer makes no mention of the fact (for understandable professional reasons, no doubt) it was to 'Old Patch's' insistence on harnessing his coach-horses to the trails of a number of royal cannon (whose drivers and teams were still largely absent) that the Royal Army owed any support from its guns at this battle. Eventually six were dragged up, one at a time, and brought into action – three against Wade from near the Guards, and three against Matthews from in front of Dumbarton's – but first all fire was concentrated on silencing the three rebel guns, which was soon accomplished by heavier pieces at such short range. Besides, by 3 a.m. both the rebel guns and the rebel infantry were fast running out of ammunition, and their fire was slackening. Only now, as the cry went up for powder and shot from the reserve, was it discovered that the handlers had fled with Grey's horsemen. The royal artillerymen grimly changed from roundshot to canister,[27] and began to pound their dimly-perceived targets without mercy, the swathes of musket-balls and metal fragments carving lanes through the ranks of the near-helpless rebel infantry. After the battle, King James awarded a grant of £40 to Sgt. Weems of Dumbarton's Foot for his skill in helping serve the guns. Thus not only·the cavalry battle but now also the firefight – both cannon and musket – had been lost by the rebels.

At this juncture two events still further prejudiced the action in favour of the Royal Army. The first was the appearance of Lord Feversham to assume command. King James II's account implies that the general had been in active control since the outset of the battle, or very nearly so.[28] Feversham had not in fact been, *pace* his royal master, 'agetting the Horse in order' and sending for the cannon. He had been, quite simply, fast asleep in Weston Court. Caution has to be exercised over this point, as many slanderous imputations were made against Feversham after the Glorious Revolution of 1688 in order to put Churchill's role in the battle into an even better light, and also to discredit a commander who, like Churchill a Protestant, had, unlike Churchill, stood loyally by James II in his hour of crisis, and shared his fate of being forced into exile. Allowing for Whig propaganda against King James's most loyal soldier of senior rank, it nevertheless seems that Lord Feversham was indeed abed for at least part of the battle. The reason was not, however, connected with *insouciance* or idleness. As mentioned above, Feversham had some years before received a severe blow to the head from a falling beam whilst helping at a fire. Although he recovered from the accident, one long-term effect may have been to make it almost impossible to wake him from a deep slumber until he emerged naturally to consciousness. He had been out visiting his outposts until after midnight; earlier he had dined and drunk well with his guest, Bishop Mews; small wonder that he was deeply asleep by 1.15 a.m. when the first alarm was raised. We have the not unengaging picture, therefore, of Feversham's valet and other servants desperately trying to shake their master awake – did they try a pitcher of cold water, one wonders? – whilst anxious aides and staff officers awaited the pleasure of his orders for the battle at the door of his bedroom. By three o'clock Feversham had regained his senses, and within a further fifteen minutes he was dressed (it is unlikely, *pace* the Whig tale, that he spent twenty minutes preening himself before a hand-glass, adjusting his cravat and combing his full-bottom wig), mounted, and in effective command. His first two instructions were eminently sensible. He approved the steps taken by Churchill in his absence to extend the line of battle to the right, and he positively ordered that the royal infantry was on no account to start to cross the ditch to come to close grips with the rebels, however spasmodic and faltering their fire was becoming, until the light had increased to a point where every soldier could see exactly what he was about.[29]

The second propitious event was the timely arrival – by way of the Bridgwater road – of a distinctly anxious Col. Oglethorpe and his sizeable patrol. After missing both the march of the rebel army at about midnight and – even more surprisingly – the departure of the rebel baggage train and fourth gun towards Puriton and Bath (although this must have passed just below him on his vantage point above the mist provided by Knowle Hill above Bawdrip village), the commander of the Blues had belatedly sent a patrol towards Bridgwater to gain confirmation that Monmouth was still snug in the town. To his consternation, the returning officer reported that there was no sign of a single rebel in the town. It being about two at this juncture, it is probable that the sounds of battle must now have reached his ears from the direction of Westonzoyland – which at least reassured Oglethorpe that he would not stand charged with having allowed the enemy to escape unnoticed towards Keynsham, as was probably his first thought. But it was high time for him to rejoin his commander-in-chief and the main army – which he duly did after a difficult ride through the remaining mist after skirting Bridgwater town to the south in order to reach the road. The arrival of approximately a quarter of his regular cavalry – however belatedly – came as a welcome development for Lord Feversham, who was now drawing up his plan for delivering the *coup de grâce* against Monmouth's army, as the light of day steadily grew.

Monmouth up to this moment had behaved well. Once surprise had been lost, he had made the only possible decisions – to send ahead his cavalry and to press forward with his infantry and guns behind them with all speed to try and redeem something from a fast deteriorating situation. He had taken the news of the flight of his cavalry with aplomb, and kept Lord Grey at his side. He had stood, half-pike in hand, at the head of his infantry during much of the firefight, and taken counsel with Wade and others as to the best course to pursue. But now, with the failure of his ammunition resupply, and the approach of broad daylight, he knew he was beaten. 'All the world cannot stop those fellows,' he sadly remarked to Lord Grey. 'They will run presently.'[30] And he proceeded to set them an example. Removing his armour, he took a purse of 100 guineas from his servant, Williams (later hanged), and accompanied by Lord Grey, Anton Buyse and the young Dr Oliver, he rode off towards Chedzoy and thence to the Polden Hills. He was, it seems, encouraged by his key advisers to adopt this course on the grounds that if Protestant England was to lose its leader, all would indeed be lost – but the desertion of his supporters at such a moment can only leave a bitter taste.

Still the royal guns roared out at regular intervals, doing particular

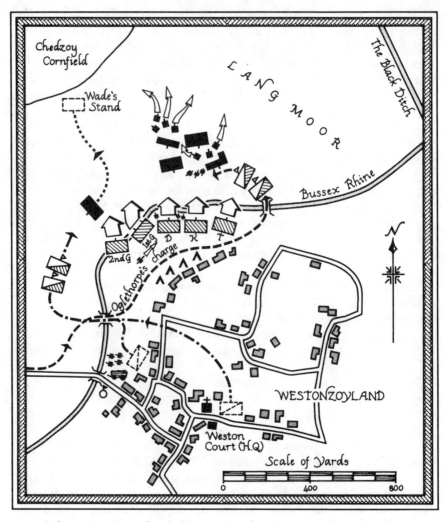

7. Sedgemoor 5: Feversham's Counter Attack at approximately 3.30 to 5.00 a.m.

damage to the Green and White Regiments – the last-named only now appearing on the scene in column, and thus presenting a tempting target in the gathering light. The royal cannon, King James noted, 'played the Reb. very hard, and did good execution.'[31] Dummer also noted, after observing that 'six of our nearest gunns were with the greatest diligence imaginable advanced . . . and did very considerable execution upon the enemies. They stood near an hour and a halfe with great shouting and courage, briskly firing.'[32] By now several leaders were down. Col. Holmes, with a broken arm, lay on the near side of the Bussex Rhine for some time unnoticed, and was eventually picked up, wandering in a daze through the royal tent lines.

After conducting a forward reconnaissance, Lord Feversham was now ready to pass from the defensive to the attack. Refusing to consider employing the militia in any active role, he ordered the repentant Oglethorpe to take his own men and Capt. Upcott's fifty troopers from the gun park behind the battle line to join more of the Blues and other cavalry and dragoons near the Upper Plungeon. The remainder of his cavalry – including troops of Life Guards and Mounted Grenadiers and two more troops of regular cavalry and dragoons – were told to prepare to cross the Lower Plungeon, ready to attack the right of the rebel infantry. It was about half-past three.

Oglethorpe was somewhat precipitate. Hoping no doubt to restore his reputation, he prematurely attacked the Blue Regiment on the farther side of the field and was repulsed with some loss for his pains – sure indication that the men of Taunton at least had still more fight left in them. His force also encountered in the gloom some unidentified rebel horsemen, which gave him cause for caution lest the enemy had somehow produced reinforcements at the eleventh hour. Shortly before 4 a.m. however, Feversham was satisfied. The cavalry trumpets sounded the charge, and lines of royal horse and dragoons, riding

11. The two men of Chedzoy watch the last stages of the fight

knee by knee several lines deep, thundered forward and proceeded to sweep in on the flanks of the rebel regiments of foot and overwhelm their silent three cannon. It was the beginning of the end. Feversham still kept his infantry straining at the·leash until he saw the body of pikes belonging to the Green Regiment 'begin to shake, and at last open',[33] sure signs of a formation beginning to dissolve. Then he gave the signal. With a roar of fury the red-coated infantry swarmed over the Bussex Rhine, reformed their ranks, lowered their pike-points and plug-bayonets and swept forwards for the kill. For Monmouth's army, it was the end. Small groups continued to fight to the last, but most turned and fled as best they could towards Chedzoy cornfields. Wade found himself fighting a rearguard action back to the Langmoor Rhine – 'a ditch a great way behind us, where we were charged by a party of horse & dragoons & routed; about 150 getting over the ditch, I marched with them on foot to Bridgwater, where I mett with 2 or 3 full Troops of horse that had rannaway out of the feild without striking stroke.'[34]

Some miles away in the Polden Hills, Monmouth reined in his horse 'up the hill wch. overlooks the moore as you go towards Bristol, and from thence looked about and could see his Ffoott still firing, and continued on his way to the top of the Mendip Hills'.[35] Minutes later, the last cohesive resistance of the rebel army broke under the combined pressures. As a horde of fugitives fled the field, each man for himself, the royal pursuit got under way.

The last battle to be fought, mercifully, on English soil, was over. The dreadful aftermath was about to begin.

BATTLE DATA TABLE
MONMOUTH'S REVOLT IN THE WEST OF ENGLAND: THE BATTLE OF SEDGEMOOR

1. DATE: 6 July 1685
2. OBJECT OF THE ACTION: the royal forces were seeking to destroy the rebel army; the rebels were hoping for a success to rally more support, and to march on Bristol, there to absorb its munitions, before marching on London to place Monmouth on the throne.
3. OPPOSING SIDES:
   a) The Earl of Feversham and John, Lord Churchill in command of the Royal Army of King James II, and of several militia regiments.
   b) James Scott, Duke of Monmouth, and Lord Grey of Warke, in command of the West Country rebels, made up of Protestant supporters and a few adventurers and mercenaries.
4. FORCES ENGAGED:
   a) *The Royal Army*: 6 infantry battalions, 4 cavalry squadrons, 26

guns. Total: 2,850 (excluding approximately three regiments of militia kept in reserve).

b) *The Rebel Army*: 5 infantry 'regiments', 600 cavalry, 4 guns. Total: 3,610 (excluding two troops of horse on detached duty who were not involved in the battle).

5. CASUALTIES:

a) *The Royal Army*: approximately 80 soldiers killed and 220 wounded.

b) *The Rebel Army*: approximately 1,000 rebels killed, 500 taken prisoner (including many wounded) and 3 guns lost.

6. RESULT:

The total destruction of the rebel army as a fighting force and the collapse of Monmouth's cause, leading to his execution. In the longer term, the outcome of Sedgemoor encouraged James II to become tyrannical, and thus helped to lay the seeds for the Glorious Revolution of 1688 when he was overthrown and replaced.

Chapter Three
NOTES AND SOURCES

1   Wade, *op.cit.*, f.280.
2   *ibid.*
3   Godfrey was illegitimate, and was therefore known by both his father's and mother's surname.
4   See p. 112.
5   J. N. P. Watson, *op.cit.*, p. 242, citing Oldmixon, *op.cit.*, Vol. 2, p. 703.
6   The original, with Paschall's short account on the reverse, is at Hoare's Bank in London. A copy hangs in St Mary's Church, Westonzoyland.
7   See maps p. 62 and 68.
8   Each bandolier had twelve powder-charges hanging from the belt, hence the name.
9   Kennet, *op.cit.*, Vol. 3, pp. 430–1, cited by Watson, p. 242.
10 Wade, *op.cit.*, f.281.
11 J. Oldmixon, *op.cit.*, Vol. 1, p. 703.
12 See C. Dalton, *English Army Lists and Commission Registers* (London, 1899), Vol. 2 introduction; and J. Childs, *The Army, James II and the Glorious Revolution*, 66. *op.cit.*, pp. x–xiii.
13 *Correspondance de Napoléon 1er*, (Paris, 1870), Vol. XVIII, No. 14707, p. 218.
14 This point is made by Paschall in his account.
15 Today there is no sign of the Langmoor Rhine or Stone, but Paschall's map allows an approximation to be worked out for the position of the former. See Illustration 13.
16 *Historical Manuscripts Commission*, 12th Report, Appendix V, Ch. ii, p. 90.
17 Heywood, *op.cit.*, p. xliii.
18 Paschall, *op.cit.* (and see p. 108).
19 *ibid.* (and see p. 109).

20   D. Defoe, *Tour through England and Wales in 1724* (Everyman edition), Vol. 1, p. 269.

21   Paschall, longer account *op.cit.*, p. xl, records that 'A Captain Hucker is said to have owned it at his trial, as done by him, to give the King's army notice.'

22   A. H. Burne, *The Battlefields of England* (London, 1950, reissued 1973), Ch. xix, p. 278.

23   See Paschall's account, p. 109.

24   King James II's account in Harleian MSS. 6845, f.289–96 – reproduced below, p. 114.

25   *Memoirs of Thomas Bruce, 3rd Earl of Ailesbury*, pp. 118–19.

26   Wade, *op.cit.*, f.281.

27   Roundshot were solid cannon-balls; canister rounds were hessian bags filled with musket balls, stones and small metal fragments, much used for close-range firing.

28   See p. 114.

29   A. H. Burne, *op.cit.*, pp. 271–91.

30   Heywood, *op. cit.*, p. xliii.

31   See p. 115.

32   See p. 129.

33   For James II's account see p. 116.

34   Wade, *op.cit.*, f.281 (reverse side).

35   James II's account.

4

Retribution

It will never be known exactly how many rebels died immediately after the battle, or indeed during the engagement itself. Perhaps 400 were killed on the battlefield, and up to 1,000 more on the swords of the royal horse and dragoons or the pike-points and plug-bayonets of the royal foot, supplemented by the enthusiastic Wiltshire Militiamen, now at last allowed to enter the action.[1] Many of the rebels were caught at the Langmoor Rhine, where some were cut down and more drowned. Others were hunted through the standing corn beyond, and some bodies lay undiscovered until the harvest. On the first of his two maps, Paschall notes in Chedzoy 'East field Corn', 'hear the flight & pursuit, 42 killed', and on a corner: 'slain in the Moor and buryed in one pit, 195'. Adam Wheeler of the Wiltshire Militia mentions seeing 174 bodies in one pit, and claims that the countryfolk who gathered the dead for burial accounted for 1,384 corpses in all. The majority of the dead were heaped into pits in what is still known as 'the Gravefield', adjacent to the memorial off the modern Langmoor Drove. As for those killed in action on the moor, it would seem that the Blue Regiment of Col. Bovet sustained the heaviest casualties as it arrived into action at the moment when the three preceding regiments broke and fled, and thus was exposed to the full fury of Oglethorpe's charges (although it repulsed the first).

There were also many prisoners taken. Wheeler, stationed in Westonzoyland churchyard, recorded seventeen batches of captives brought in to a total of 238 souls, and by the end of the day perhaps the church held twice as many. Five died the first night of their wounds, and one escaped – having forced a small door while the guards dozed.[2] The plight of many of the captives was pitiful, and nothing seems to have been attempted to treat the rebel wounded or feed the prisoners. Some twenty-two rebels were summarily executed the day after the battle – including the Dutch gunner whose cannon had wrought such havoc and a deserter from the Hampshire Militia; four of these victims were hanged in chains. Conditions within the church of St Mary's rapidly deteriorated, and the interior had to be fumigated, as the churchwarden's accounts reveal, when at length the prisoners were transferred to Taunton. The dead were the more fortunate.

The Royal Army seems to have lost some eighty killed in battle –

most of them from Dumbarton's Regiment – and perhaps 200 more wounded in varying degrees; once again we have no accurate figures – as even King James's account has left a blank at the critical point, with a marginal note vainly requiring Mr Blathwayt, Secretary-at-War, to supply the figure. The casualties – whatever the correct figures – were suffficient to raise the blood-lust of the soldiery, who now sought revenge and compensation far and wide – although perhaps not on quite such a scale as local legend and Whig propaganda later claimed. Nobody would emerge with a worse reputation than Col. Kirke – whose name became a byword for sadistic cruelty and ruthlessness. It was he who, reputedly, after escorting the main convoy of prisoners (the wounded in wagons) from Bridgwater to Taunton on the 9th surrounded by 500 troops, had nineteen hanged without trial within two days to terrorise the population of the county town, and ordered his regimental drummers, fifers and hautbois to play the while, taking the time from the twitching of the victims. It was also Kirke who is credited with having accepted the offered favours of an inn-keeper's daughter at Crewkerne in return for the life of her father; but when next morning she went to the window it was to see his corpse dangling from the inn-sign.[3] On the other hand, there is the very different local story of what happened to Mary Deare. This young girl was a witness to an officer of Kirke's 'Lambs' attempting to rape her mother; snatching up his sword, she ran it through his body and killed him. His enfuriated comrades dragged her before their colonel, but instead of hanging her – or worse – he ordered her release and presented her with the sword as a keepsake.[4] Such a tale is hardly in character with the earlier stories. Similarly, we do know that later Kirke was in correspondence with Blathwayt in London, seeking clarification of the powers he could employ to punish looters and murderers amongst his own men. Without a doubt many 'war-crimes' were committed by the soldiery and militia in the days and weeks after the battle, but these were rough times, and it is clear that King James II was prepared to use terror – however unwisely, as 1688 was to prove – to extirpate the last traces of rebellion amongst his subjects. At the same time, however, he would later order strict enquiries into alleged illegal acts against innocent townsfolk during the period of military occupation to which the region was now subjected.

That occupation had begun on the morning of the 6th, immediately after the battle, when Lord Churchill rode into an apprehensive Bridgwater with the cavalry. Lord Feversham meanwhile marched towards Wells at the head of the three battalions of Guards and the Wiltshire Militia, spending a night at Glastonbury en route, where six rebels were hanged from the sign-board of the White Hart, as Wheeler and others recorded. Kirke entered Taunton on the 7th, followed by his prisoners two days later, as already mentioned. For the next six weeks he controlled the mopping-up operations conducted by the men of the two Tangier regiments – his own and Trelawney's Foot, being subsequently reinforced (and then relieved) by new regiments sent down at the King's orders.

Meanwhile news of the outcome of the 'trial by battle' had been carried far and wide; loyalists rejoiced – and secret sympathisers of the Monmouth party hastily reorganised their order of priorities. Amongst the former category was the Rector of Chedzoy, who had reached Honiton 'where we met the good news given that morning in this place'. He at once hastened back with his family, and 'the next day we through danger rode safe home, where, using my best diligence to learn the truth of that great and important action [of Sedgemoor] . . . I attained that notice of it, which I think to be pretty near the truth, and which I am in the next place to present you withall.'[5] The result of his enquiries were the two accounts and accompanying maps that were written down within days of the battle. In London the church bells rang out to salute the news of the success, and Parliament hastened to congratulate their monarch on the happy resolution of the crisis.

In the West Country, meantime, the grim tasks of burying the newly dead and hunting down the living amongst the rebels were getting into full swing. The men of Chedzoy found time to complain of the expense they had been put to erecting gibbets for the execution of rebels immediately after the battle. There were rumours of pestilence spreading through the countryside from the shallow gravepits, and from the festering wounds of untreated wounded. Some, on the royal side, were accorded proper and ceremonious burial. In Middlezoy church, for example, there is a brass plate set in the chancel floor. 'Here lyes the body of Louis, Chevalier de Misier, A French gentleman who behaved himself with great courage and gallantry 18 years in the English service, and was unfortunately slain on the 6th July 1685 at the battel of Weston, where he beheaved himself withall the courage imaginable against the King's enemies, commanded by the rebel Duke of Monmouth.'[6]

The main army, the Tangier regiments excepted, soon began to disperse. The Guards set off back to the capital. The Tower train of artillery travelled from Westonzoyland to Devizes by way of Glastonbury, Wells, Emborough and Norton St Philip. At Devizes the Wiltshire Militia was disbanded and the men were sent back to their homes. The bye-train, accompanied by Dummer, after two days' rest at Wells made its ponderous way to Frome and thence to Amesbury, whence on the afternoon of the 12th it headed for Portsmouth. The day before, Dummer tells us, 'the Scotts [marched] to Devizes. The

Kings Battallions to Warminster and encamp. Lord Churchill, Lord Feaversham and the Duke of Grafton to London.'[7]

John Churchill was selected to ride ahead bearing Feversham's official despatch. 'As he had anticipated (and was only right) the lion's share of rewards were lavished on Feversham, who received the Garter and other marks of royal favour. But Churchill was not forgotten; in August he was awarded the lucrative colonelcy of the Third Troop of Life Guards in succession to Feversham (who received the First Troop) and the London Gazette of 18 July [OS] duly described how he had "performed his part with all the courage and gallantry imaginable." '[8]

For the royal hierarchy, then, there were the rewards of a grateful sovereign. For the commander of the rebel host, another fate was impending. We left Monmouth in the Polden Hills, riding from the scene of battle in the early morning of 6 July. With a price of £5,000 placed on his head there is small wonder that the hue and cry was conducted with enthusiasm by law-officers, militiamen and ordinary citizens alike. After leaving young Dr Oliver to head for Uphill near Weston-super-Mare, from which town he later escaped to Holland after amazing adventures, Monmouth and his small party rode fast northwards along the Mendips, and swung south-east past Wells to Downside, where a few hours' rest was snatched at the 'safe' house of Edward Strode. Once darkness returned, the fugitives hurried on through Somerset, passing Selwood Forest before entering north-east Dorset near Gillingham, thereafter keeping deep within Cranborne Chase. The declared aim was now to reach Poole, there to seize a ship and escape to the Continent, and to help them on their way they enlisted one Richard Holyday as guide. Continuing past Berwick St John in Wiltshire, they came to Woodyates Inn, where Monmouth, Buyse and Grey disguised themselves in country clothing, the Duke exchanging clothes with an astonished shepherd. Near Wimborne St Giles, having covered some forty miles, they turned loose their exhausted horses and pressed ahead on foot, splitting into two pairs. Grey and Holyday had reached within six miles of Poole before they were spotted and arrested by members of Lord Lumley's Sussex Militia. Monmouth and Buyse made slower time, but stayed together until they reached Woodlands in Horton parish, near Blandford Forum, where they separated to hide. Ravenously hungry, Monmouth gathered some peas from a field before concealing himself in a ditch. Unbeknown to them, they had been observed by Amy Farrant – and when a patrol of Sussex militiamen came by, she reported the recent presence of strangers acting suspiciously nearby. The search intensified, and early on 8 July Buyse was discovered. A little later and Militiaman Parkin found the dishevelled Monmouth in his ditch

12. Monmouth captured near Woodlands in Dorset

beneath 'Monmouth's Ash'.[9] His identity was in doubt until Lord Lumley arrived soon after, when the discovery of the 'lesser George' (part of the insignia of the Order of the Garter) and his pocket-book about his person cleared up the matter once for all.

The prisoner was held at Ringwood for two nights, whilst news of Monmouth's capture was rushed to London. On 10 July he was moved under close escort to Winchester, and next day to Farnham Castle and thence to Guildford. By this time he was writing a stream of letters to the King and other influential figures, imploring the royal forgiveness and hinting that he was in a position to make some important revelations to him alone. On Monday the 13th he was brought to London through Lambeth, where he crossed the Thames by boat to the privy stairs at Whitehall. There he was seen by his friend, Lord Aylesbury. 'I, coming from the city by water, unfortunately landed at the same moment, and saw him led up the other stairs on Westminster side, lean and pale, and with a disconsolate physiognomy, with soldiers with pistols in their hands. The Yeomen of the Guard were posted, and I got behind one of them that he should not perceive me, and I wish heartily and often since that I had not seen him, for I could never get him out of my mind for years, I loved him so personally.'[10] Monmouth was promptly lodged in the Tower. Within two days he would be dead at the hands of the executioner, Jack Ketch.

Jubilant that he had secured the arch-traitor his nephew, James hastened to distribute largesse. The two messengers who brought the news of his capture were awarded £100 each, Amy Farrant received £50. The remainder of the offered reward was, at Lord Lumley's suggestion, split between all members of the Sussex Militia. The reflections of Militiaman Parkin about this liberality are not recorded.

News of other important captures soon arrived thick and fast. Although Cols. Matthews and Foulkes escaped to Europe, whence Venner had preceded them, the three remaining commanding officers (or, in Wade's case, acting-colonel) were taken. The one-armed Holmes had been captured in the royal camp on the 6th. The other Cromwellian, Richard Buffet or Bovet, was captured two weeks later by one of Kirke's patrols at Stoke St Gregory. Nathaniel Wade was secured on 22 July after considerable adventures. We left him in Bridgwater on the morning of the 6th, whence he had retreated in good order at the head of the 150 survivors of the Red Regiment from the Langmoor Rhine below Chedzoy cornfields. There he had found, to his disgust, much of Grey's runaway cavalry. 'I gott my horses and wth. about 20 officers and others, amongst wch. was Ferguson, I went westward to meett 2 troops of horse who were gone to Minehead to fetch up 6 peices of canon, being Capt: Hulins and Capt: Caryes Troops. With part of ym. amounting in all to neare 50, wee went to Ilfordcombe [Ilfracombe] and seized on a vessell wch. wee victualed and put to sea but were forced ashoare by 2 fregatts cruising on the coast; after wch. wee dispersed & fled into the woods. I for my part was alone from that time to the time I was taken coming out of the house of one John Birch in the parish of Brendin [Brendon] in the county of Devon.'[11] In fact he was sheltered by John Birch at Fairleigh with two other rebels after being found nearby in an exhausted condition and befriended by one Grace Howe. However, the local Rector, the Rev. Richard Powell, became suspicious when he found the best ale at the inn being reserved for an anonymous and invisible stranger, and after forming a small posse he surrounded Birch's house. When Wade and the others tried to make a run for it from the back door he was fired at, severely wounded in the back, and made prisoner. His two companions escaped. Wade at first tried to pass himself off as John Lane, but admitted his true identity the next day.[12] As an officer who had accompanied Monmouth from Holland he was excluded from the original General Pardon, but once he had recovered from his wound after a severe illness and delirium, he began to dictate and then write the most celebrated account of the rebellion by a participant on Monmouth's side. Moved in due course to the Tower of London, he was informed that he would only be spared if he revealed all he knew. According to a family tradition, he smuggled out a letter hidden in his laundry to a friend, requesting the names of all known to have been killed at Sedgemoor or afterwards. The list in due course safely reached him, hidden in the pleats of his shirts.[13] He subsequently took great care to mention only those he knew to be dead, already taken or escaped overseas. It seems that he did not fully fool James II, who acidly remarked that 'All your friends, Mr Wade, appear to be dead', but this co-operative attitude earned him the royal favour. He was moved to Windsor Castle, where he dictated his account of the events of 1685. To earn a full pardon, he was subsequently required to turn King's Evidence against Henry Booth, Lord Delamere and other Cheshire supporters, but Delamere, after acquittal by his peers in the Lords in January 1686, was eventually released for lack of evidence. In August 1686, when James II paid a personal visit to view the battlefield, Wade was taken along as guide – and subsequently became Town Clerk of his native city of Bristol, but only until the Glorious Revolution.

Other leaders made good their escapes. Ferguson 'the Plotter' slipped away to Holland. Fletcher of Saltoun – after killing Dare at Lyme – reached Spain. George Speke – a close friend of Monmouth's during his 'great progress' in 1679 – and his father-in-law, John Trenchard, former M.P. for Taunton and another supporter, for whom warrants had been issued in late June, also made good their way to the United Provinces. Most of these gentry would return to England in 1688 during or after the Glorious Revolution.

There were others amongst the gentry of the south-west who also had lucky escapes for themselves and their tenantry. Although Monmouth had been bitterly disappointed by the failure of the landed classes to rally to his standard, at least one titled family had been on the move to join his army when news of Sedgemoor caused an understandable change of mind. Dunster Castle contains the papers of the Luttrell family, whilst Churchill College, Cambridge, holds the correspondence of Erle of Charborough Park in Dorset. Although the Luttrells hesitated for several critical weeks in declaring their hand, by early July they had at last made up their minds, and set out at the head of what was reputedly a force of several hundred well-armed tenants to join Monmouth. They were still on the road when tidings of what had transpired on the night of 5/6 July outside Westonzoyland reached them – probably from fugitives heading for their Dorset homes. The column lost no time in turning itself around and heading back whence it had come. A story is told that at the approach of Royal Dragoons in hot pursuit of fleeing rebels the Luttrells told their apprehensive tenants to conceal their arms, take their horses into neighbouring fields and there adopt convincing agricultural postures! So well was this simulated agrarian activity put on, that they all got away with it. The red-coated hue and cry passed them by, and the family was never seriously investigated as possible malignants by James II's commissioners in the following months. Matters would be very different in 1688. Although Jeffreys' treatment of the West Country broke the spirit of Somerset, and no sizeable number of local people rallied to the cause of the future William III during the Glorious Revolution, the Luttrells raised a complete regiment for the Orange cause in a record three days – and Francis Luttrell became the first colonel of the 19th Foot, later known as the Green Howards, with a commission dated 28 February 1689 but backdated to run from 20 November the previous year. He also served as M.P. for Minehead from 1679 to 1690.

Of those who fell into James's II's hands, a number survived besides Wade and Lord Delamere. Lord Grey of Warke earned a pardon by providing information and by paying Lord Rochester, the King's brother-in-law, who certainly had a personal stake involved in his fate, a bond worth £40,000. Edward Strode of Downside was let off with a fine. Maj. John Wildman (sent to raise London) and Monmouth's chaplain, the Rev. Nathaniel Hook (who became a Catholic), both got off in the end. Many another lesser figure also proved able to compound for money.

But for many more there would be no mercy whatsoever. The Earl of Argyle had been executed, as already mentioned, in Edinburgh on 30 June. Col. Richard Rumbold of the Scottish rebellion already condemned for high treason during the Rye House Plot of 1683 suffered the full fate of a traitor. Col. Holmes and Bovet were executed, as were Capt. John Jones and a number of other subordinate officers. As will be seen, the main suffering fell upon the hapless rank and file, deprived of influence, money or friends – but they were by no means the only victims who could expect scant mercy. When Hannah Hewling went to Court to petition the monarch on behalf of her two brothers – Benjamin and William, rebel officers and Baptists both – John Churchill, standing by the mantelpiece in the antechamber, 'assured her of his most hearty wishes of success to her petition, "but madam," said he, "I dare not flatter you with any such hopes, for that marble is as capable of feeling compassion as the King's heart." '[14] Both were subsequently hanged.

What chance was there, then, for James Scott, Duke of Monmouth, earning a reprieve? Of course there was none, and he survived his arrival in London by barely two days. Sadly, he spent many of his last hours abjectly pleading for his life on any terms. He would reveal the names of all his fellow-conspirators, become his uncle's most loyal subject, even become a convert to the Roman Catholic Church. It is possible that James II might have been impressed by the third offer and interested by the first; but he was not impressed by the second, as Monmouth had spoken in the same terms at the time of his proven complicity in the Rye House Plot just two years before. Indeed, he agreed to see Monmouth on 14 July – and many believed this was a sure sign that a reprieve might be forthcoming. Doubtless so Monmouth hoped, and he was prepared to sob and grovel at his uncle's feet, his arms bound behind him with a silken cord, in the hope of achieving a pardon. He was to be disappointed, however. He may unwittingly have dashed his last hope by offering to reveal the names of all who knew of his plotting. Sunderland – possibly chargeable with double-dealing – may have intercepted some of Monmouth's more interesting missives before they reached the monarch, and according to Lord Aylesbury – but no friend of the Secretary of State's was he – the minister (eager to clear his own name) whispered in the royal ear that 'there could not be two kings', so the final die was cast. James II asked Monmouth, according to Sir John Bramston, how he could expect clemency after making 'me a murderer and poisoner of my dear brother, besides all the other villainies you charge me with in your declaration?'[15] As the King wrote the same day to William of Orange, Stadtholder of the United Provinces (who was himself not a little implicated in double-dealing, as we have already remarked), 'The Duke of Monmouth seemed more concerned and desirous to live, and did not behave himself so well as I expected nor as one ought to have expected from one who had taken upon him to be King. I have signed the warrant for his execution tomorrow.'[16]

'So he was sent to the Tower,' continued Ailesbury, 'and in forty hours after was executed, by virtue of the Bill of Attainder [which made a trial unnecessary] . . . the day my dearest son died, and tis by that the day is so fresh in my memory.'[17]

It is pleasant to be able to record that Monmouth regained some dignity in his last hours. He saw his estranged wife, and their three children, and signed a written statement to the effect that his father, King Charles II, had always told him that he had never been married to his mother, Lucy Walters.[18] On the 15th he was brought to Tower Hill, where he resisted with patience the repeated attempts by two bishops in attendance to persuade him to make good his 'very imperfect repentance' by publicly declaring it to be a heinous sin to rebel against the King. He did apologise from the heart for all the trouble he had caused – particularly to his erstwhile supporters – and declared his undying affection for Lady Henrietta Wentworth – but further than that he would not go.[19] With that the divines had to be content. On the scaffold, Monmouth gave the executioner a sum of money, and promised him more through his servant if he made a quick, neat job of his duty. It was, alas, not to be earned. Jack Ketch barely broke the skin of the neck with his first blow. To the horror of the vast and sympathetic crowd, after four more hacks the head was still on and Monmouth alive (though hopefully stunned). At this, Ketch threw down the axe and refused to continue the ceremony, but the Sheriff of London with a few short, succinct words persuaded him to return to his duty, which he then carried through with the aid of a knife. Monmouth's body was brought back to the Tower, the severed head in a red bag lying alongside the body in the coffin, and there the Duke of Monmouth was buried in the chapel of St Peter ad Vincula. 'Thus died ignominiously', wrote Aylesbury, 'the finest nobleman eyes ever saw as to his exterior, and that was all, save that he was of the most courteous and polite behaviour that can be expressed. He had served in the French army, as a Lt. General, and he was brave and a good officer.'[20]

The agony of James Scott was over, but that of his closest friends and supporters was about to begin. Prominent amongst them was Lady Henrietta Wentworth, his devoted mistress, who had sold her jewels to help raise money to hire shipping and purchase arms. The news of her lover's end came as a horrendous shock, and according to some sources she never recovered from it but entered into a decline that led to her death, following her return from the United Provinces, in Bedfordshire in April 1686. She had been cheated and defrauded by several agents the previous year, and is a tragic figure.

Meanwhile, in England and Scotland the hunting down and punishment of Monmouth's supporters was fast reaching a peak. As there were rewards to be gained, the hue and cry was often pressed with undue enthusiasm and lack of scruple – and many an old score was paid off by the perjured denunciations of rivals and old enemies. The Government attempted to regularise the proceedings, and as a preliminary for what was to follow required the constables and local officials of the counties of Somerset, Dorset and Devon – supervised by Commissioners – to prepare lists of all men absent from their homes during the rebellion. Most of the returns still exist, and the names recorded total 1,832 for Somersetshire, 494 for Devon and 295 for Dorset – but of course not all absences were indictable – far from it.[21] There were already some 1,500 former rebels held in West Country jails, and a few in London, and the number was increasing daily as escapees or wrongly-charged citizens were brought in.

Of course, there had been numbers of escapes by rebels immediately after the battle. In the confusion and terror of the immediate follow-up to Monmouth's defeat, not a few slipped away or bluffed their way to freedom. The single escape from St Mary's, Westonzoyland, has already been mentioned. Another that has entered folklore was that of Jan Swayn (or John Swain in other versions). This rebel, apparently a native of Shapwick, reached his home after the battle only to be arrested by the Militia. He was marched off, followed by his grieving wife and children, towards Bridgwater. The story goes that Jan Swayn asked his escorts to allow him to demonstrate his prowess as a long-jumper to his family just one more time, and surprisingly they agreed. The young man, however, proceeded to make three gigantic leaps, not one, and disappeared into the woodland. To this day in Loxley Wood besides the main road are to be seen three stone markers, separated by distances of 13 ft. 8 in., 13 ft. 3 in., and 14 ft. respectively at the reputed site of this achievement. The local scholar, Mr W. MacDonald Wigfield, has found reference to a John Swayne captured after the Bloody Assize was over, tried at Dorchester early in 1686 and eventually pardoned by Royal Proclamation.[22] This might have been the same man.

However, for the vast majority of rebel prisoners the midsummer period of 1685 involved a long and anxious wait to see what fate held in store for them amidst the appalling conditions of the local prisons and bridewells. Many of the sick and wounded died awaiting justice, which still further confused the issue, enabling not a few condemned rebels to pass themselves off as men already dead and thereby cheat the gallows. The authorities were equally aghast at the prospect of having to arrange the trials of 1,500 souls – but the King was adamant that an example had to be made. To ease the problem, strong efforts were made – and with some success – to induce many of the rebel prisoners to agree to plead guilty in large batches in return for promises of leniency.

As this book is mainly concerned with the military aspects of the Western Rebellion it is only proposed to summarise the grim story of the Bloody Assize. The name of Lord Chief Justice George Jeffreys, First Baron Jeffreys of Wem, has become the target of local hatred for three centuries and national obloquy for almost as long. No doubt he deserves most of the denunciation he has received, but once again party propaganda has exaggerated the picture. 'The Devil in Wig and Gown' has in recent years received a measure of re-examination and even exoneration from certain historians, in much the same way as King Richard III has been rescued from the worst distortions of Tudor propagandists (amongst whom we must certainly list William Shakespeare). Care has to be taken to find a middle course between the 'ogre' and the 'misunderstood' images.

Jeffreys was aged forty in 1685, and had a notable, if controversial, legal career already behind him before James II appointed him to conduct, with four other judges, the special Assize on the Western Circuit in August that year. Educated at Cambridge and trained as a barrister at the Inner Temple, he had taken silk in 1668, and nine years later had become Solicitor-General to James, Duke of York. In that year he was knighted. It was as Recorder for the City of London – a post he held from 1678 to 1680 – that he first rose to full public notice, by the severity with which he dealt with the trials associated with the Popish Plot – including that of the notorious perjured denunciator, Titus Oates. In due course, indeed, he was reprimanded by the House of Commons for his excessive zeal, and forced to resign his London appointment. He moved to a legal post in Chester, and again became the centre of controversy for his bullying cross-examinations from the Bench. Although King Charles II had no great liking for him, he was appointed Lord Chief Justice in 1682 and a year later a Privy Councillor. He was well thought of by the King's ministers for his ability to procure the desired verdicts in certain state trials after the Rye House Plot.[23]

A notably handsome man, there is no doubting that he had a wide circle of friends and acquaintances who admired his witty conversation and broad knowledge, and particularly his penetrating mind. But he was also a seriously sick man, tortured by a stone in the kidney, and when he was subject to an excruciating attack of pain his attitude became transformed into that of a hectoring bully, whose savagery and brutality of manner in the courtroom became a byword. He was 'a man of great and fiery passion, and did more ill things out of his natural temper, which was insufferable, than out of a design to render the King odious'. It should be mentioned, however, that it was the normal custom for seventeenth-century judges to take a far more active part on the side of the prosecution than would ever be tolerated today, and he was determined that the royal cause should win.

Such was the 'lion under the throne' who travelled down from London in his coach to alight at Winchester on 25 August, ready to open the legal proceedings which have left a scar on the reputation of English justice. Over the following weeks, the assize circuit would take Jeffreys and his four colleagues from Winchester to Salisbury, Dorchester and Exeter, and finally to Taunton and Wells. The first major case was the most notorious of all (and the best recorded) – that of Dame Alice Lisle on 27 August. Charged with harbouring two rebels, John Hickes and Richard Nelthorpe, she was a widow of over eighty, and had scant sympathy for the cause of Monmouth; of the former, she believed him to be only a dissenting minister; of the latter, she knew nothing at all. Jeffreys produced an appalling virtuoso performance from the Judge's Bench, and bullied and confused witnesses until after a six-hour trial he extracted the verdict he wanted

13. Dame Alice Lisle before Judge Jeffreys at Winchester

from an unwilling jury, even though Hickes had not been proved to be a rebel.[25] 'Had she been my own mother, I would have found her guilty', he commented to the cowed jury, before sentencing Dame Alice to be burnt at the stake, the penalty for women convicted of high treason. A five-day postponement of execution was eventually agreed, and the King was persuaded to substitute a sentence of beheading with the axe. She died at Winchester on 2 September, it was noted in Hansard's second volume of *State Trials* 'with a great deal of Christian resolution'. Another eyewitness recorded that 'she was old and dozy and died without much concern'.[26] There may have been others tried at Winchester on lesser charges, such as rumour-mongering, for when he came to pass sentence the Lord Chief Justice addressed 'Alice Lisle and you the several prisoners now at the bar, you have been severally indicted, arraigned and now stand severally convicted of crimes that by the laws of the land are to be punished with death'.[27] However this may be – and the transcript was made some time later and has, in detail, been questioned for complete authenticity – there is no doubt that Lady Lisle's case was the 'show trial' the Government required to set the tone for all the legal proceedings that were to come. If a shudder of horror went through the land as news of

Dame Alice's fate spread, it would be as nothing to what was soon to follow.

The judges – who included William Montagu, Sir Cresswell Levinz, Sir Francis Wythens and Sir Robert Wright besides Baron Jeffreys of Wem – re-entered their coaches and, properly escorted, moved on to Salisbury. There a light list awaited them – not a single rebel charged with treason, only six to be tried for seditious utterances and one for spreading false information. Sentences of whipping and the imposition of fines sufficed. On again moved His Majesty's Commission of *Oyer* and *Terminer* to the town of Dorchester, where on 5 September, in the large Oak Room at the Antelope Hotel, the really serious work of the Western Circuit began. Here no less than 320 souls awaited trial as suspected rebels, besides another 17 (including two women) for making seditious utterances. Clearly, a full trial of those accused of treason – if tried one at a time at an average of (for lesser folk) three hours apiece – could have extended (supposing a fifteen-hour 'working day') for sixty court days at Dorchester alone. Jeffreys had no such intention, and proceeded to try the prisoners in large batches. His agents had already been moving through the crowded jails of the south-west softening up the miserable captives with half-promises of leniency in return for pleas of guilty, and now the Lord Chief Justice set his seal upon the work. The first group of 34 rebels brought before him were carefully selected for their obduracy in insisting upon entering pleas of not guilty. Jeffreys spent the whole morning on these unfortunates, and by the midday break had obtained 30 verdicts of guilty and had sentenced 29 (one was reprieved) to suffer death for high treason – hanging, drawing and quartering – on the following Monday. The message was quickly absorbed in the cells – and throughout the prisons of the West – and in the afternoon all 69 captives put up pleaded guilty. Their cooperative spirit earned them little, for all were condemned to death (although in the end a majority had their sentences commuted to transportation as indentured labour to the West Indies). As Jeffreys wrote to Lord Sunderland that night, 'I this day began the trial of the rebels at Dorchester and have despatched 98.'[28] As will be seen he would soon beat this record. Certainly this form of mass-justice from the Bench outdistanced the capabilities of the executive arm of the law. On 7 September, Ketch, despite the enlisted services of a butcher, was only able to carry out the sentence of the law with all its grisly rituals on a mere 13 unfortunates.

That same day only 2 out of 103 rebels tried attempted pleas of not guilty, and it was clear that Jeffreys had won his procedural point. By the time his work was done at Dorchester after five days of hearings, almost 300 had been sentenced to death (of whom 74 would actually pay the supreme penalty at locations throughout the county[29] and a further 175 be transported beyond the seas). Of the rest 27 were able to produce certificates proving that they had laid down their arms during the period of amnesty, 28 were recommended for mercy, 15 remained in custody (probably to serve as witnesses at future trials) and as many more were fortunate enough to be discharged for want of evidence.

When the Assize was opened at Exeter on the 14th there were no less than 494 names on the presentment rolls but only 28 actually present to stand trial for treason, 12 on 'seditious words' charges and 2 accused of helping a rebel escape. Such a bill of arraignment presented few difficulties to Jeffreys and his team, and a single day sufficed to clear the list. Four pleaded not guilty and 2 of them were executed the same day; 24 pleaded guilty, and 10 were sentenced to death. Of the rest, 5 were reprieved, 7 sentenced to transportation and 2 to be whipped. What Jeffreys had to say about the '343 at large' is not recorded, but it is clear that some of the listed rebels had already been dealt with at Dorchester and others had died at Sedgemoor itself.

September 18th found the Justices at Taunton – the hot-bed of revolt in the eyes of the Government. Again there are discrepancies between documents, but between 514 and 534 prisoners appear to have been dealt with in the two days that followed. As usual a small minority insisted they were guiltless – and received three death sentences for their pains (the fourth actually won a reprieve). By the end of the court a further 146 had been sentenced to hang (2 were later reprieved) – not to forget a further 15 on a separate list 'omitted in the Warrant for Execution altho designed to be executed';[30] 284 were to be transported; 20 had produced magistrates' certificates, 22 were recommended for the royal prerogative of mercy, 2 were granted bail, and 33 were returned to jail for later consideration.

There remained one more port of call – the cathedral city of Wells. The Gaol Delivery there is dated 22 September and contains 543 names, 527 charged with capital offences. By the end of the Assize, 99 had been condemned to death (1 then being reprieved), 383 sentenced to transportation, 6 freed on certificates, 26 more recommended for mercy, a further 5 to be executed but left off the main list in error, 10 still held in custody against future disposal, 5 sentenced to be whipped and 1 to be fined. Once again, the figures do not exactly tally, and there are a number of anomalies.

At this juncture – there being no prisoners held at Bristol in connection with the late rebellion – the judges ended the Assize and headed gratefully for London. Jeffreys visited Windsor Castle to wait upon the King, with whom he had been in constant touch over the number of sentences of death or transportation desirable, and on 28 September received the Great Seal of the office of Lord Chancellor from his grateful monarch. So ended the Bloody Assize, although a fair number of cases were dealt with on the next visitation to the West early the following year.

The cold statistics totalling 333 sentenced to death and 814 listed for transportation during the short space of thirty days almost beggar belief. The impact of such severity was immense, as it was expected to be by those that oversaw it. Even the King 'afterwards protested to me [Ailesbury] that he abhorred what had passed in that Commission'.[31] A terrible lesson was meted out to crush, once for all, the temptation to rebel. And it is true that the south-western counties did not rebel again, and for good reason, although the revulsion felt throughout the land at large would contribute in no small measure to the events of three years later. Yet there were those at the time who pointed out the moderation of the King's revenge. James II had not visited wholesale fire and the sword on the dissident areas as King Louis XIV did twice to the Palatinate or as the Hanoverians inflicted during the Highland clearances of the mid-eighteenth century. He did not even allow his rough soldiery free licence – but had his servants busy themselves with hundreds of compensation cases for damage and losses sustained during the rebellion and its immediate aftermath. It could also be claimed that the very presence of 1,500 prisoners in the jails that late August was an indication of royal and military moderation. A travesty though the appearances of trial before the law proved in so many cases, at least there was a pretence at legal forms: most other monarchs of the day would have not expected full prisons at the end of an unsuccessful rebellion – suspicion of complicity in such an act would alone have been deemed justification for instant rough justice. But that, thank goodness, has never been England's way, as the outcry the Bloody Assize evoked illustrates.

Of course not all those sentenced to death or to transportation actually suffered either fate. Some of the former category died of sickness or won reprieves and lesser sentences; some of the latter were able to escape or simply buy themselves off. 'The rich escaped', noted Aylesbury.[32] These were cynical times, and the Government, with perennial economic problems to face, was aware of the need to recoup what it could of its expenses, which included the military costs of suppressing the rebellion, the rewards offered for important captures and the claims for compensation. The sale of some one thousand estates of proven rebels was a help. Lord Grey's pardon cost him £40,000, and that of Edward Prideaux of Ford Abbey all of £14,500 (a sum that went into Jeffreys's own pocket by royal largesse). The wish to raise further sums explains in part the large number of death sentences commuted to transportation. Some ransoms could be purchased for £60 a head, but the potential value of a fit young indentured labourer in the labour-starved West Indian colonies was put by the Lord Chief Justice at between £10 and £15 a head. These were, perhaps, optimistic figures, but even half that sum – gained by selling a rebel to a middleman, who would have the responsibility for shipping him to the auctions over the Atlantic – would represent a profit, whilst the costs of executing a man for high treason were not negligible, and would represent a loss. In fact James II largely ignored these hard-headed arguments, and instead of recouping what was available for the Government insisted on giving batches of convicted rebels to the Queen and other favourites. Some had to pay a consideration, it is true, but not all. Great hopes, for example, were expressed by the agent for the Queen's ladies-in-waiting who were awarded the 40 or so Maids of Taunton. As negotiations with their Whig parents went along slowly, they were specifically excluded from the General Pardon of March 1686 to win a little more time. In the end an asking price of £7,000 was beaten down to £2,000 for all the girls.

The fate of the 750 or so rebels who reached the West Indies alive was mixed. Some had been able to purchase the status of free labourers – but many of these found themselves swindled by unscrupulous contractors and ships' captains, who took their money with fair words and promises and then reneged at journey's end. The sentence of transportation was not for life but for a minimum period, in effect, of ten years. In fact the auction only sold indentured labourers for four years, but King James instructed his colonial legislatures to ensure that no one, for whatever reason, was to be allowed to return in under a decade – on pain of a £250 fine on any person aiding or abetting an indentured person to do so. That applied equally to those who were free labourers.

The colonies were delighted at this influx of cheap, often skilled, labourers, and the governors proved very unwilling to let such a windfall go even after the abdication of James II and the direction by William III and Mary II – in January 1690 – that free pardons were to be given 'for such as desire the same'. They were far too valuable to colonial life and economies. A compromise was eventually reached whereby the authorities in Jamaica, the Barbados and the Leeward Islands were constrained to free all the Monmouth rebels, but these were only to leave the islands of their present employment with specific royal permission in each individual case.

It is uncertain how many made their way back to their homes. Some escaped; a few individual cases are well known, and it has been estimated that perhaps 148 came back from Jamaica in due course. It is unlikely that more than a quarter of the 750 or so who actually arrived in the West Indies ever returned. Of the remainder a great many would have succumbed to the notorious sicknesses of the tropical islands – particularly the feared yellow fever. A fair number, however, elected to stay. Some prospered and became established figures in island society. Many more swelled the ranks of the 'poor white' elements, particularly in the Barbados – where the authorities provided no help to return home even after the ten-year period was expired. Here the Monmouth rebels removed into a remote valley beneath Pico Tenerife in the north of the island, and thanks to the arrival of a shipment of female orphans from the Poor Houses, they were able to keep their community white. As W. MacDonald Wigfield has described,[33] they built themselves cabins in a recognisably West Country style, and erected dry-stone walls. And so they swelled the ranks of the poor white communities – known as the 'Redlegs' or 'Red-shanks' from their sunburned legs – which included Cromwellian exiles (and later added Highland exiles after the revolts of 1715 and 1745 in Scotland), and which still exist today. All knowledge of their origins have disappeared, and the practice of in-breeding has caused some deterioration, but some surnames have survived, and it is said that the distinctive intonation of Somerset speech can still be detected. Modern research has shown up a number of myths and exaggerations, but there is no doubt that some of the 'Redleg' communities draw a substantial part of their origins from the West Countrymen sent into distant exile in late 1685.[34]

By March 1686, King James II was eager to encourage the return of his country to normalcy. His General Pardon issued in that month, although it excluded those who had accompanied Monmouth from Holland, who had known of the conspiracy in England before the event, who were deserters from the militia, or who had accepted commissions in the rebel army, offered amnesty and oblivion to an estimated 2,000 rebels who were still at large in the West. Their services were desperately needed if the local economy was to begin to recover. The Maids of Taunton, we have seen, were also temporarily excluded from the pardon, but not for long. The royal generosity was even extended to rebels living in the United Provinces with some alacrity when, as Peter Earle recently discovered, there was a danger of a group of English exiles setting out to establish a serious rival manufacturory of English cloth over the Channel. The threat this potentially represented to what was still England's staple export was sufficient to secure them very favourable terms of pardon, the exclusions announced in March notwithstanding. By June 1686 a number had availed themselves of the royal offer of clemency, and the enterprise was closed down.[35] Economic pressures, then as now, can overcome political pronouncements.

By August 1685 the situation had so far returned to normal that King James II was able to pay a visit to Bridgwater and Taunton in person, accompanied by the Yeomen of the Guard and his helpful adviser, Nathaniel Wade, late acting-commander of the rebel Red Regiment. There were no signs of hostility – indeed, James was at the peak of a somewhat spurious (and short-lived) popularity following his issue of a Declaration of Indulgence the same April, which had benefited Roman Catholics and Protestant Dissenters alike. It is true that the authorities of Bridgwater only expended the princely sum of 2s in advance of the royal visitation to clear some of the litter from the main streets, but the loyal parishioners of Westonzoyland laid a plank bridge over one of the Rhines to facilitate the royal inspection of the battlefield.[36] Some versions claim this was the work of the men of Chedzoy, but an inspection of the Westonzoyland church accounts would seem to show that the latter village at least shared in the scheme.[37] Traditionally, they wasted their time and effort, for the King preferred to show off his horsemanship by jumping the obstacle (some say he feared a booby-trap).

Superficially, at least, James seemed to have reaped the benefit of his strong policy in the autumn of 1685. His policy at this time was certainly acceptable in the West. 'Trade he had much at heart,' wrote his strong critic, Lord Aylesbury, 'and his topic was liberty of conscience and many hands at work in trade.'[38] It is also noteworthy that when all had gone amiss by late 1688, and his other relation, William of Orange, invaded the realm at the invitation of a group of influential Whig noblemen, the newcomer found no true support in the area although he deliberately placed the early stages of his march from Torbay towards London through part of the rebel region of three years before. But appearances can be deceptive. James's severity had cowed the West, and they were not prepared to risk a repetition of the horrors of the Bloody Assize: they had taken their moment centre-stage, and lived to regret it. Yet James had hardly won what we would today call the local 'hearts and minds' campaign. The lasting scars of the events of the summer and autumn of 1685 were in the hearts and memories of men long after the return of apparent normalcy to the area. After the General Pardon there was considerable, if generally low-key, local feeling between the loyalists and the former rebels. The society of the West had been sundered in a way even the Great Civil War of the 1640s had failed to do. The poet John Dryden reflected in part of his poem Hind and Panther the superficial and conventional approval of Sedgemoor's outcome, claiming that the Northern Lights symbolically gilded the murk of the mist banks that early July night:

Such were the pleasing triumphs of the sky
For James's late nocturnal victory,
The pledge of his almighty patron's love,
The fireworks which his angels made above.

The messenger with speed the tidings bore,
News which three labouring nations did restore;
But heaven's own Nuntius was arrived before.[39]

The reality of the suffering caused, however, is far more movingly expressed in the following excerpt from a folk ballad of *c.* 1692.

Oh Lord, where is my husband now –
Where once he stood beside me?
His body lies at Sedgemoor
In grave of oak and ivy;
Come tell me you who beat the drum,
Why am I so mistreated?
To stand alone, a traitor's wife,
My will to live defeated.
He swore to me he would be gone
For days but two and twenty –
And yet in seven years or more
His bed lies cold and empty.
The scars upon my body have grown cold;
To spin the broken remnants of my soul.[40]

There, in the final analysis, lies all the tragedy of war – and above all of civil strife. Such memories leave traces that even the passing of 300 years have not finally eliminated – for the scars of the Western Rebellion and the battle of Sedgemoor and all that they led to continue to linger. Today there are probably, it has been estimated, over a million descendants of the rebels of 1685,[41] the great majority of them doubtless unaware of their forefathers' fates, so perhaps little by little memories do fade.

It is some indication of the blessed fortune of England that we should be in a position to commemorate the tercentennial of the last battle to be fought on our native soil. No other country of the developed world can make such a proud claim, and we must fervently hope – and ensure – that this record will never be broken in the future. That, when all is said and done, is the real lesson of the events of 1685 in the West.

Chapter Four
NOTES AND SOURCES

1 See p. 133–5 for Wheeler's full account of his experiences on 6 July.
2 Hence the entry in the Churchwarden's Accounts for repairs. See p. 105. The belief that he escaped from a narrow window has been disproved as it post-dated the battle.

3 As reported by Ailesbury, *Memoirs*, Vol. 1, p. 213. He was, however, a noted Whig, who lost few opportunities to attack the reputation of James II and his army.

4 The sword was presented to the Blake Museum in Bridgwater by the last direct descendant of Mary Deare, and may still be seen there with other relics of the time.

5 Paschall's second account, *op.cit.*, p. xxxv. For the condensed version, see p. 105–10.

6 'Misier' is probably a reference to 'Mezieres'. Nothing else is known of this officer. 'Weston' is of course 'Westonzoyland'. Although the battle was in fact fought on Langmoor, it became known as Sedgemoor as this was the name of the overall area.

7 Dummer – see p. 130.

8 See D. G. Chandler, *Marlborough as a Military Commander* (London, 1973), p. 21.

9 The stump of the tree, with a small brass plate, is still to be seen.

10 Ailesbury, *op.cit.*, Vol. 1 p. 119.

11 Wade, *op.cit.*, f.281 (rear).

12 The full account of Wade's capture is in Rev. Thomas Axe's papers, Harleian MSS. 6845, f.260 et seq. (British Library).

13 As recounted to W. MacDonald Wigfield; see *The Monmouth Rebellion*, p. 77.

14 W. Prime, *Remarkable Passages in the Life of William Kiffin* (London, 1823), p. 147.

15 Sloane MSS. 4194, f.404 (British Library).

16 W. Turner, *James II* (London, n.d.), p. 279.

17 Ailesbury, *op.cit.*, Vol. 1, p. 120.

18 Alan Fea, *King Monmouth* (London, 1902), p. 366. But also see Appendix D below.

19 Monmouth's dying speech is given in *The Oxford Book of English Talk* (Oxford, 1956).

20 Ailesbury, *op.cit.*, Vol. 1, p. 120, who, however, gives the date wrongly as 16 July.

21 W. MacDonald Wigfield, *op.cit.*, Chapter 10 *passim*. His new work names and identifies the rebels.

22 *ibid.*, p. 76 and fn 20 (p. 130).

23 See entry in the *Dictionary of National Biography*, Vol. 29, p. 277. This erroneously gives Jeffreys's dates as 1648–1689. In fact he was born in 1644.

24 Ailesbury, *op.cit.*, Vol. 1, p. 121.

25 A good account of this trial is in M. Hardwick, *The Verdict of the Court* (London, 1964) pp. 35–63 and 86–9.

26 Hardwick, *op.cit.*, p. 62, citing Hansard's *State Trials* Vol. 2 and J. G. Muddiman, *The Bloody Assizes* (London, 1929), p. 28.

27 Hardwick, *op.cit.*, p. 61.

28 *Calendar of State Papers (Domestic)*, 5 September 1685 (Public Records Office).

29 See Appendix C for an analysis of these aspects and of transportation.

30 Lord Jeffreys Report, Add. MSS. 90,337 (British Library); and see W. Mac-Donald Wigfield *op.cit.*, pp. 82–95 and P. Earle, *op.cit.*, pp. 161–187, for good modern analyses.

31 Aylesbury, *op.cit.*, Vol. 1, p. 121.

32 *ibid.*, Vol. 1, p. 122.

33 W. MacDonald Wigfield, *op.cit.*, pp. 111–13.

34 'Redlegs – Myth and Reality', an article by Jill Shepherd in *The West Indies Chronicle*, May 1974, pp. 144–5, is particularly interesting on the overall picture.

35 See Peter Earle, *op.cit.*, pp. 156–60.

36 B. Little, *The Monmouth Episode*, *op.cit.*, p. 239.

37 See p. 106.
38 Ailesbury, *op.cit.*, Vol. 1, p. 103.
39 John Dryden, *Hind and Panther*, Part II, lines 654 et seq. See *Dryden's Poetical Works*, ed. W. D. Christie (London 1874), p. 252.
40 Modern ballad based upon a seventeenth-century lament.
41 *The Harbinger – News from the County of Somerset* (ed. R. Gouldsworthy), No. 2, July 1984, p. 1, reporting the Rebel Ancestry Tracing Service of Sherborne and Taunton.

PART TWO

5

Contemporary Witnesses

The historian seeking to cast new light on a subject of the past places his greatest reliance on various sources of documentary evidence of contemporary origin. First come records of various types – letters, official reports, documents of all kinds. These primary sources are supported by the examination of as many contemporary descriptive accounts by participants or eye-witnesses as can be discovered. The official records are inevitably vital to establish the basic facts whenever this is possible, and the further one goes back in time the more difficult this tends to prove. Contemporary accounts are of the greatest importance if the atmosphere of the time is to be recaptured, and a little life breathed back into long-past events. Of course great care has to be observed in checking such sources for accuracy. With the best will in the world, errors creep in – sometimes blatant ones for political or other purposes, but more often because of human fallibility and lack of complete knowledge. It is well known that two or more witnesses of the same happening will never agree on every detail of what they saw – and the longer the time that elapses between an event taking place and the evidence of spectators being formally recorded, the greater the number of inaccuracies, disagreements and distortions will become.

This is certainly the case with history, which has been well described by an eminent Dutch historian as 'an argument without end'. In that lies much of the subject's attraction – and also a great deal of the frustration it can engender.

Here, however, we are concerned to illustrate a selection of contemporary evidence relating to the Revolt in the West in general and the battle of Sedgemoor in particular. Most of the extracts that follow were written within a short period of the events described – one or two within a couple of days, but a few are impossible to date with absolute accuracy.

To illustrate the official documentation, we begin with an extract from the *London Gazette*, covering a bulletin issued from Whitehall in the early days of the rebellion. Although there were still no newspapers as such, the *Gazette* and various news-sheets were reasonably widely circulated to local government officials and for public consumption to coffee-houses and taverns. As a government source of information, the *Gazette* was not above being used for dissemination of official propaganda as well as hard facts – as the reference to the 'loyal' citizens of Bristol makes clear. This is followed by two Proclamations – Monmouth's of 20 June and James II's of a week earlier.

So much for Court-inspired evidence, based on the reports of Lords Lieutenant, Justices of the Peace, government agents and official pronouncements. At the other end of the spectrum – but no less interesting for that – come the records maintained by village church wardens. To represent these, we reproduce entries from the St Mary's, Westonzoyland, Parish Register and extracts from the Church Wardens' Account Book for 1685 and 1686. Here is the small, incidental detail of history – the day-to-day repairs and disbursements to the bell-ringers on special occasions grimly interspersed with entries concerning the fumigation of the church once the 300-or-so prisoners incarcerated there after Sedgemoor had been removed elsewhere to await trial at the hands of the feared Judge Jeffreys during the Bloody Assize. This entry is a telling comment on the horrors of those insanitary times – and gives some slight idea of the sufferings the captives underwent awaiting their fate. The following year we have a glimpse of King James II's visit to view the battlefield, with plank bridges being set up over the 'broad ryne' (presumably the Bussex Rhine) to facilitate the royal tour's progress. We know from other sources that the King was accompanied by Major Wade, who had commanded the Red Regiment in action so effectively, and who subsequently, following his capture, turned King's Evidence and thereby earned a royal pardon. Of this visit the relevant *London Gazette* records under 'Bridgwater. Aug. 27' that 'His Majesty parted from Bristol about six this morning. About 5 this afternoon his Majesty arrived here viewing in his passage Weston Moor. The Mayor and Aldermen of this place [i.e. Bridgwater], in their formalities [or robes], attended his Majesty, and the people followed his Majesty with continued acclamations' – as well they might, if somewhat anxiously, considering their record in 1685.

As might be expected of seventeenth-century village-folk, the entries are full of misspellings and other inaccuracies. On the other hand, our third contemporary extract – the account of Andrew Paschall, Rector of Chedzoy – is the work of an educated man. The Rev. Mr Paschall wrote his account down a day or so after the battle, and sent it, together with a surprisingly good sketch map, to a friend in London. Later on he wrote a second, longer account, which is preserved in the British Library, but it is his original document that is reproduced here. Paschall was a loyal subject of King James II, and did all he could to keep his parishioners from joining the revolt: and it would seem with some success. He did not spend the night of the battle with his flock at Chedzoy, however, but prudently moved with his family to Honiton. Next evening, however, he was back in his own village, questioning his parishioners, who had, some of them, watched events from a neighbouring windmill. The Paschall narrative is particularly interesting and vivid. It was discovered in an ancient deed-box at Hoare's Bank in the City of London earlier this century, and is a most valuable piece of evidence. Some of the additional points in the fuller version have been incorporated in the chapters forming the first part of this book.

For our fourth contemporary document we go to the furthest imaginable point in the social scale – namely the King himself. James II, however ill-judged many of his policies as monarch, had been a soldier and a sailor of no mean experience during the years of his exile following the execution of his father, Charles I, and clearly preserved the intense curiosity of a professional military man. Accordingly he took great pains to assembly all information on what had transpired during the revolt which had attempted to drive him from his throne. He then wrote down – with a number of gaps where he was not sure of his facts – his own summary of what had taken place at Sedgemoor, basing much of his account on Lord Feversham's reports. He perpetrates at least one error – in ascribing his erring nephew's failure to ignorance of the presence of the Bussex Rhine – a point which has been repeated by many another historian, but in general terms the royal account is as accurate as can reasonably be expected. The King himself admits the problems involved in gaining an accurate impression of what happened in a battle fought under conditions of near-darkness in a dense mist. It is also interesting to note that His Majesty's spelling is not markedly superior to that of his subjects, but then the English of the late seventeenth century was very much a 'living' (or developing) language.

From the King we go on to reproduce 'an Anonymous Account' which was first printed four years after the battle or thereabouts. Although we cannot be absolutely sure, it is highly probable that this was written by Lt. Col. Samuel Venner, the original commander of the Red Regiment in Monmouth's army (under the Duke himself). Samuel Venner was a Cromwellian captain, and possibly a relation of the leader of the Revolt of the Fifth Monarchy Men, who was hanged in 1661. He commanded the rebel foot under Lord Grey at Bridport on 14 June, where he was wounded in the belly. As a result, Menmouth appointed Wade to acting-command of the Red Regiment, and kept Venner on his staff. From what is written in this account – if it was Venner's – it is clear that the author was against Monmouth proclaiming himself King at Taunton, and he clearly became most pessimistic about the outcome of the rebellion, advising the night march to Frome after the 'victory' of Norton St Philip, and then advising Monmouth to abandon his army and retire back to Holland through Poole. We do know that the Duke for a time agreed to this course of action, and that Venner and a Major Parsons set off forthwith before Monmouth changed his mind again. It was given out that the two men had been sent on a mission to buy arms in Holland – but this was probably a statement designed to dissuade other officers from following their example and leaving the army, in which desertions had begun to spread amongst the ranked file following news of King James II's offer of amnesty. The rest of the 'Anonymous Account' from this point on must be hearsay if it was indeed compiled by Venner – but doubtless he met other escaped rebels who fled after Sedgemoor. The author was clearly not at Sedgemoor, for he states that the royal camp was 'within a mile and a half of the town' [Bridgwater] which was a major miscalculation, and other aspects of his brief description of the battle are confused. On the other hand it is strange that Venner makes no mention of his wound sustained at Bridport, although he was chosen to climb Keynsham church tower when the alarm went up on 25 June, unless his wound had been very slight (as may well have been the case as Wade speaks of his riding off back to Lyme from Bridport after having given the order for a general retreat). At best, then, the evidence as to authorship of this passage is conflicting, but it is clearly by an officer on Monmouth's staff who travelled from Holland with him, helped raise the original troops at Lyme, and played a part at Taunton and Norton St Philip, if not at Sedgemoor. All we can safely say is that the author may have been Venner, who certainly escaped to Holland, returned to England after the Glorious Revolution in 1688, and may have been appointed to Col. Dering's Regiment of Foot in 1691. But this is a case of our having to 'see through a glass darkly'.

By far the best rebel account was Nathaniel Wade's narrative provided for King James – a lengthy document giving a considerable amount of detail. However, owing to its length and to the fact that it was reprinted in full as recently as 1980 in W. MacDonald Wigfield's, *The Monmouth Rebellion: a Social History*, it would clearly be superfluous to reproduce it again here. Nevertheless, Wade has frequently been cited in the earlier chapters of this book.

The next two extracts are by royal soldiers who took an active part in the military operations. Capt. Edward Dummer of the Board of Ordnance is generally considered to have written the best royalist participant's account – which was clearly written for the most part on a daily basis as events unfolded. He is regarded as reliable, but it is clear that he is covering up the flight of the civilian drivers of the artillery train when he claims that 'six of our nearest gunns were with the greatest diligence imaginable advanced' – in fact it was only due to Bishop Mews, as we have seen, that any of the royal guns got into action at Sedgemoor at all. Still, his reticence on this point is understandable. The second account is by an Other Rank – and therefore extremely rare for this period – namely Drummer Adam Wheeler of the Wiltshire Militia. Clearly this part-time soldier was a man of letters – he even tries his hand at some Latin – and so he may have been a schoolmaster. Apart from this account of his experiences in 1685 nothing is known about him, although a man of the same name, possibly his father, is listed in the rate-book of St Edmund's Parish, Salisbury for 1661. In one respect his *Iter Bellicosum* is misleading. Although the days of the week he cites are correct throughout, he is one day out from the start of his account to 30 June. Thus his first Wednesday should be the 17th, not the 16th as in his original text. From Wednesday, 1 July, however, he is quite correct with his dates. The Militia was the ancient constitutional force that drilled one day a month and was often used in the maintenance of law and order and the local enforcement of government edicts. For reasons that become apparent from what he writes, the Militia of the various shires was not particularly highly-regarded as a fighting force by Feversham and Churchill, but Wheeler's account gives every appearance of having been written down at the time or very shortly thereafter and thus it is of some importance as well as overall interest.

Finally in this chapter, we have included a short transcript of part of the most celebrated trial of the Bloody Assize – that of the septuagenarian Dame Alice Lisle, held at Winchester on 27 August 1685. She was tried for giving lodging – in all innocence – to two rebels, John Hickes and Richard Nelthorpe. The full proceedings are to be found in *State Trials*, Vol. II. Here only one series of exchanges is given – between Lord Chief Justice Jeffreys and a witness by the name of James Dunne. Something of the style of Judge Jeffreys's bullying of witnesses comes clearly from this extract, and although this is appalling by any standards it should be understood that in the seventeenth century many judges conducted much of the examination of witnesses from the Bench, and also that Jeffreys was at the time suffering a great deal from a stone in the kidney. Jeffreys duly secured his desired verdict of guilty from the jury, and sentenced Dame Alice to death by burning at the stake. However, he was persuaded with difficulty to grant her five days' respite of execution, and direct appeals to the King resulted in the sentence being commuted, on royal instructions, to death by beheading – and the execution was duly carried out on 2 September. Many another would suffer a similar fate for participation, however minor, in the west country rebellion, but this single extract must suffice to represent the witch-hunt that followed the collapse of the revolt as the King's servants carried out his vengeance with a ruthlessness that still horrifies us 300 years later – and indeed contributed to his loss of his people's trust and thus his throne in 1688.

I. THE CONTEMPORARY VIEW – AS GIVEN IN THE PRESS

THE LONDON GAZETTE

PUBLISHED BY AUTHORITY[1]
From Monday, 22 June to Thursday, 25 June 1685[2]

Whitehall, June 24. The Rebels, according to the last account we have, were about *Glastonbury.* My Lord Churchill observing them very narrowly with part of the Kings Forces; he sent out the 22d. instant a party of 40 Horses from *Langport,* who met a squadron of the Rebels of double the number and beat them into their Camp. The Duke of Albemarle (who hath put three companies into Lyme) was with the Militia of Devon at *Wellington* about five miles from *Taunton.* The Duke of Somerset was with the Militia of that County at Bath. The Duke of Beaufort with the Militia of *Gloucestershire* and some of the adjacent Counties at *Bristol,* where all things were in a very good posture, and the inhabitants very forward and zealous to express their Loyalty to his Majesty.[3]

PROCLAMATION AND COUNTER-PROCLAMATION – THE PROPAGANDA WAR

A. *Monmouth proclaims himself King, Taunton, 20 June 1685* (Harleian Mss 7006, B.Lib.)
Whereas, upon the decease of our Sovereign Lord, Charles the Second, late King of England &c., the right of succession to the Crown of England, Scotland, France and Ireland, with the dominions

---

[1] *The London Gazette* was (and still is) the official organ for announcing government news of importance. It would have been circulated to cities and towns, and copies would be consulted in the inns and public houses.
[2] These dates are Old Style – i.e. not of the modern form of the calendar. 'Old Style' dates were ten days earlier in the seventeenth century – i.e. 24 June (NS) was 14 June (OS).
[3] In fact Bristol had a large 'disaffected' party – hence Feversham's eagerness to reach it with regular troops as early as possible. It later received a visitation from Judge Jeffreys, and it was no coincidence that the 'repentant' Major Nathaniel Wade, late of the Red Regiment of Monmouth's army, was appointed Town Clerk from 1687.

and territories thereunto belonging, did legally descend and devolve upon the most illustrious and high-born Prince, James, Duke of Monmouth, son and heir apparent to the said King Charles the Second; but James Duke of York (taking the advantage of the absence of the said James Duke of Monmouth beyond the seas)[1] did first cause the said late King to be Poysoned, and immediately thereupon did usurp and invade the Crown, and doth continue so to do. We, therefore, the noblemen, gentlemen[2] and Commons at present assembled, in the names of ourselves and of all the loyal and Protestant noblemen, gentlemen, and Commons of England, in pursuance of our duty and allegiance, and for the delivering of the Kingdome from popery, tyranny and oppression, do recognise, publish, and proclaim the said high and mighty Prince James Duke of Monmouth, our lawful and rightful sovereign and king, by the name of James the Second[3], by the Grace of God, King of England, Scotland, France and Ireland, Defender of the Faith, &c. God save the King.

B. *The Government's Proclamation of 13 June 1685, Denouncing Monmouth's Invasion*

By the King – a Proclamation . . .

Whereas we have received certain information that James Duke of Monmouth, Ford, late Lord Grey outlawed for High Treason, with divers other traitors and outlaws, are lately landed in a hostile manner at Lyme in our County of Dorset, and have possessed themselves of our said Town of Lyme. And have sent and dispersed some of the traitorous complices[4] into the neighbouring countreys to incite them to join in open rebellion against us;

We do hereby, with the advice of our Privy Council, declare and publish the said James Duke of Monmouth and all his complices, adherents, abettors and advisers to be Traitors and Rebels. And so command and require all our Lieutenants[5], Deputy Lieutenants, Justices of the Peace, Mayors, Sheriffs and all other our Officers, Civil and Military, to use their utmost endeavours to seize and apprehend the said James, Duke of Monmouth, Ford, late Lord Grey, and all their said confederates and adherents. And all and every other persons that shall be aiding and abetting the aforesaid Traitors and Rebels; and the

---

[1] Monmouth was in disgrace for complicity in the Rye House Plot.
[2] In fact Monmouth had only a single nobleman, Grey, and very few gentry in his party.
[3] The obvious confusion with his uncle, the crowned King, caused the rebels to call their leader 'King Monmouth'.
[4] i.e. accomplices.
[5] i.e. Lords Lieutenant – the senior royal officials in the counties and shires, who commanded the militia.

said persons and every of them to secure until Our further Pleasure be known, as they will answer the contrary at their utmost peril.

Given at our Court of Whitehall this 13th day of June 1685 and in the First year of our Reign.

JAMES R.   God Save the King.

II. WESTON ZOYLAND CHURCH RECORDS

A. Extract from the *Parish Register* (as reprinted in *Somerset & Dorset Notes & Queries* Vol. XIX, Part clxii). On the last page of the Baptisms, Weddings and Burials Register which begins in 1682 is the following, some of it faded and rubbed:

'Ann account of the ffight that was in Langmore[1] the six of July 1685 between the King's Army and the D. of M (text obscure)

'The Jniadgement[2] began between one and two of the Clock in the morninge. It contineued near one Hour and halfe. Their was kild upon the spott of the King's souldiers sixtenn: ffive of them Buried in the Church: The rest in the Church yeard: and they had all Christian Buriall. One Hundred or more of the King's Souldiers wounded of wch. wounds many died: of wch. wee have no certaine account. Theire was kild of the Rebils upon the spott about 300: Hanged with us: 22[3]: of which 4 weare Hanged in Gemmacess[4]: About 500 prisoners brought into our Church, of wch. there was 79 wounded and :5: Of them died of thire wounds in our Church.

'The D. of M. beheaded July : 15 : A.D. : 1685.'

There is no signature for this entry, although elsewhere in the Register the entries are attested by

'Tho. Perratt   Vicar.

Thomas Croker
Richard Alford   Churchwardens.'

[1] Langmoor was technically the correct description of the battlefield; but the overall area and especially that east of Westonzoyland was known as King's Sedgemoor – hence the derivation of the battle's name.

[2] i.e. Judgement – a reflection of the ancient belief that 'trial by combat' or battle revealed God's will or judgement on the rival causes and participants.

[3] Some commentators have used this phrase to assert that some rebels were hanged from the Church-tower of St Mary's. This is unlikely. It appears that a number were executed on trees adjoining the churchyard – and probably as many as twenty-two in all were hanged in the village area (hence 'with us'). Had executions taken place within the church or from its tower, reconsecration would have been necessary, and of this there is no mention in the church records.

[4] i.e. in irons or fetters; it was the practice at the time to leave such malefactors or victims to rot where they hung as a dire warning to others.

There is a claim that the passage was written by Richard Alford.[1] A native of Westonzoyland who lived from 1641 until 1693, it seems that he was a cousin of Gregory Alford, Mayor of Lyme Regis at the time of Monmouth's landing in June 1685, whose famous ride to Honiton to give the alarm has already been mentioned.

B. Extracts from the *Church Wardens' Account Book*, which is incomplete, and runs from 1669 to 1752. Many pages are missing, but fortunately the entries for 1685 have survived intact. It is important to note that entries were made retrospectively at the end of the year without strict attention to correct chronological sequence, and that few are dated.

ENTRIES. THE YEAR OF SEDGEMOOR. 1685.

Expended upon the ringers the 10th of February being the day King James was proclaimed (Charles II died Feb. 6)	o	8	o
Paid for the King's pocklamason [proclamation] and frame	o	1	o
Paid the apparrator ffor bring of the procklaem	o	1	o
Expended upon Middellsoy parish [indistinct] when they went through Weston a prison [indistinct]	o	2	6
Expended the 29th May upon the ringers[2]	o	7	6
Expended when Monmouth was taken upon the Ringers	o	8	8
Paid Ben Page ffor mending a seat in the church	o	1	6
Paid Andrew Newman for mending of the Clocke and righting of the Key of the North Dore[3]	o	1	9
Paid Ben Page ffor laying of the stones in the Church[4]	o	5	o
Paid John Jones and Andrew Elroy ffor cleansing of the Church	o	10	6
Expended upon the ringers this Crounnason day being the 23 day of Aprill	o	17	6
Paid ffor ffranckenssence and peivey and resson[5] and other things to burn in the Church after the prissoners was gon out	o	5	8
Expended upon the day of . . . (erased) Thanks given after the ffight upon the ringers	o	11	8
Expended when we viewed the winddows wither John Fransis had done his werks well	o	o	6
Paid John Fransis ffor 10 Pds of soder[6]	o	10	o

---

[1] *Alford Family Notes* (privately published, 1908). Richard Alford and Laetitia (or Lettice) his wife have a memorial slab in the floor of the nave aisle.
[2] i.e. Oak Apple Day – commemorating Charles II's escape after Worcester.
[3] This may relate to the escape of one Scott through 'the little north door'. See p. 73.
[4] Probably over the five royal soldiers buried within the church.
[5] i.e. saltpetre and resin needed for fumigating the church interior.
[6] i.e. solder.

Paid John Franses 2 dusson and halfe of quarrells ffor mendg. the Church windowes[1]	(no sum given) 1686[2]		
Pd. the appertor for the King's proclaymation[3]	o	I	o
Expendd. upon the ringers the 6 of July in remembrance of the great deliverance wee had upon that day in the year 1685	o	7	o
Pd. Ben Page, John Keyser, Thomas Cole, James Somers [indistinct] and John Tugbeard ffor ringing when the King was in the more[4]	o	5	o
Pd. ffor writting our presentmt.[5] at Bridgwater when the King's Commis. was there	o	I	6
Pd. Richard Cole, Antho. Evens and James Somers taking up the planks wh. was laid over brod ryne when the King was in the more	o	5	o
Expended then in beere on the next day when the King came through Weston[6]	o	8	10
Pd. Rich. Hoared (indistinct) ffor carrying the planxes down to broad ryne	o	I	o

III. THE NARRATIVE OF ANDREW PASCHALL, RECTOR OF CHEDZOY, 6 JULY 1685

AN ACCOUNT OF THE D. MONMOUTH'S LANDING & HIS SUCCESS

The Duke of Monmouth landed at Lyme in Dorset with 82 men, Thursday June 11, 1685, at night. He ordered his affairs so in those parts as that he was able to enter in a triumphant manner into Taunton, June 18, being the Thursday following, with an army of about 3,000 men. At Taunton, Saturday, June 20, he was proclaimed 'King' and the next day, Sunday June 21, he marched into Bridgwater with about 5,000 men – armed about 4,000, unarmed about 1,000 – and encamped on the north side in Castle Field. Monday June 22, he marched by Westonzoyland over the moor to Glastonbury, his soldiers boasting that by Saturday night next they would be in London and place the

[1] It would appear that the church had sustained some damage during the battle and its aftermath.
[2] Entries with a bearing on the events of the previous year have been extracted.
[3] The Declaration of Indulgence granting pardon to unapprehended rebels on 10 Jan. 1686.
[4] James II visited the battlefield on 27 August 1686.
[5] Each village throughout the West was required to list absentees on 6 July 1685.
[6] Presumably on his way from Bridgwater to Taunton on 18 August OS (or 28th NS). The village was clearly and understandably keen to demonstrate its unswerving loyalty.

'King' upon his throne. But, the difficulties which he met in his motions eastward, and the hopes he had of great additions from the Clubmen[1] rising in the Marsh Country, gave the occasion of his return to Glaston.; and thence by Westonzoyland back to Bridgwr. into which town he came Thursday July 2. He was about to fortify that place, and to that purpose summoned in Pioneers, but the townsmen disapproving it, he desisted and dismissed the countrymen.

On Sunday July 5, the King's army, consisting of about 4,000 in all, marched from Somerton. About noon they encamped in Zog, in the parish of Chedzoy under Westonzoyland. Two thousand lodge in the camp, 500 horse quarter in the town, 1,500 militiamen quarter in Middlezoy and Othery. Benjamin Newton[2] of Bridgwater parish, sees the manner of their encamping, goes into the town to the Duke of Monmouth, tells him all, gives account of the way through Northmoor and had a guinea for his pains. The Duke forthwith goes up to the church tower[3], there spends a considerable time viewing all with a perspective glass. He calls a Council of War and, with consent, in the evening he marches forth, the townsmen being unwilling he should stay there, as fearing the King's army would fire down the town. He did not take the nearest way to Westonzoyland, by which he went June 22 and returned July 2, but he took the Long Causeway in which way, some being in the trees and hedges by, heard him animating his men with great zeal. He left the way through Chedzoy by the Short Causeway, though that was the nearer and more convenient; probably that was to avoid the danger of being discovered. But he went by Bradney Lane, which lane he also soon left to avoid being too near to a loyal man's house, as thought likely, so by Marsh Lane which is further about and less commodious, he led his army into Northmoor[4].

About sunset a party of the King's Horse[5] came to Langmoor Stone from the camp, and taking with them the Guard there (about 12 or 16 Horse) went by Northmoor into Bawdrip and afterwards up the hill towards Bristol road. They passed the Long Causeway to Bridgwater's town's end and so round the next way to Westonzoyland. While they were about Bawdrip, the Duke's army marched into Northmoor with great silence, standing still till the Guard party of horse[6] was gone, for they were within view of them. This party is supposed to be Colonel Oglethorpe's.

[1] Local bands of countrymen who clubbed together for mutual protection.
[2] Other accounts call him Godfrey, a servant of one Sparke.
[3] Of St Mary's church, Bridgwater. The turret is still there.
[4] By way of Peasy Farm.
[5] In fact this confuses Compton's patrol (Chedzoy) with Oglethorpe's Blues riding through Bawdrip.
[6] Col. Oglethorpe at the head of the main body of the Blues.

About midnight (probably while the Duke of Monmouth was in Northmoor) another party of the King's Horse came from Zog (tis said the Lord General rode with this party)[1] by Langmoor stone and step stones to Parchey Gate, so they marched quite through Chedzoy and round, as is supposed, to the camp again, yet though they were so near to the enemy marching towards the King's Army, those Horse made no discovery of them. Guards and sentinels were placed in the avenues in and about the nearer way from Westonzoyland to Bridgwater and in the other and farther way about by which the enemy designed to come. But all were gone (particularly that most necessary guard at Langmoor Stone and the sentinels that stood near it) before bedtime.[2] A watch of eight Chedzoy men was set at Chedzoy Crossing. Two persons (friends to the Duke) who had seen his army march as far as Bradney came and told them that the army was marching and that there would be a fight and said they were going in haste that nearest way to the mill to see it. But these men in the watch, whether thinking it might be too late for them to go with safety to give notice to the camp; or from country dullness and slowness, did not, as they might and ought to have done, inform the Royal Army of the extreme danger in which it then was.

The King's Camp in Zog consisting of five regiments – the Scots, the King's, Lord Grafton, Colonel Trelawney, Colonel Kirke[3] was at rest in the tents, the muskets and pikes standing up against them. The Lord General was on his campaign bed set up in the parlour at Weston Court. Col. Kirke lodged in the Vicarage; Bishop of Winchester Peter Mews at one Baker's house; the 500 Horse in the town; the 1,500 militiamen in neighbouring parishes. Countrymen, hearing that the Duke was moving, informed divers of the officers and of the King's soldiers of it. J. W. avers that he himself spoke of it to above 500 of them but none would believe it. While those lay there in security[4] and utmost danger, the Duke placed his 42 wagons in Bristol road with orders to drive on towards Axbridge when they would hear the guns. He then leads his army through the by-lands into Northmoor. He committed 500 horse to the Lord Grey with this design: they should march about quarter of an hour before the main body of the army directly to the Upper Plungeon[5] and, in going over, they should silently get up behind the camp, seize the officers in their beds as also

[1] In fact Feversham was at dinner with Bishop Peter Mews in Westonzoyland, but later he inspected his outposts.
[2] Probably sun-down in the countryside. 'To bed with the sun, to rise with the lark'.
[3] Royal Scots, 1st Guards, 2nd Guards, the Queen's Regiment, North Lancashire Regt.
[4] i.e. insecurely.
[5] One of two crossing places over the Bussex Rhine.

1. James Scott, Duke of Monmouth and Buccleuch

2. James II

3. Monmouth depicted on horseback at a battle, reputed to be Sedgemoor but probably one of the engagements he attended when serving as a young man with Louis XIV.

4. Ford, Lord Grey, who commanded Monmouth's cavalry at Sedgemoor and later cheated the executioner by compounding for a large sum.

5. Henrietta Maria, Lady Wentworth, Monmouth's mistress

6. John Churchill, the future Duke of Marlborough, who as Feversham's second-in-command distinguished himself at Sedgemoor.

7. Louis Duras, Earl of Feversham, the French-born soldier who commanded the Royal Army during the Campaign in the West.

8. Monmouth's pocket book, showing the damaged cover and a page describing a cure for 'The Bloody Fluxe'.

boile them together to the thi-
-ckeneß of a salve and lay it on
so hot as you can suffer it.

For the Bloody
    Fluxe.

Take beane flower minglit
w:th Malmsey and make a
yeast therof and beake it
in an ouen like a Cake
but not to hard, and lea i
upon the navel of the belly
as hot as it can be suffer'd
and wet it over w:th Malmsey
and kepe it warme. it
will help in three days.

The late D. of M. & other Rebells taking shipping for England

Two of y Rebells Ships laden with Powder & Armes taken at Lime by Cap! Trevanion

9. Some of the playing cards printed in 1685 which depict scenes from the ill-fated rebellion of Monmouth and Argyle

Rebells Marching out of Lime

the godly Maids of Taunton presenting their Colours upon their knees to y D. of M.

10. More of the 1685 playing cards

ESTONZOYLAND FROM THE LEVEL

11. Two postcards, probably published in the 1920's, which show the battlefield of
Sedgemoor much as it must have appeared in 1685.

E. SEDGEMOOR BATTLEFIELD WESTONZOYLAND

12. The Coldstream Guards c. 1680

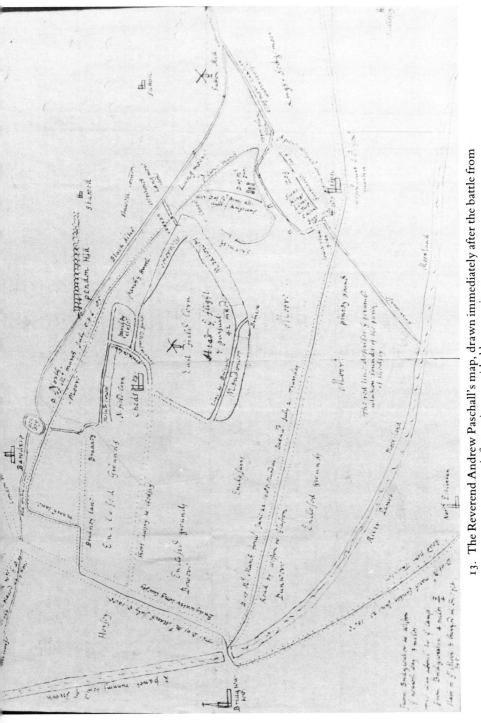

13. The Reverend Andrew Paschall's map, drawn immediately after the battle from information provided by eye witnesses.

14. Monmouth's letter to the Queen, Mary of Modena, begging her to intercede for his life.

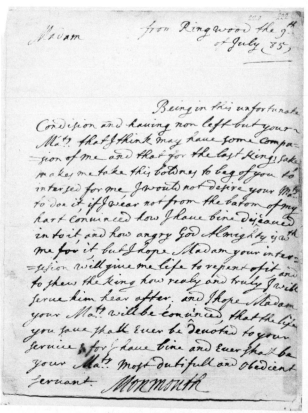

15. Monmouth prostrates himself before an unmoved James II.

16. Judge Jeffreys; handsome, able, but suffering acute pain from a kidney stone throughout the Bloody Assizes.

18. The treachery of Colonel Kirke. A Victorian version of the story, almost certainly apocryphal, that Kirke demands a young maiden's virtue in return for her rebel father's life, only for the wretched girl to discover next morning that her father's body is hanging outside the window.

17. Kirke's 'lambs' arrest Dame Alice Lisle for harbouring rebels in her home.

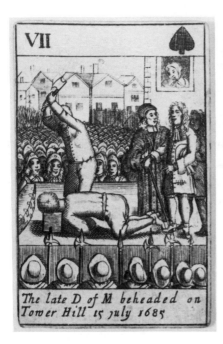

The late D of M beheaded on
Tower Hill 15 july 1685

Severall Rebells tryed
in the West.

19. More of the 1685 playing cards

Major Holmes and 2 other
Rebells Hanged in Chaines

Bonfires made the 26 of Iuly
att night being the thanksgiving
for the Victory 1685

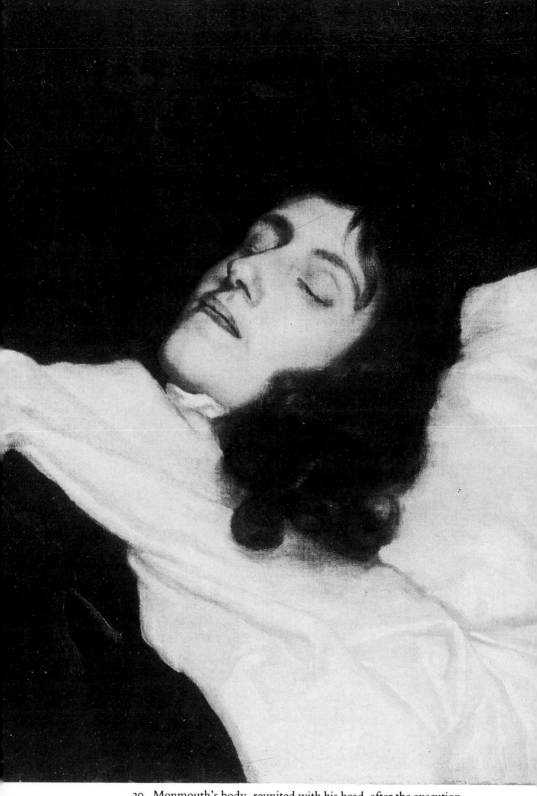

20. Monmouth's body, reunited with his head, after the execution.

the 18 guns and 160 wagons standing all together and, if occasion were, turn the guns, as they might have done easily, upon the King's Camp and thus give them a terrible alarm on that side. The known ways being very convenient for doing all this.

While all this was to be in the doing, the Duke, with the body of his army, was to make the onset. These were commanded to march with all possible silence. Their first orders were to fire and run over the ditch[1] within which the camp was, it being presumed that the Lord Grey with his 500 Horse would have drawn the army in the camp into the town, by the alarm designed to be given from thence. When all this was just putting into execution and the Duke's army was marching after midnight into Langmoor with great silence, a pistol was discharged about step stones or Langmoor Stone. Immediately an 'unknown' trooper rides from that place-ward full speed to the camp, calls with all imaginable earnestness, 20 times at least, 'Beat your drums, the enemy is come. For the Lord's sake, beat your drums.' He then rode back with the like speed the same way he came. Among some of the King's soldiers, particularly the Scots, there was expectation of the enemy before this, yet all continued quiet. Now the drums beat, the drummers are running to it, even bare-foot for haste. All fly to arms. All are drawn out of their tents and in five battalions stand in the space between the tents and the ditch, fronting the ditch, not having their clothes or arms all on and ready. Thus were they expecting the enemy.

The Lord Grey, with his 500 Horse, missed the Upper Plungeon. Falling below it, they marched on by the outside of the ditch, seeking a way over, which was not to be found for the Horse, though the ditch was then dry enough for the foot to have got over. When (these) last were come so far as the Scots Battalion, they were demanded who they were for. They pretend they are friends and from the Duke of Albemarle. They are believed by the Scots and let past. At length they are discovered and fired at, and march off. Those wheeling towards the rear of the Duke's army are fired at by their own with some execution, they supposing them to be the enemy coming from the left wing of the King's Army. Thus a consternation went into the hinder part of the Duke's army which, by the narrowness of the lanes retarding them, were not come up. The front being also somewhat sooner engaged than was intended by reason of the alarm given.

A quarter of an hour after this march[2] of his Horse, the Duke having planted his three guns north of the King's Camp, brings up his army in

---

[1] The Bussex Rhine was clearly dry in the area of Westonzoyland and the Royal Camp.
[2] Or rather flight.

three bodies, two greater, one lesser (which lesser body might be intended to follow the Lord Grey's Horse, if they had gone over the plungeon into Westonzoyland). This lesser body after a time joined itself with one of the greater bodies when, as before, they were commanded to run over the ditch, now they are commanded not to do so upon pain of death.

The assault made was chiefly upon the Scots[1] (of whom 'tis said that the Duke of Monmouth was made to believe that they were disposed to come over to him and this by a drummer who ran from them to him in Bridgwater the night before). The fight was very sharp for about half an hour. At length the Scots (who had but four officers in their regiment of 500 men that were not killed or wounded) were made to give ground. They are seasonably reinforced by three troops of Horse of the King's who are also said to have taken the Duke's three guns.

Three of the King's guns were brought [probably by Bishop Mews][2] at length to the place where the Scots were fighting. They play with case shot[3] which made lines amongst the rebels who were not seconded by their own rear. And now[4] the King's men fortuned to give a shout. 'Tis said the enemy had as great reason to do so, which if they had happened to do, 'tis thought the King's Army had been utterly routed. This was followed immediately with a total rout of the Duke's army.

IV. KING JAMES II's ACCOUNT OF THE BATTLE OF SEDGEMOOR[5]

The D. of Mon. marched from [blank][6] to Bridgwater on the [–] of June,[7] from whence he sent his orders to the neighbouring villages to send in provisions to him, and to send in men with whatever tooles they had, as if he intended to fix there and fortify himself. But whether he designed it then, as tis likely he did, in expectation that there should

[1] Largely because the Royal Scots were posted directly opposite the three guns, and were easy to distinguish in the dark by their glowing matches.

[2] 'Old Patch', a soldier of distinction during the Civil Wars, finding that the civilian horse-team leaders had fled at the start of the battle, reputedly used his own servants and coach-horses to draw the three cannon to the battle line from the extreme left. Maj.-Gen. John Churchill also acted wisely in transferring two battalions from the left of the line to extend the exposed right wing (this is not mentioned by Pascall). Feversham only appeared on the field at about 3 a.m.

[3] Case-shot was canister – musket balls in hessian bags, used for close-range fire.

[4] The proverbial English Army's cheer before charging with the pike and bayonet. The time was approximately 5 a.m.

[5] Punctuation has been adjusted to preserve the sense throughout.

[6] Several blanks appear on the Manuscript. Insertions in square brackets are my own.

[7] The King uses Old Style dating; ten days need to be added to convert to New.

be a rising in London, he sending Major Manley[1] and his Chaplin from thence to the Citty, to call upon his friends to do it; or that he intended by sending those orders to the villages only to make Ld. Feversham beleive he designed it, that he might the better give him the slip, and once again endeaver to gett a Cansham bridge[2] before him, with designe to march towards Cheshire whence he had great hope that many men of estate and quality as well as great numbers of common people would joyne with him; but whether this were so or no, or that he altered his mind after the departure of Mr. Manley is not known, he began to march out of Bridgwater on the [–] of June being [blank], with all his army about three in the afternoon, passing the bridge, and drew them all up in a meadow wth. intention to begin his march for Corsham as soon as it should grow dark in order to his getting into Cheshire. But as his men were passing the bridge, having intelligence that the King's troops were come to Weston that afternoon, and that the foott were camped on the moore just under the village, and the horse quartered in it, and asking the spy[3] if they began to entrench, and being told they did not, wch. being confirmed to him a second time, he altered his mind, and instead of marching Northwards, resolved to attacque Ld. Feversham where he lay, hoping to surprise him, to wch purpose he began to march as it grew night, taking his way about by the head of the moore, leaving Chedzoy on his right hand; hoping by taking that compas[4] to surprise the King's troops, who he believed would not expect him that way, it being also the best way he could take to attaque them the straight way, being a perpetual defile and all. They were very neare the Weston camp to wch. place Ld. Feversham had advanced with the Kings troops, wch. were about 1,800 foott, in six small Battalions and some 700 horse and dragoons on the [blank], leaving the Earl of Pembroke att Middlesee[5] and villages agacent[6], with the militia horse and foot wch. consisted of [–] Regts. of Foott and [–] troops of horse.

The post of Weston was a very well chosen one for such a small body of men, and very secure, the foott being camped with their reare to the village, and had their front covered by a ditch wch. serves for a draine to the moore[7]; and as it was then a dry season was not to be by

[1] Maj. John Manley, who led the cavalry attack on Bridport, was accompanied by his son.
[2] Keynsham.
[3] Godfrey.
[4] i.e. compass or direction.
[5] Middlezoy.
[6] Particularly Othery.
[7] The Bussex Rhine. It is now considered doubtful that Monmouth was wholly unaware of this obstacle; what defeated him was Lord Grey's failure to take the crossing.

past by horse but in one or two places – and t'was this draine deceived the Duke of Monmouth, for he not knowing of it thought the foott lay open, and consequently the whole quarter.

And now Lord Feversham, being advertised that the Rebells army were past over the bridge and drawn up in a meadow by the riverside[1] close by it, juged their designe was to see if they could give them the slip, and gett to Cansham Bridge before him; and because his Horse and Dragoons had been much harrassed by their perpetual marching, [he] thought it best not to draw them out of their quarters, but to lett them remaine there, that they might be the fresher to march after the Rebels the next day, in case they should march northward; but [he] left a garde of one hundred horse commanded by Sir Francis Compton and fifty dragoons upon the moore, the way the Rebels came, wch. had an advance garde and senterys before them to give notice if anything came their way. He placed another garde of fifty horse on the highway wch. comes from Bridgwater, and fifty foot in a sheepfold on the moore to help to make their retreat in case they should be pushed; and to be advertised of the enemy's motion he sent Major Oglethorpe and a part of [–] horse to crosse bothe the roads wch. go toward Bristol and Cansham, that if they were marched that way he might know it, and was out himself[2] till neare one after midnight at the horseguard on the moore towards Chedsea, expecting the return of his party and to heare the noyse of the enemys march in case they did – it being a very still night – and then returned back to his quarters.

In the meane tyme the Rebells were marching, and the Oglethorpe crost both the roads, as he was ordered, beyond the end of the moore. He fell not into their march they not coming quit as far as he was, nor did he heare them; and so returning back in the moore went through Chedsea and crost to the other road which goes from Bridgwater to Weston; and halting there within half a mile of that towne sent fower horsemen to go if they could as far as a barricade that was neare the bridge. The sentinel challenging them, they pretended to be of their men, and answered 'Monmouth' and then asked where he was. He replyed was marched with the whole army and had left only a gard there. Upon wch. they returned back to their party, and Oglethorpe made what hast he could back to the Camp to give notice of it. In the meane tyme the D. of Mon. was upon his march towards Weston, taking the compas, as I have already said, by the waye of the moore, and ordered what bagage and carriges he had[3] with a small garde, when he turned off into the moore to go on the roade to Axbridg, and to stay there till further orders and continued his march to attaque the

[1] Into Castle Field, having crossed the River Parrett.
[2] i.e. on the ground inspecting outposts.
[3] The Rebel Army had some 127 waggons; it also detached a fourth gun.

King's troops. He had two defiles[1] to passe after he was in the moore –
the one presently after he came on it and the other about a mile from
the camp. He drew up in two collomns after he had past the first, the
foot on the right and the horse on the left, and so marched till he came
to the seconde. There his Horse past over first wch. were some eight
squadrons; his canon wch. were but three small iron gunns marched
over after them at the head of the Foott, wch. consisted of five great
Battallions, each of wch. had one Company of at least 200 sythmen[2]
instead of Granadiers.

The Horse was commanded by Ld. Grey, with the title of Lt. Genll.
The first Reg. of Foot by Wade, Lt. Col. to the D. of Mons own Reg;
Matthews commanded the next, then Holmes, Bussett and Foulks. As
they were passing the last defile, the advanced sentery of the horse
guard discovered them and galoped back to advertise Sir Fr. Compton
of it, who immediately gave the allarum to the Camp, and stayd in his
post till he received a faint charge from an advanced party of some of
the Rebels Horse, who after having fired their carbines[3] and received
some shott from his party, went off, on their side, and he drew back to
the camp on the right hand of our foott behind the ditch.[4] Whilst this
past, the D. of Mon. hearing the allarum was given the men in the
Kings Camp, ordered Ld. Grey to march fast on with the Horse to fall
in amongst the tents of the foott, and to take them by the flanke, not
knowing anything of the ditch wch. covered them;[5] and told him he
would march after him with the foott as fast as he could. And now in
the Camp so soone as they had the allarum, the foott stand to their
armes, and were in a moment drawn up in battele[6] at the head of their
tents in very good order, and the Horse were drawing out of the
village as fast as they could. The foot were in six battalions, the first on
the right was comprised of five companies of Dumb.[7] one of wch.
were granadeers,[8] commanded by L. Col. Douglas; next to wch. were
two Batt. of the first Reg. of Gards of six comp. in each being one
Comp of Gran. of that Reg. At the head of the first of wch. was the D.
of Grafton, their Col., and Eaton the Major of it was at the head of the
other. Next to them was a Batt of the second Reg. of G. of six comp.
and another of Gran., at whose head was L. Col. Sackfeild. Then five

[1] i.e. narrow bottlenecks: the second was the need to cross the Langmoor Rhyne.
[2] Rebels with scythe-blades affixed to poles.
[3] A carbine was a shortened form of musket, used by mounted troops.
[4] i.e. to the Upper Plungeon or cattle crossing.
[5] This is unlikely as Monmouth had twice marched near Westonzoyland on earlier
days.
[6] i.e. in line of battle.
[7] Dumbarton.
[8] Grenadiers were elite troops armed with hand-grenades and axes as well as muskets,
bayonets and swords. One company was attached to each regiment of foot.

comp. of Trelawny, one of wch were Gran, comm. by L. Col. Churchill. On the left of all was another such Batt composed as the former, com. by Col. Kirke. As for the Horse, there were 150 commanded out of the the three troops of [Life] Gards, and sixty Gran. on Horseback com. by [blank] Villars; seven troops of the Kings Reg. of Horse and fower of Dragoons, the Horse com, by Sir F. Compton and the Drags. by Ld. Cornbury, one of which last was at Lanport com. by Cap. Coy to secure that passe and to gett intelligence in case the Reb. should march Westward. The Traine of Artillery consisted of sixteen feild pieces under the Conduct. Mr. Sheirs.

And now whilst the Kings Horse were getting into order, the Reb. Horse in persuance of the orders they had received marched on to put them in execution, and meetting with the ditch came along by it; and being chalenged by Douglas who they were, some one answered 'Albemarle', at least he understood it so, and lett them passe without firing at them. Then, coming up to the first Batt. of the Gards, Cap. Berkeley – who comd. the right wing[1] of the musketeers of it, asked who they were for. They answering 'the King' he called to them 'What King?' They answered 'Monmouth and God with us', wch. was their [pass-]word. He then sayd 'Take this with you!' and made his wing fire at them. So did the other wing of that Batt. as also the next Batt. of the same Reg. and half that of the 2 Reg. of G, upon wch. that party of the Reb. Horse ran away, leaving some of their men and horses on the ground by the fire they had received. But to this day it was not known certainly whether twas only part or ther whole Horse[2] that came up to the ditch, or whether it was part of them or a fresh party of them wch. were charged some tyme after by a party of our Horse.

As this happened, Ld. Feversham, that had been agetting the Horse in order[3], and sent for the cannon, came to the Foott and ordered them to keep their fire till the enemy came closse up to them. Some [time] after this the Reb. Foott came up, but not in good order, for the D. of Mon, would not stay, after they had past the last defille, to draw up in line of Battalle, but made them march on in their ordinary way of marching, Batt. after Batt., guiding them by the matches[4] of Douglas (wch. was the only Batt. of the Kings Foott had matchlocks), as soon as they came in sight of the camp, and did not begin to forme their Batt. till they came within about 80 paces of the ditch, intending to come as their line was drawn up to have attaqued the Kings Foott. But according to the account Lt. Col. Wade has given, before the three first

[1] A regiment drew up in two 'wings' of musketeers with the 'body' of pikes between.
[2] It was the great majority.
[3] i.e. preparing the cavalry to attack over the Bussex Plungeons.
[4] Used to fire matchlock muskets.

were quite gott up upon line, he being the right hand batt., Mathews, wch. was the next to him, without orders from their commander began to fire; then his and Holmes's, wch. was on Mathews left, did the like. After wch. they could never make their men advance one foott, but stood firing as they were. And then they thought that their right was over against the Kings left, they were mistaken, for the right reached no farther than the first Batt. of the Gards. And then three smal guns were advanced as neare as would be just before the interval wch. was betweene Mathews and Holmes, and were very well plyd[1] and did great execution on Douglas and the first foot Batt. of the gards – wch. two indeed bore all the brunt of the Reb. fire and lost many officers and souldiers, and most of them by the cannon; for tho' the Reb. fired hard, their men, being new, shott to high, and they continued firing at least three quarters of an hour. And except Douglas, who fired a little, the rest never fired a shott but boore the Reb. shott both small and great with great order and stedynesse. Only the Kings cannon wch. came sone up[2] in the intervals of the Batt. played the Reb. very hard, and did good execution.

Tis a hard matter to give a very exact account of such an action as this, wch. began in the night and was ended by break of day, and to do right to all the General officers and other commanders, who behaved themselves with great steadynesse and resolution in their severall posts and stations, as appeared by the success they had. Whilst this was passing bettweene the Foott, Ld. Feversham ordered Villars with all the Horse Gards and Gran. on Horseback (except that party of them wch. had been out with Oglethorp), Cap. Aderly's troop of Horse and one troop of Drag., to passe over the ditch on the left of the Foott[3] and to draw up on the enemys right – but not to charge them. And meeting Oglethorp who was but then come back with his party of Gards and Volunteers from towards Bridgwater, and Cap. Upcot, with his small gard of fifty horse, brought them with them behind the Foott to the right. Where, finding the rest of the Horse and Dragoones drawne up in the last next the Foott – and the Horse on the right of all – orderd them to passe over the ditch; and Oglethorp who was with his party over first, mett with a body of the Reb. Horse. What their number was the darknesse of the night and their runing so soone made it not to be known, so that instead of pursuing them they were ordered to halt. And after they had stood some tyme fronting that way, Ld. Feversham ordered them to wheel to the left and to keep their ground, not knowing what was become of all the Reb. Horse – not judging it

---

[1] 'plied'.
[2] No mention of Bishop Mew's part.
[3] By the Lower Plungeon.

proper then to lett them charge their Foott. Only Oglethorp with his party tryed one of their Battalions[1], but was beaten back by them, tho they were mingled amongst them,[2] and had several of his men wounded and knocked off of their horses; amongst wch. number was Cap. Sarsfield who was knocked downe by the butt end of a muskett, and left for dead upon the place.

I forgott to give an account of one thing wch. happened before the Horse and Dragoons past over the ditch – wch. was that Holmes's Batt., firing at the Ld. Cornburys troop of Drag. His Lieut. Warde who was standing by him called out to that Batt. not to fire more at them for that they were friends, wch. they thinging [sic] to be true, did – and not only that but Holmes himself, taking them for friends, came up on horse back from the head of his Batt. to the very ditch behind wch. they stood; and the same Lieu. calling to him, 'Who are you for?' and being answered 'For who but Mon.', the Lieu. and one of the Sergeants fired at him, killed his horse under him and brock his arme – and there he lay. Sone after wch. Lord Churchill passing over the ditch there when that wing past over, seeing him hold up his head as he lay, asked him 'Who art thou?' He answered he was not in a condition to tell, and lay still. But afterwards gott up and was taken by some straggling men amongst the tents of the Foott.

And now, as things were in this condition, Ld. Churchill went to the left of the Ffoot and ordered the two Tangier Batt. to march from their post, there being no enemy against them, and to march behind the other Batt, to draw up on Douglas his right. But as I take it just as they gott thither, the day begining to breake, Ld. Feversham, who was with the Horse on the right, seeing no appearance of any more of the Reb. Horse, and that the pikes of one of their Batt. began to shake and at last open[3], ordered the Ffoot to passe over the ditch to charge them. Wch. they did – wch. the Reb. seeing, ran before they came to bandy blows, and the five comp. of Grans. were ordered to follow the persute, and some of the Horse and Dragoons fell in with them and did execution on them till they gott off of the moore into the enclosures,[4] wch. they sone did, the moore being but eight hundred yards broad in that place from ditch to ditch. And there was the greatest slaughter of the Reb. in that ditch wch was deep and boggy, and in a corn feild wch was on the other side of it; and there they took and gave quarter to about 1200 of them.

As for Mon. himself, he brought up the Foote and then went to his

---

[1] Probably the Blue Regiment of Taunton men.
[2] Usually cavalry amongst men on foot would have a great advantage, but it was dark.
[3] Once the tight bunch of pikes began to waver it was clear the unit was breaking.
[4] 'Chedzey Corn' as marked on Paschall's map.

cannon to see them well plyd, as indeed they were, by a Dutch gunner[1] he had brought over with him. But some tyme after his Horse were all gone, and that Williams a servant of his told him he might see the King's Horse on their flanques, going as he believed to encompass them, he put off his arms, and take one hundred guineas from his servant, left his Ffott still fighting, and went away with Ld Grey (who came to him after his Horse were all disperst or gone), one [blank] a Brandenburger[2] and one or two more, and went up the hill wch. overlooks the moore as you go towards Bristol, and from thence looked about and could see his Ffoott still firing, and continued on his way to the top of the Mendip hills, where he disguised himself, and altering his course took his way towards Ringwood, designing to gett into the new Forest – wch. if he could well have done he looked on himself as safe, Ld. Grey being well acquainted there. And then it would have been easy for him to have found some imbarcation[3] to have carried him beyond sea.

But to return to his beaten troops, Bessetts Batt. suffered the most[4]. They were all of the towne of Taunton, and were for the most part killd or taken. The rest were all dispersed tho' they suffered not so much; only Wade with some two or three hundred Ffoott of his Batt. gott in a body into Bridgwater where he found three of their troops of Horse wch had run away in the night drawn up in good order in the markeyt place com. by Cap. Alexander, Cap. Hucker and one Tucker. At first they would not owne they were beaten to the people of the towne, but after they had consulted a little amongst themselves thought the best they could do for self preservation was to disperse. Wch. they did – every one shifting for himself; so that when Ld. Feaversham, marching towards Bridgwater, sent before him a trumpeter to summon the towne, expecting that those who had escaped from the battel might be rallied there to defend it, found them all gone.[5]

As for the number of the slaine on the Kings side they amounted not in all to above [in margin: Mr. Blath.[6] to give a list] and some [blank] wounded. On the Reb.(side) they lay about two hundred of them dead on the moore; what were slain in the ditch and the enclosures in the persut is very uncertain; they were about [blank] hundreds of them taken, amongst wch. very few officers.

Tis very hard to give an exact relation of such a right peece of

[1] Buyse.
[2] Still unidentified.
[3] i.e. a boat.
[4] The Blue Regiment.
[5] Most accounts say Churchill was first to Bridgewater.
[6] Mr Blathwayt, Secretary-at-War.

surmise as this was, so that tis not to be wondred if one dos not give so particular an account of the behaviour of the Gen. Officers, and indeed of all the officers of the severall bodys of Horse, Foot and Dragoons, who tis certain behaved themselves with great steadyness and temper as well as resolution, and shewd themselves to be old troops; and what difference there is between such and new raised men. And here I cannot chuse but make this remarke, that as God Almighty has been pleased to be some tyme called the Lord of Hosts, as has many and many a tyme made his power to be known upon such occasions as these, and as he commanded Gedion[1] to send away all his army but three hundred chosen men, that the stiff-necked might owne his power, so he has in our days saved from toatal ruine and destruction, with a handfull of men, not only these three Kingdoms but France itself in 1652[2] when nothing but the considerate hand of God could have preserved that Monarchy from being utterly destroyed by rebellious subjects and foraine enemys.

The Kings Account of the Battle of Sedgemoor.[3]

V. AN ANONYMOUS ACCOUNT PRINTED IN 'THE BLOODY ASSIZES'[4]

To begin then, May 24, old style, we left Amsterdam about two of the clock, being Sunday morning, and in a lighter sailed for the Texel, our vessel being sent before us thither, but meeting with extreme cross winds all the way we arrived not till Saturday [30 May] night, and then went all on board. Here our man of war with about 32 guns, where the Duke's person was, was under an arrest by order of the States of Amsterdam, on the complaint of our Envoy, they presuming we had been clear, but we broke through our arrest,[5] and Sunday morning [31 May] at break of day set sail for England. We had in all three ships; that of 32 guns carried most of our men, the other two were for our ammunition. We met with exceeding cross winds, most part of the

---

[1] Gideon.

[2] A reference to the two *Frondes* – risings against the infant Louis XIV. It is curious that King James placed this piece of information at the end of his account of Sedgemoor – evidence of his close association with France.

[3] On the spine of the document.

[4] This short 'Anonymous Account' first appeared in a book entitled *The Protestant Martyrs or the Bloody Assizes* (1689), which went through several editions. The most recent, edited by Muddiman, in 1939, places the narrative between pp. 164 and 170. For a discussion of its probable authorship see the introduction to this chapter. It may well have been written by the rebel Col. Venner after his escape.

[5] An indication of the intrigues around the venture: William of Orange was playing a double game.

time we spent upon the seas and arrived not at Lyme until Thursday, June 11 [OS], so that from Amsterdam to Lyme we wanted but two days of three weeks.[1]

We landed without any the least opposition, and were received with all expressions of joy imaginable. The Duke, as soon as he jumped out of the boat on Land, call'd for silence, and then desir'd we would join with him in returning God thanks for that wonderful preservation we had met with at sea, and accordingly fell on his knees on the sand and was the mouth of us all in a short ejaculation, and then immediately well armed, as many as we were,[2] entered the town.

Friday the whole day was spent in listing of men, which flocked to us so fast that we could scarce tend them with arms.

The like on Saturday also; and then about ten of the clock at night, 300 of our men were sent to Bridport, about six English miles off, to storm that town betimes in the morning [14th, Sunday]; which we did accordingly, taking many prisoners out of their lodgings. And had not our soldiers been a little too eager of plunder, we had made a good day's work on't, but there lying about a wood some of the King's forces, we were forced to retreat, losing three or four men and killing several of theirs and taking eight prisoners. This was the first action that we had.

Sunday also was spent in listing, and Monday morning, but in the afternoon we marched out of Lyme for Axminster, a little town four miles off. Our party was near 2,000 foot and 300 horse, though we landed not full a hundred men. And all these in the space of four days. About two miles from Lyme we espied the Duke of Albemarle, with about 4,000 men, designing that night to quarter in the same town, which we had news of in the way. Yet we marched on in good order and came into the town, lined all the hedges, planted our field pieces and expected nothing more than that we should give 'em battel, they being not an English mile from the town. They made towards us as soon as they heard that we were there, but the Duke of Albemarle finding his men to be all Militia men of the County of Devonshire, and that they had no stomach to fight against Monmouth, retreated when he came within a quarter of an English mile of the town. He came from Exon[3] with these forces, intending to lay a siege against Lyme, presuming we could not be ready in so short a time. But, finding us so well prepared to receive him, he wisely retired, his men being in great disorder and confusion, supposing we had pursued them, which was debated. But the Duke said it was not his business to fight yet, till his

[1] This 19-day delay doomed effective cooperation with Argyle in Scotland.
[2] About 80 in all – see above p. 3.
[3] Exeter.

men had been a little disciplined, but rather to make up into the country as fast as possible, to meet his friends, not questioning but there would have been in several parts of the kingdom some action on the news of his success. But this in the end proved fatal to us, for had we but followed them, we had had all their arms, several more men, and might have marched in two days with little or no opposition, to the very gates of Exon, the country troops resolving not to fight us. And several came to us that night with their arms. But missing this opportunity, we marched to Taunton, lodging at several small towns by the way, which received us as kindly as possible. And all the way met with the loud acclamations of the country praying God to succeed our arms.

Thursday we came to Taunton, about twenty miles from Lyme. To give a particular account of our reception here would be too tedious; the streets so thronged with people, men could scarce enter, all endeavouring to manifest their joy at his coming, and their Houses, doors and streets garnished with green boughs, herbs and flowers, all emblems of prosperity.

The next day, twenty-six gentlewomen, virgins, with colours ready made at the charge of the townsmen,[1] presented them to his grace; the Captain of them went before with a naked sword in one hand, and a small curious bible in the other, which she presented also, making a short speech, at which the Duke was extremely satisfied and assured her, he came now in the field, with a design to defend the truths contained therein and to seal it with his blood, if there should be an occasion for it. Nothing could now content the country but he must be proclaimed king, which he seemed exceeding averse to; and I really am of opinion from his very heart.[2]

They said the reason why the gentry of England moved not was because he came on a Commonwealth principle. This being the cry of all the Army he was forced to yield to it, and accordingly Saturday morning he was proclaimed. In the afternoon, came out three proclamations, one setting a sum of money on the Kings head, as he had done before on the other. The second declaring the Parliament of England a seditious Assembly; and if they did not separate before the end of June, to give power and authority to any that would attempt to lay hold on them as traitors and rebels. The third, to declare the Duke of Albemarle as a traitor (who now lay within six miles of us, having had time to rally his men) if he laid not down his arms. Forthwith also a message was sent to command him; but he sent word that he was a subject to James the Second the late Kings brother and that he knew no other Lord.

[1] The myth has it that they were made from petticoats, but Taunton was a cloth town.
[2] Venner was a staunch republican from Commonwealth days.

We tarried here till Sunday morning [21 June], and then march'd for Bridgwater, seven miles from thence. We were now between four and five thousand men, and had we not wanted arms[1] could have made above ten thousand. We were received here as in other places, but did little more than read our declaration, which we did also in all other towns, the magistrates standing by in their gowns, and likewise our proclamations, and so march'd forward for Glassenbury.[2] From Glassenbury we design'd for Bristol, three days march from that place, designing to attack it. Accordingly we arrived at Cansham-bridge[3] a little town, three miles English from Bristol, intending to enter next morning, the Duke of Beauford[4] being there with a garrison of about four thousand men. Being here lodged in the town we were on a sudden alarm'd with the noise of the approach of the enemy,[5] being in no small confusion on this unexpected news. The Duke sent me up the tower to see whether he could discover them marching. As soon as he came up, he saw them at the very entrance into the town fighting with our men. Here we had a small skirmish, our men being in the fields adjoining to the town, refreshing themselves. But it lasted not long, for before he could bring word, they were fled, being not above sixty horsemen. They did us mischief, killed and wounded about twenty men, whereas we killed none of theirs, only took four prisoners and their horses, and wounded my lord Nubery,[6] that it was thought mortal. They came thither, thinking it had been their own forces, and had not our undisciplined fellows been too eager, and suffer'd 'em to come a little farther on, they would have entered the town, and we must have had every man of them. Their infantry was following, but on their return came not forward. These forces being so near and Bristol being so well mann'd also, the Duke was loth to pass the bridge for Bristol, though some gentlemen that came over with us, and were proscrib'd upon account of the former plot, being Bristol men, and knew the hearts of the townsmen, begg'd him heartily to proceed towards it, offering themselves to go in the head of them into the town, by some private ways which they knew, assuring him they would make no resistance, but we could not persuade him. Which, had we been possessed of, we could not have wanted money nor arms, the only things needful for us in that juncture. For had we but had arms, I am persuaded we had by this time

[1] Many weapons had been left at Lyme Regis, where they were impounded by royal troops.
[2] Glastonbury.
[3] Keynsham.
[4] Beaufort was at the head of the Monmouth and Gloucestershire Militias.
[5] The royal cavalry patrol led by Capt. Parker.
[6] Lord Newbury.

had at least twenty thousand men. And it would not then have been difficult for us to have march'd for London, with the recruit of Bristol, the King not being able to make 7,000 men for the gaining of so many kingdoms. But God saw it not fit for us, and over-ruled our consultations to our own ruin, for this was in the top of our prosperity. And yet, all the while, not a gentleman, more than went over with us, came to our assistance.

So we marched on to Bath [26 June], we lay before it in the afternoon and sent in our trumpeter to demand the town, but they refused to give us entrance,[1] having a strong garrison, it being a stout people, and a strong place. Having no mind to spend time in laying sieges, we march'd that day to a little town called Phillips-Norton and there lay that night, being now Sunday,[2] the 26th of June, old style, Saturday morning [27 June], preparing for Frome, we were drawing out our baggage for the march, and on a sudden were alarmed with the appearance of the enemy, who had entered the town, and had lined all the hedges, and began to fire upon us. Here we began the briskest recounter we yet had, and for an hour or more we had a brisk skirmish, but at last we beat them back, killing about thirty which lay in the place, and we lost about ten in all, and a few wounded. They retreating with their whole army, pitched within a mile of the town. And we went out also, and pitched near them, but out of musket shot, playing canon one on another for some hours. They killed but one man all the while, but with ours we did great execution, having the advantage of the ground. So at last they retreated, and I have been told lost some hundreds of men in the battle, both killed and wounded. So we marched on for Frome, a town where we were as well beloved as at Taunton. Where we wanted for nothing but arms, which were by a stratagem taken from them a few days before our entrance. Here came the unexpected news of Argyle's being defeated and likewise of the advance of the King's forces from London, with considerable baggage and thirty field pieces. On this news, together with our want of money and arms (not seeing which way to avoid these forces) we were at a stand and not a little non-plus'd. Twas at last agreed on, that we that came with the Duke, should get good horses that night, and so for Pool, a little seaport town not far off, where we were to seize a ship and set forth for Holland again, leaving our infantry to the mercy of the country.

This was much like that revolution of the Hollanders, in the time of the civil war with Spain, being, as we then were, in despair of making better terms, and not daring to enter Salisbury plain, because their

---

[1] And, indeed, shot Monmouth's messenger.
[2] Venner is wrong here: the date was in fact Friday, 26 June.

horse being so much better than ours, their men all being disciplined, ours not, we could not face them in so plain and open a country, so that we retreated backward, in the meantime resolving to see what London would do, having a great opportunity offer'd them, the soldiers being call'd forth, and not two thousand men to be had for their defence if they had but attempted anything. This disheartened our men, and several of them coming home to their own country, having felt by experience the hardships of war, withdrew from us.

We came well back again to Bridgwater, and were received with wonted love. We arrived here on Friday, the 3rd of July and resolved here to fortifie, so as to hold our ground till we heard from London. Saturday in the afternoon, news was brought of the approach of the King's forces within a mile and half of the town,[1] where they had encamped. The Duke went up into the tower, and there took a view of them, and seeing them so careless, and their horse at some distance from the army, in a little town, the infantry being in Sedge-Moore, he called a council on it. And it was concluded on, that we should fall on them in the dead of the night. Accordingly, having a guide to conduct us on in a private way, we march'd out at about eleven o'clock in the night, and about one fell on them in their tents. There was a ditch between but our men seeing the enemy just before them, ran furiously on, and lost the guide[2]. So that while they endeavoured to recover over that place, the enemy got on their legs, and put themselves in order. And now began as fierce a battel as perhaps ever was fought in England in so short a time. Our foot fought as well as ever foot fought, but not a horse came up; had our horse but assisted, we must have beaten them out of the field. But our horses would not stand the noise of drums and guns, so that we soon lost two of our pieces of ordnance, and we had but four in all, and then but one more in the field. Our foot flung most of their shot over, so that the men for the most part were killed in the rear. And that run but the front stood still, and had we done as much execution in the front as we did in the rear, the day had been ours, but God would not have it, their time was not yet come. By this time their horses came up, and having six or eight hundred good disciplin'd men, well mounted and well armed, ours neither; out foot having shot away all their ammunition and our baggage being not then in the field, they were forced to retreat, being all in confusion.

Having no money left, and our party thus unexpectedly repulsed, the Duke seeing he could not hold it any longer, fled with my lord Gray.

The Duke's party[3] was said to be about three thousand foot and a

[1] In fact, a good three miles.
[2] Godfrey.
[3] He means 'the Earl's party'.

thousand horse. We had more, at least five thousand men and horse, but not well arm'd, yet in the field. 'Tis said we lost not above three hundred, and they foot, but after, when we were routed, in our retreat lost a vast many more, though they pursued not in save hours after.

The most remarkable persons that were taken in this total rout were Colonel Holmes, Major Perrot, the constable of Crookhorn[1] and Mr. Williams, servant to the late Duke of Monmouth.

VI. EDWARD DUMMER: A BRIEF JOURNALL OF THE WESTERN REBELLION[2]

June 1685

11   The Duke of Monmouth, Lord Gray and one Ferguson, a phanatick priest, accompanied with about 100 more, arrived in three small vessels hyred or bought in Holland at Lyme in Dorsetshire; and from thence sent fourth their accomplices into the adjacent parts to give notice of their landing, and to exhort the people to their assistance.

12   They continued in Lyme listing associats (which every moment came to them) under their new display'd colours, which are a deep green inscribed wth letters of gold (Fear nothing but God) forming a propense[3] Rebellion; under an audacious declaration of protecting the Protestant Religion against Popery and arbetrary power.

13   They remain still in Lyme; the Mayor of the place makes his escape and gives his Matie. an account thereof.[4] The Dorsetshire Militia, and many Gentlemen volunteers are mustering themselves with all expedition to oppose them.

14   The Rebells march'd out of Lyme to a place call'd Bridgport and surpriz'd some of the King's party; among whome Mr. Strangeways and Mr Coaker (Gentlemen Volunteers) were killed. But the rest with some of the Militia get to their armes and charg'd the Rebells, kill'd 7 of them and took 23 prisoners; the rest retiring in disorder to Lyme. Duke Albemarle was now about Exeter raising the Devonshire Militia. The Rebells with a rabble of rascally people march out of Lyme towards Taunton; having with them 4 field pieces and ammunition suitable.

[1] Crewkerne.

[2] The passage is described as: 'A Journal of the proceedings of the Duke of Monmouth in his invading England; with the progress and issew [issue] of the Rebellion attending it. Kept by Mr. Edward Dummer then serving in the Train of Artillery employ'd by his Majesty for the suppression of the same.'

[3] i.e. proper.

[4] Other accounts claim the messengers were the Custom's officer and friend.

15   My Lord Churchill wth part of my Lord Oxford's Regiment of Horse are on their way to Dorchester, followed by Coll. Kirke's and Trelawney's Regiments of Foot. The Duke of Somersett who commanded theat County militia and the Duke of Beaufort the militia of Glocester Shire are on their way to those stations.

16   Monmouth is about Taunton,[1] forming his adherents into a body. Eight pieces of cannon with ammunition proportionable under the care of Mr. Shere, Comptroler[2], are this day set forward from Portsm. towards my Lord Churchill, guarded by 3 companies of Foot and 2 troops of Horse under the command of Coll. Churchill.[3]

17   The Rebells are about Taunton. No considerable action.

18   Nothing of moment.

19   My Lord Churchill arrives at Chard, sends out twenty commanded Horse under Lieutennt Monaux and a Quarter Master, who met with much about the like number of sturdy Rebells, well arm'd; between whome hapned a very brisk encounter. Twelve of the Rebells were killed and the rest being wounded fled and alarmd the body of the Rebells wch lay neare; so that a fresh party apperd and caus'd ours to retreat, leaving Lieutennt. Monaux upon the place, shot in the head and killed on the first charge. The Quarter Master wth the rest came off well, saving two or three that were wounded. This action happened within three miles of Taunton.[4]

20   Capt. Trevanion in the Suadadoes wth other of his Maties ships under his command arrives at Lyme, and there finds and secures a pink[5] and a Dogger that belong'd to the Rebells (the 3d vessell being gone[6]), together with forty barrells of powder wth. back and breast and head pieces for betwn. 4 & 5000 men in the town. The Rebells are about Bridgwater. The Duke of Albemarle at Exeter.

21   The Portsm. artillery comes to Dorchester and receives orders from my Lord Churchill to marche to Sherborne; his Lordship taking his way to Langport. The Rebells are marching towards Glastonbury; two companies of the Sommersett Shire Militia (excepting the officers) revolt to him.

22   My Lord Churchill sends out a party of Horse consisting of

[1] In fact he was at Chard.
[2] Henry Sheres, an officer of the Board of Ordnance.
[3] Charles Churchill (1656–1714), brother of John, Lord Churchill, commanding Trelawney's Regiment.
[4] In fact at Ashill, some ten miles from Taunton.[3] A small sailing barque.
[5] The 32-gun frigate *Helderenburgh*.
[6] In fact to Bridgwater; Dummer is here one day out in his knowledge of rebel movements.

about Fourty from Langport, which meets with double the number of Rebells and beats them into theire camp. The Artillery is now at Sherborne and receives orders from my Lord Churchill to march to Somerton. The Rebells are now in quarters at Glastonbury which is 12 miles from Sherborne and 6 from Somerton. My Lord Feaversham with a detachment of his Majistices Horse Guards joyne the Earle of Pembrokke with the Wiltshire Militia at Chippenham. The Duke of Grafton is likewise marching with 2000 of his Majistices Foot Guards.

23   The Artillery joyned my Lord Churchill at Somerton and quarters there, not without fear of interception; our out-guards have frequent skirmishes with those of the Rebells every moment taking some one or other. Jarvice, a feltmake of evill (a notorious fellow) was also taken, and his brother after a brisk resistance, killd. The Rebells march to Shepton Mallet.

24   The Duke of Albemarle is now at Wellington 5 miles from Taunton, having put three companies into Lyme. The Duke of Somersett is at Bath with the Militia of Somersett. The Duke of Beufort at Bristol with those of Glocestershire, joyned by my Lord Feaversham, Commander-in-chief. My Lord Churchill marches close upon the Rebells, and this night quarters at Wells. The Rebells march from Shepton Mallet and quarter at Pensford about 5 miles from Bristoll, 7 from Bath and 10 from Wells; thus surrounded lies the Rebells – without possibility of avoiding some rencounter.

25   The Rebells march to Canisham[1] 3 miles further & encamp in a meadow on the side of Gloucestershire, upon the River Avon, about midway between Bath and Bristoll. My Lord Churchill marches to Pensford. Coll. Oglethorpe advances with a good party of Horse[2] out of Bristoll, and with a detachment of 25 only, commanded by Captain Parker, attacks the Rebells in their quarters at Canisham towne, killd 40 or 50 of them with the loss but of one man; a successful but desperate attempt.[3] Duke of Albemarle continues in Devonshire.

26   My Lord Churchill marches towards Bristoll, hangs Jarvice the Feltmaker about a mile from Pensford, who dyes obstinatley and impenitently. He receives advice from my Lord Feversham to march the nearest way to Bath, the Rebells taking that way on the Somersetshire side of Avon; in the evening, the Lord Feaversham, Churchill and Duke of Grafton joyne at Bath and quarters

[1] i.e. Keynsham.
[2] Oglethorpe's Blues – or the Horse Guards.
[3] For this feat of arms, see p. 30–1 above.

with severall regiments of the Militia. The Rebells are marched to Phillips Norton 5 miles distant. The Duke of Albemarle continues in Devonshire.

27 The Army marchd early from Bath after the Rebells to Phillips Norton, whence they were dislodging. Five hundrd Foot with some troops of Horse Granadeers[1] and Dragoones were detachd under the command of the Duke of Grafton to fall upon their rear, wch. was accordingly done, but with ill success. The Rebells having posted themselves so advantageously that we lost about 50 men, besides wounded, the Duke himself narrowly escaping. Soon after the body of the Army with the Artillery came up, and having stood two houres a fair mark, shooting at hedges and shot at, in desperate rainy weather, we marched off to Bradford,[2] the Rebells to Froom Selwood. Our own damage was certain, but that of the Rebells could not be guessed at. We left our morter ps.[3] and shells at Bath.

28 We rested at Bradford, the Rebells at Frome. Here we receivd advice that the enemie in the late action receivd considerable damage.[4] Duke Albemarle continues in Devonshire. The great Traine of Artillery from London is at Marlborough.

29 We marchd early towards Westbury under the Plaine, having advice that the Rebells were marching to Warminster. But our near approach causd their returne to Shepton Mallet, and so to Wells and Bridgwater. We quarterd at Westbury. The Duke of Albemarle is in Devonshire, the Great Traine of Artillery at the Devizes.

30 This morning early the great Traine of Artillery joyn'd the army at Westbury and then march'd for Froome.

July

1 Rested at Froome, and first encamp'd, nothing extraordinary; confirmation of much damage done the Rebells at Phillipsnorton, and that they had done a great deal of spoyle to the town of Wells. Duke of Albemarle is still in Devonshire.

2 The Army march'd to Sheptonmallet and encamp'd. Nothing else of moment, the Rebells [being] at Bridgwater.

3 The Army march'd to Somerton and encampt; had advice of the Rebells making show of fortyfying Bridgwater, having summon'd in the country[-folk] to assist them therein. Our party are confirm'd by the countrey people of the like intentions.

4 Rested at Somerton. Capt. Coy with a strong party of Horse

---

[1] Part of the Life Guards.
[2] Bradford-upon-Avon.
[3] i.e. a 'mortar piece'; mortars were guns with a high trajectory, firing bombs.
[4] Only 18 killed.

being this morning within ½ a mile of Bridgwater, met with a greater party of Rebells, charg'd through them and broke them without any considerable damage on either side. We are now within 10 miles of the enemie. Orders sent to bring away the morter piece from Bath towards Bridgwater.

5   We marched into the levell,[1] and in the evening[2] encampt at Weston in Sedgmore about 2 miles from Bridgwater, with the village on one side, and bequirt[3] with a dry (but in some places mirey) ditch on the other, fronting the moor; a place copious and commodious for fighting. In our march hither we understood that the Rebells had given out they would fight in this place. In the evening Coll. Oglethorp advanced with a strong party of Horse to Bridgwater, to discover the motion of the Rebells who were said to be drawn out from thence and in their march towards Bristoll (as they would have us believe).[4] We securely went to sleep, the Foot in camp, and the Horse in quarters at Weston and Midlesea[5], saving some outguards of Horse upon our right and left.[6]

6   Att 2 o'clock this morning (securely sleeping) our camp was rouzed by the near approach of the Rebells – a dark night and thick fogg covering the Moore. Supineness and preposterous confidence of ourselves, with an understanding of the Rebells that many days before had made us make such tedious marches, had put us into the worst circumstances of surprize: Our Horse in quarters, some near, some remote; our Artillery distinat[7], and in a separate post to that of the camp – neither accomodable to a generall resistance. Thus we rec'd the alarme from Sir Francis Compton upon the right, whose successfull charging the whole body of the Rebells Horse commanded by the Lord Gray, with his single party of 150 Horse and Dragoons, broke their body of near 1200[8] and routed them. From this alarme there seems to be 2 minutes distance to a volley of small shot from the body of the Rebells Foot,[9] consisting of about 6,000 (but all came not up to battell) in upon the right of our camp, followed by 2 or 3 rounds

[1] The marshes.
[2] The slow-moving artillery would be last into camp – hence the evening arrival.
[3] i.e. 'begirt' or 'surrounded'.
[4] This was discovered only after midnight.
[5] Middlezoy.
[6] See p. 51 for Feversham's precautions.
[7] i.e. distant – placed to cover the Bridgwater to Taunton road on the extreme left – the most obvious enemy line of approach.
[8] Most accounts agree 800.
[9] Dummer, in the heat of action, probably refers to the first volley fired by the Royal Foot into Grey's horsemen riding along the ditch far-side.

from three pieces of cannon brought up within 116 paces of the ditch, ranging our battalions. Our friendly Artillery was near 500 paces distant, and the horses and drivers not easily found[1], through confusion and darkness. Yet such was the extraordinary cheerfullness of our Army that they were allmost as readily drawn up to receive them as a preinformed expectation could have posted them, tho' upon so short and dangerous a warning. Six of our nearest gunns were with the greatest diligence imaginable advanced,[2] three upon the right of the Scotts[3] and three in the front of the King's first battalion (of Guards), and did very considerable execution upon the enemies. They stood near an hour and a halfe with great shouting and courage, briskly fyring; and then, throwing down their armes, fell into rout and confusion. The number of the slaine with about 300 taken, according to the most modest computation, might make up 1,000, we losing but 27 on the spot and having about 200 wounded. A victory very considerable, where Providence was absolutely a greater friend than our own conduct. The dead in the Moor we buried, and the country people took care for the interment of those slaine in the corn fields.[4] Coll. Oglethorp was dispatch'd to give his Matie. intelligence of this action. My Lord Feaversham hastens to Bridgwater[5], where it was reported that the remn't of the Rebells were gone to Axbridge;[6] to which place their baggage, waggons and one gunn (three being taken in the field) had been sent, before they attack't us, assuring themselves such success in our ruin as that it would little hinder their intended march to Bristoll; it being most probable (had not God Almighty by an express Providence order'd otherwise) they would have directly gone. This evening Capt. Parker was detatched with a party of Horse to Wells and so to Axbridge after the baggage. Expresses are sent to the King with the particulars of this action. Rested at Weston.

7 We march'd to Wells and quarter'd, leaving Coll. Kirke's and Trelawnye's Regiments to march to Bridgwater[7] and the Great Traine of Artillery to the Devizes. Two Rebells were hanged this morning before the Army; the one a Dutch gunner, the other a

[1] It seems that most had fled.
[2] He makes no mention of Bishop Mew's role.
[3] Dumbarton's Regiment.
[4] To the South of Chedzoy.
[5] Most accounts say he sent Lord Churchill in the first instance.
[6] On the Somerset River Axe, not to be confused with Axminster on the Devon and Dorset river of the same name which figured in the early days of the Rebellion.
[7] In fact Col. Kirke marched his troops to Taunton on 7 July.

deserter from Capt. Eely. Six more hanged at Glassenbury in our march.

8   Rested at Wells and publique thankes returnd for our victory. The Bishop of Winchester[1] preach'd. At night we had news of Monmo. and Gray's being taken near Ringwood. Many volunteers depart for London.

9   Rested at Wells. Nothing of moment.

10   Our Foot march'd to Froome and encampt, & our Horse to Warminster and quarter'd.

11   The Scotts to Devizes. The Kings Battallions to Warminster and encamp. Lord Churchill, Lord Feaversham and the Duke of Grafton to London.

12   Coll. Sackvill,[2] commandr. in chief marches to Aimsbury[3] and the [Bye-]Traine of Artillery in the afternoon towards Portsmo, all going to their respective posts.

VII. ADAM WHEELER, DRUMMER IN THE WILTSHIRE MILITIA

ITER BELLICOSUM[4]
or
A Perfect Relation of the Heroick
March of his Maties Truely Loyall Subject
and Magnanimous Souldier, Colonell *John
Windham Esquire*[5], With his Regiment of Foote
into the Western Parts of England for
the Suppressing of *James Scot* and his
Accomplices in theire Rebellious
Insurrection. Together with
some remarkable Occur-
encies happening in
that Expedition
Faithfully set down by Adam Wheeler
one of the Drums of his Honors owne Company
Ano, Christt 1685.

[1] Bishop Mew, now also sometimes known as 'the Gunner'.
[2] Dismissed as a Non-Juror at the Revolution in 1688, but later employed by Marlborough for secret missions.
[3] Amesbury.
[4] 'The Path of War'. The original is reproduced in the *Camden Miscellany*, Vol. 12, 1910, pp. 159–66. Adam Wheeler's spelling has been retained throughout.
[5] Col. John Wyndham of Norrington, MP for Salisbury in 1681 and 1685.

1685
June 16
(in fact 17th)

Being Wednesday, I was summoned by a comand from his Honor to appeare in the Market-Place of New Sarm[1] in the County of Wilts by eight of the Clocke in the Morning in his Regiment compleatly armed according to my place as a *Drum*[2]. Where the Regiment being drawne together was dischardged till the next morning. When againe it being the siventeenth day, they were dischardged untill Friday the eighteenth [19th] of June; and they mustered by Satturday; the Regiment was exactly compleated by his Honor and accomodated fitt for Warr according to Military Discipline, and that day by his Comand, about sixe of the clock in the Evening, the Drums beating and the Colours displayed, leaveing the Citty, wee directed oure March to Wilton, being about Two Miles distant and Quartered there that night, where his Honor ordered his carridge and Ammunicon to be brought to him.

June 20
(21st)

The next day being Sunday on wch. day in the afternoone leaveing the Towne of Wilton, we continewed oure March to Market Lavington.

June 21
(22nd)

Early the next morning his Honor marched to the Devizes, and there refreshed his Regimt. for the Weary and hard Afternoones March they sustained the day before.

In the afternoone by Beate of Drum the Regimt. marched as farre as Chippenham and June 22 [23rd], being Tuesday, They marched from Chippenham to the Citty of Bath, where they Quartered that night.

June 23
(24th)

The Regimt. leaving the Citty of Bath as farre as Bradforde[-on-Avon]. *That Night* being very darke there was an Alarum. By reason of which the Regimt. could not unite into a Body till they came to Trowbridge[3], wch was Where, for the better security of his Honors Carridge, I desired some assistance being Resolved to hazzard my life by Ball or Sword, rather than loose any part thereof; here the whole Regiment lay.

[1] 'New Sarum' or Salisbury.
[2] A regiment would have a dozen drummers.
[3] Clearly the regiment ran away – and took some time to rally.

June 25   The Rt Honrble thé Ld. Lieutent Earle of
(26th)   Pembrook[1] gave comand for some of the Regimt.
          and some of the Militia Horse to gow wth him to
          Froome, where he forced the Rebells to lay down
          their Armes, and brought away with him the
          Constable[2] of that Towne to Trowbridge who
          proclaymed the Duke of Monmouth King, and
          severall cruell and New invented murthering
          Weapons as Sithes and the like. *Here* There was
          One of the Colonells Regiment belonging to
          Lieutent. Colonll. Young accidentaly hurt by
          dischardging a Musquett which rent his hand in
          peaces, and soe became the Occasion of his Death,
          for he lived not many days after.

June 26   We continued our march from Trowbridge to
(27th)   Kingsdowne, where divers other Regimts met.[3]
          Here his Honors Regiment was by his *Grace* the
          Duke of Grafton and the Rt. Honrble the Earle of
          Feversham set in Batalia, as if presently to engage
          the Enemy. Thence we marched to Bath.

June 27   From Bath the Regiment was led by his *Honor
(28th)   Coll. Windham* to Trowbridge. Where they made
          stay but Marched forwards into Bratton Lane, and
          there by an Alarum of the Enemies being neare[4]
          caused the Regimt. to incampe in that Landsend
          and the Blew Regiment alsoe, and the yellow
          Hampshire Regimt.[5] encamped in a ground neare
          the said Lane.

June 28   Dislodging from thence, wee marched into
(29th)   Froome; Where the Kings Maties. Gracious
June 30   Pardon was proclaimed to all such as had taken up
(in margin) Armes against him, if in 7 daies They would come
          in and accept thereof. Some Persons merely
          excepted, who were therein mentioned.

July 1st Being Wednesday, his Honors Regimt. tooke
(correct) theire March to Shepton Mallet; Here not farre
          from the Towne, a Ground was shewn which lay

[1] Thomas Herbert, 8th Earl of Pembroke (1656–1733), Lord Lieutenant of Wiltshire.
[2] An ancient official, like the Reeve of the Middle Ages. This man was hanged.
[3] The concentration of regular and militia regiments was between Keynsham and Kingsdown at Bathford.
[4] There was a possibility that Monmouth's Army might try to break into Wiltshire following their failure to reach Bristol by way of Keynsham Bridge on the 25th.
[5] The Hampshire Militia wore yellow coats.

within Prospect where Monmouth and his Army
was drawne up and exercised.[1]

July 2   Being Thursday, we marched from Shepton
Mallet to Glastonbury, and from thence wee
removed and went towards Sumerton. In which
March wee had the sight of Kings Sedgemoore
being about One Mile distant from us; And here
Wee received a comand to Returne and March to
Charleton.

[There is no entry for Friday, 3 July]

July 4   From whence wee Marched to Kings Sedgemoore,
marching Eight Miles in the Moore so farre as
Middlesey; Where being Alarumed[2];

[There is no entry for Sunday, 5 July]

July 6   The Rht. Honorble the Earle of Pembroke Lord
Lieutent in great hast came rideing to the house
where his Honor *Colonll Windham* was quartered,
it being betweene Twelve and One of the Clock in
the Mornening, calling out 'Colonl Windham
Colonll Windham – the Enemy is Engadged,' and
asking for his Drums[3]; The Colonll answer was
that he was ready, and soe forthwith prepared
himself.

There being then noe Drum in the house but
Adam Wheeler, who opened the doore and
answered his Lordhp. that he was ready to obey his
Comand; soe his Lorp. immediately comanded
him to beate an Alarum, wch. he presently
performed. (Although some of the Regimt. did
endeavor to have the Credite of that peece of
Service ascribed to Themselves; One saying it was
I that did first beate the Alarme; Another in like
manner saying the same, soe that Wheeler may
justly complaine as the *Poet Virgil* did concerneing
his, *Sic vos non vobis*, and somewhat after The same
manner as he spoke, superscribe, *Hos Ego
Versiculos feci tulit alter honores.*[4]

[1] i.e. where Monmouth's Army had been drilled on either 23 June (during his advance)
or on 30 June (during his retreat): they left Shepton Mallet early on 1 July.
[2] This was of course caused by Monmouth's attempted surprise night attack on 5/6
July.
[3] Drums and Colours were used to give signals and pass orders in the days before
radio.
[4] 'Yours but not yours'; 'I have made the effort myself but the honours are borne by
another' – very close to a remark made by John Churchill at this time.

When the *Alarum* was beaten by Adam Wheeler in
Middlesey according to the Lord Lieutents
Comand; The Regimt marched through Weston[1]
into Weston Moore with as much expedicon as
possible could be, where They were drawne up
Three deep in order to engadge if Occasion
required.[2]

The Aforesaid Sixth of July, the *Fight* began very
early in the morening which Battell was over
within the space of Two Howers, and the Enemy
received a totall Rowte.

Here Adam Wheeler (being then at his post) was
one of those of the Right Wing of his Honor
Colonll Windhams Regimt who after the Enemy
began to run desired Leave of his Honor to get
such Pillage in the feild as they could finde; But his
Honors Answer and comand was; That uppon
Paine of Death not a Man of his Regimt should
move from his post saying; That if the Enemy
should rally together againe, and the Regimt. be in
disorder, every man of them might loose his Life.

The *Battell* being over the Right Honorble the
Earle of *Feversham*, Generall of his Maties Army,
came to the Head of Colonlls *Windhams* Regimt
and gave him many Thanks for his readynesse,
Saying, his Matie should not hear of it by Letter,
but by Word of Mouth; and that he would certify
the Kinge himself of it.

An Account of the Prisoners that were brought along
by the Right·Wing of his Honor Colonll
Windhams Regimt to Weston Church as they were
tyed together; Adam Wheeler writeing them
downe on his Drumhead as they passed by.

The first Number was fifty and five, most of them
tyed together.

The Second Number was Thirty and Two tyed in
like manner.

The Third was two wounded in their Legs,
crawling uppon the Ground on theire Hands and
Knees to Weston Church.

---

[1] i.e. Westonzoyland.

[2] In fact Feversham and Churchill were careful to keep the unreliable militia regiments
in reserve.

The Fowerth was Thirty seven in number, many
of them tyed and pinacled together.

The Fifth was One alone being naked, onely his
Drawers on.

The Sixth was One single one more.

The Seventh was one more running, being forced
along by Two Horse Men with Blowes, and
rideing close after him.

The Eighth Number was Fowerteene most of
them being tyed together.

The Nineth was Forty Seven most of them tyed as
the former, such of Them as had a good Coate or
any thinge worth the pilling[1], were very fairely
stript of it.

The Tenth Number is Eight, tyed by Two
together, Arme to Arme.

The Eleventh was Twelve tyed and pinnackled.[2]

The Thirteenth one more.

The Fowerteenth in Number were Seven more.

The Fifteenth, one more.

The Sixteenth, one more.

The Seventeenth was One more. Hee was very
remarkable and to be admired, for being shot
thorow the shoulder and wounded in the Belly,
Hee lay on his Backe in the Sun stript naked, for
the space of Tenne or Eleven Howers, in that
scorching hot day to the Admiration of all the
Spectators; And as he lay, a greate Crowde of
Souldiers came about him, and repraoched him,
calling him, *Thou Monmouth Dog* How long have
you beene with your Kinge *Monmouth*? His answer
was, that if he had Breath, he would tell them:
Afterwards he was pittyed, and they opened round
about him, and gave him more Liberty of the Aire,
and there was One Souldier that gave him a paire
of Drawers to cover his Nakednesse; Afterwards
haveing a long Stick in his hand he walked feably
to Weston Church, where he died that Night, and
two wounded men more.

The Number of the Prisoners that were led by the

---

[1] i.e. the pillaging.
[2] i.e. manacled.

Right Wing of his Honors Regiment did amount to 228.[1]

The County men that gathered up the Dead slayne in that Battell gave an Account to the Minister and Church Wardens of Weston of the Number of One Thousand Three hundred Eighty and Fower; Besides many more they did beleive lay dead unfound in the Corne.

Where Adam Wheeler saw of dead men lying in One Heape One Hundred Seventy and Fower; which those that were digging a Pit to lay them in gave the number of.[2]

From Weston Moore the Regimt. marched to Weston, and thence to Middlesey, and from Middlesey againe to Weston[3], and thence to Weston Moore *where* a Dutch Gunner, and a Yellow-coate Souldier that ran out[4] of his Maties Army to Monmouth were hanged on a tree in Western Moore not farre from the Church.

This Day *Adam Wheeler* went into the Campe[5] and tooke an Account as neare as hee could of his *Maties Carridges* and Great Guns wch. were neare One Hundred and fifty of them; Of these there nineteen Guns some having sixe Horses, some seven, and some eight Horses a peece to draw them.

Here his *Honor Coll Windham* received Orders to Guard his Maties Guns and Carridges with his Regiment; from Weston Moore to the Devizes, it being a peece of service of noe small Trust and Credite, and soe much his Honor was pleased to inform his Souldiers of.

This afternoone an Accident fell out to be lamented. One of his Honors owne Souldiers[6], being in Exercise, and quitting his Armes, A musquett went off as it lay on the Ground, and shot him thorow both of his legs, soe he died in a short time after.

[1] In fact 238 in all.
[2] This mound was later levelled but was in the Grave field.
[3] No doubt after collecting their kit.
[4] i.e. deserted.
[5] i.e. the Royal Camp just north of Weston Zoyland behind the Bussex Rhine.
[6] i.e. belonging to the Colonel's own company (one of twelve in the average regiment).

From the Camp in Weston Moore his *Honor Coll. Windham* marched with his Regimt. to Glastonbury: Heare at the signe of the White Hart a Duell was fought between Captain Love and Major Talbot. The Major Fell, and Captain Love fled for it.

Heare alsoe were six men of the Prisoners that were taken hanged on the Signe Post of that Inne who after, as they hung were stripped naked, and soe left hanging there all night.

Heare Alsoe at this towne of Glastonbury there was an Alarum, where uppon the Regimt. was comanded to the Abby Cloyster.

His honors Regimt. Marched from Glastonbury (where there six men were left hanging on the Signe-Post) to Wells, Thence they marched to Embetch[1] and soe to Philps Norton.

The Regimt. left Philps Norton, and Marched to the Devizes (guarding his Maties Carridges and Guns) where his Honor was dischardged of that Trust, And heare his Honor dischardged the Regiment likewise, till the next Summons by Beate of Drum.[2]

9 July — This is the best account I can give yor Honor[3] of that successful March: and doe humbly beg yor Honors pardon for this Presumption, and with leave subscribe my Selfe Sir,

Yor *Honors* most dutifull *Drum*, and most humble
and
Obedient Servant.
Adam Wheeler.

Anglorum vivat semper Prolesque Jacobi,
Rex; fugiant Hostes non remorante pede.
Atque diu vivat stirps Nobilis inclyta Wyndham
Detque Deus pueris Gaudia Multa suis.[4]

---

[1] Embetch is today the village of Emborough.

[2] Wyndham (the father of Thomas, Lord Wyndham, later Chief Justice of the Common Pleas) was accorded a triumphal march past in Salisbury, the bells of St Thomas's, Salisbury, being rung in his honour for the sum of 5s.

[3] Clearly Wheeler wrote this account for the information of his Colonel.

[4] A rough translation might be: 'Long live our James of England and its peoples King,
His enemies with relentless foot do flee.
Also long life to the noble family Wyndham named
And may God to his brave sons much joy accord'.

VIII. THE BLOODY ASSIZE

LCJ JEFFREYS. And this is as much as you know of the business?

DUNNE. Yes, my lord, that is all that I remember.

LCJ. Well, and what hadst thou for all thy pains?

DUNNE. Nothing but a month's imprisonment, my lord.

LCJ. Thou seemest to be a man of a great deal of kindness and good-nature; for by this story, there was a man that thou never sawest before (for I would fain have all people observe what leather some men's consciences are made of) and because he only had a black beard, and came to thy house, that black beard of his should persuade thee to go twenty-six miles, and give a man half a crown out of thy pocket to show thee thy way, and all to carry a message from a man thou never knewest in thy life to a woman whom thou never sawest in thy life neither; that thou shouldst lie out by the way two nights, and upon the Sunday get home, and there meet with this same black-bearded little gentleman, and appoint these people to come to thy house upon the Tuesday; and when they come, entertain them three or four hours at thy own house, and go back again so many miles with them, and have no entertainment but a piece of cake and cheese that thou broughtest thyself from home, and have no reward, nor so much as know any of the persons thou didst all this for, is very strange.

DUNNE. My lord, the man that came to desire me to go on this message said that Hicks would reward me, and pay me for my pains.

LCJ. But why wouldst thou take the word of a man thou didst not know?

DUNNE. I was forced to take his word at that time, my lord.

LCJ. There was no necessity for that neither; no body could force thee to do it. Alack-a-day! thou seemest to be a man of some consideration: I mightily wonder thou shouldst be so kind to people thou didst not know, without any prospect of recompense whatsoever.

DUNNE. All the reason that induced me to it was, they said they were men in debt, and desired to be concealed for a while.

LCJ. Dost thou believe that any one here believes thee? Prithee what trade art thou?

DUNNE. My lord, I am a baker by trade.

LCJ. And wilt thou bake thy bread at such easy rates? Upon my word then, thou art very kind. Prithee tell me, I believe thou dost use to bake on Sundays, dost thou not?

DUNNE. No, my lord, I do not.

LCJ. Alack-a-day! thou art precise in that; but thou canst travel on Sundays to lead rogues into lurking holes. It seemeth thou hast a particular kindness for a black beard, that's all thy reason for undertaking all this trouble. Thou hast told me all the truth, hast thou?

DUNNE. I have, my lord.

LCJ. But I assure thee thy bread is very light weight, it will scarce pass the balance here.

DUNNE. I tell the truth, and nothing but the truth.

LCJ. No doubt of that; but prithee tell me, whose horse didst thou ride when thou wentest first?

DUNNE. The man's horse that came to me to desire me to go the message.

LCJ. How came he to trust thee with his horse?

DUNNE. The Lord knows, my lord.

LCJ. Thou sayst right, the Lord only knows, for by the little I know of thee I would not trust thee with two-pence. Whose horse didst thou ride the second time?

DUNNE. My own, my lord.

LCJ. And where didst thou put thy horse when thou camest to my Lady Lisle's?

DUNNE. In the stable, my lord . . .

LCJ. Was the stable-door lock'd or open?

DUNNE. The stable-door was latch'd, and I pluck'd up the latch.

LCJ. How came you to know the way to the stable then?

DUNNE. Because I had been there before, my lord.

LCJ. Thou hadst need to know it very well, for it seemeth thou wentest without a candle or anything in the world, and put in thy horse. Didst thou see that man Carpenter the bailiff that thou spokest of?

DUNNE. Mr Carpenter gave my horse hay.

LCJ. Now prithee tell me truly, where came Carpenter unto you? I must know the truth of that. Remember that I give you fair warning, do not tell me a lie, for I will be sure to treasure up every lie that thou tellest me, and thou mayst be certain it will not be for thy advantage. I would not terrify thee to make thee say anything but the truth; but assure thyself, I never met with a lying, sneaking, canting fellow but I always treasure up vengeance for him; and therefore look to it that thou dost not prevaricate with me, for to be sure thou wilt come to the worst of it in the end.

DUNNE. My lord, I will tell the truth as near as I can.

LCJ. Then tell me where Carpenter met thee.

DUNNE. In the court, my lord.

LCJ. Before you came to the gate, or after?

DUNNE. It was after we came to the gate, in the court . . .

LCJ. Now upon your oath, tell me truly who it was that open'd the stable door – was it Carpenter or you?

DUNNE. It was Carpenter, my lord.

LCJ. Why, thou vile wretch, didst not thou tell me just now that thou pluck'd up the latch? Dost thou take the God of heaven not to be a God of truth, and that He is not a witness of all thou sayst? Dost thou think because thou prevaricatest with the Court here thou canst do so with God above, who knows thy thoughts? And it is infinite mercy that for those falsehoods of thine He does not immediately strike thee into Hell! Jesus God! there is no sort of conversation[1] nor human society to be kept with such people as these are, who have no other religion but only in pretence, and no way to uphold themselves but by countenancing lying and villany! . . .

DUNNE. My lord, I am so baulked, I do not know what I say myself; tell me what you would have me to say for I am clutter'd out of my senses.

LCJ. Why, prithee man, there's no body baulks thee but they own self; thou art asked questions that are as plain as anything in the world can be: it is only thy own depraved naughty heart that baulks both thy honesty and understanding, if thou hast any. It is thy studying how to prevaricate that puzzles and confounds thy intellect; but I can see all the pains in the world and all compassion and charity is lost upon thee, and therefore I will say no more to thee.

[1] i.e. intercourse, dealings with.

6

The Historians' Interpretation

Every historical writer owes a debt to his predecessors in the field he is examining. Although his main attention will be taken up by the various forms of contemporary evidence discussed and illustrated in the last chapter, he will also read the accounts, analyses and opinions of other historians if only to agree or take issue with them as he develops his own particular lines of thought which he hopes will contribute something new to the knowledge of the subject. There are, evidently, certain perils awaiting the unwary who may be tempted to accept as fact an earlier opinion which has been much repeated. 'History never repeats itself,' runs an adage, 'but historians seldom differ.' It is therefore vital for the writer to return wherever possible to primary sources and check for himself. A case in point from the battle of Sedgemoor is the oft-repeated idea that the Rebels were unaware of the existence of the Bussex Rhine until they stumbled on to it that foggy night of 5/6 July. As we have seen, King James II is partly responsible for the creation of this myth – loyally repeated by historian after historian whose belief in 'the Divine Right of Kings' apparently extended to an acceptance of their infallibility as historians – most unwisely in this case. Similarly, even modern writers accept without question that Monmouth was able to inspect in some detail the dispositions of the Royal Army in the vicinity of Westonzoyland from 'Monmouth's turret' on St Mary's churchtower at Bridgwater, and thus corroborate through his telescope the message sent by hand of Godfrey from Farmer Sparkes of Chedzoy. How many, one wonders, have taken the trouble to ascend the dark and twisting stairway to Monmouth's vantage point to look out towards Westonzoyland? Even on a fine, clear day without a trace of mist, it is hard to pick out Westonzoyland church-tower, despite its commanding height, through modern binoculars. How then, *pace* many writers, could Monmouth reputedly have picked out the regiments he once fought alongside in happier years abroad despite their six-foot square regimental and company colours? Still less, '. . . ranging his spyglass along the Royalist lines, he noted that the horse were widely separated from the foot . . .'[1] No, the role of much-repeated myth, however

[1] J. N. P. Watson, *Captain-General and Rebel Chief* (London, 1979) p. 241.

lovingly enshrined in the minds of successive generations, has to be taken with a large pinch of salt.

With the passage of three hundred years, it is hard to establish exactly what took place that dark, early Monday morning. One assembles, studies and tests the available contemporary and secondary evidence, tries out what one can on the ground, and then writes what one's own mind, experience (academic and military) and conscience – having weighed up all the surviving evidence – believe to have been the case, falling back when all else fails on what Col. Alfred Burne – a fine battlefield historian of the 1940s and 1950s – called 'Inherent Military Probability'.

There is no such thing as wholly objective history; or rather, when this is attempted (as in certain Common Market handbooks, for instance) the result is anodyne, flat and desperately dull. Every historian in each succeeding generation has therefore tended to put his own particular gloss on the story of 1685, reflecting the prejudices, political convictions and personal biases and attitudes of his own time. To illustrate this, three examples are published below – selected from over seventy accounts available – to secure a reasonable spread of treatment. They date (in terms of publication) from 1723, 1848 and 1932.

To introduce the three representative excerpts, a quick examination of their authors is necessary. Bishop Gilbert Burnet (1643–1715) wrote his account years before it appeared in print, some time after his death. He was an Episcopalian Scot, a native of Edinburgh and later of Aberdeenshire, who studied law, history and divinity. His lawyer father and strictly Presbyterian mother did not share his religious convictions, which may be described as middle-of-the-way, and from 1663 he spent as much time south of the border as in Scotland. He was for long an intimate of Charles II's somewhat notorious minister, Lauderdale, and this probably earned him preferment. Used to negotiating with both the die-hard and moderate Presbyterians, he was appointed professor of divinity at Glasgow University in 1669, and later became an intimate of the Duke of Hamilton, whom he induced to accept Charles II's religious compromise. This earned him a Royal Chaplaincy, but his opposition to his old patron Lauderdale's extreme measures in Scotland and his public preaching against the Merry Monarch's profligate habits in 1673 earned him the disfavour of the authorities and cost him his Chaplaincy. He continued to preach in London from 1675 to 1684, and although he was no admirer of Roman Catholics he deplored their persecution during the Popish Plot of 1678–80, and thus earned the dislike of both the Court and the extreme Protestants. At times he had to withdraw abroad, and in 1684 he was deprived by the King's order of both his Chaplaincy of the Rolls and lectureship at St Clements Danes which he had held since 1675. On Charles II's death, Burnet applied for leave to travel abroad, and this was granted. He knew well that the Protestant party might go to extremes (he was a friend of Lord Delamere), and wished no part in it. 'So I was to go beyond the sea, as to a voluntary exile . . . I perceived, many thought the constitution was so broken into by the elections of the house of Commons[1], that they were disposed to put all to hazard. Yet most people thought the crisis was not so near, as it proved to be.'

Burnet, then, took no part in the events of 1685 in the West, but toured Paris, Rome, Geneva, Strasburg, Frankfurt, Heidelberg and Utrecht for a year, and thus viewed events as a strongly pro-Whig historian. In 1687 he was outlawed by James II and thereafter played an important role in the Glorious Revolution. He drafted William III's *Declaration*, accompanied him to Torbay in 1688 and thence to London, preached the Coronation sermon, and was elevated to the see of Salisbury as a reward for his efforts in 1689. He remained very much to the fore in public life through the next two reigns, championing the Protestant claim of the House of Hanover.

Besides his largely autobiographical *History of his own Times*, he published volumes of sermons and a much-acclaimed (at the time) *History of the Reformation* (1697–1714).

A century later, and we come to our second historian, also a Whig or Liberal by political persuasion, and therefore also certain to be anti-Jacobite. Thomas Babington Macaulay, Lord Macaulay (1800–1859), was, after Thomas Carlyle, the most celebrated historian of the mid-Victorian period. Educated at Trinity College, Cambridge, he became a barrister in 1826. The previous year he had published his first article (on John Milton) in the *Edinburgh Review*, this proving the first of many. He entered Parliament in 1830 as M.P. for Calne, and then for Leeds. He had a distinguished career in the Indian administration and legal service, but in 1838 returned to London and became totally committed to writing and politics. He began work on his *History of England* (from which one extract appears below) in 1839; he became M.P. for Edinburgh (1839–1847, and 1852–1856), and was Secretary of War (1839–1841). His famous historical poems, *The Lays of Ancient Rome*, appeared in 1842 and the four volumes of the *History* appeared in 1848 and 1855. In Parliament he was responsible for the Copyright Bill, whereby a published work remained in copyright until forty-two years after its author's death. He became Lord Rector of Glasgow University (1849), and was created Baron Macaulay of Rothley in 1857. He is buried in Westminster Abbey.

Macaulay is widely regarded as a writer of strongly Whiggish

[1] It was reputedly 'packed' with James II's supporters.

sympathies, who hated speculation and all forms of peculation and corruption. His historical writings were not invariably accurate in every detail, but his style and underlying sentiments were clear and understandable by the ordinary reader – his zest for picturesque detail creating much popular interest. He regarded the Glorious Revolution of 1688 as the determinant event in English (and thus British) history, together with the Great Reform Bill of 1832. In his writings he was severe on Whigs and Tories alike if they fell short of his standards of public probity – which were prosaic and even simplistic, allowing nothing for the contemporary standards and public attitudes of the seventeenth and early eighteenth centuries. He made a god of William III and represented James II as a fiend incarnate. He regarded Marlborough as 'a fallen angel', because of his moral failings (real or supposed) making charges which Sir Winston Churchill was determined to refute in his great work, *Marlborough, his Life and Times*. But if Macaulay's repute suffered after his death for the great popularity he had enjoyed in his lifetime, he was well described by Lord Acton as 'in description and in narrative . . . the first of all writers of history'. Above all, he introduced the study of history to the general public.

But not all worthwhile historiography comes from the pens of the great alone. The Muse of History can inspire smaller men (in terms of national or academic standing) to no less good effect, and to make the point we lastly turn in this chapter to the writings of a local Somerset historian, Mr Maurice Page of Bridgwater. 'Grass-roots' historiography is an important source of much excellent work, for the local resident, with an historical bent, some literary ability and a deep regard for the area where he lives in terms of both its past and present, can often tap streams of local consciousness which are hard for the library- and study-based historians fully to appreciate. Born four years before Winston Churchill, Maurice Page lived his life in the Somersetshire he loved. He attended Dr Morgan's Grammar School in Bridgwater, and in 1883 joined his family's printing and stationery business in that town, with its strong historical connections not only with Monmouth but also in the preceding generation with the great parliamentarian General-at-Sea, Robert Blake. Indeed, the town withstood a siege and a great fire in July 1645, and Oliver Cromwell and Sir Thomas Fairfax were all but drowned at Dunwear on a reconnaissance, when they were caught by the tidal bore of the River Parrett. So the young man doubtless absorbed much local history. He never married, but lived most of his life over the shop, latterly sharing a house with another local historian, T. Bruce Dilks, when his health began to decline. It was here, at East Gate Post Office, that he died in 1940. His series of 'Bridgwater Booklets' were well received, emanating from the East Gate Press, and none received greater acclaim than his study of Sedgemoor, which Churchill was amongst the first to recognise as of great value. Maurice Page inspired apparently the first systematic search of the Westonzoyland Parish Records, and the results were important. In recognition of his historical work he was elected a Fellow of the Royal Historical Society.[1] He lies buried in the churchyard of St Mary's, Bridgwater, the town of his birth. For an evaluation of Page's contribution to the history of our subject, let us turn to Winston Churchill. 'Much the best account of Sedgemoor is written by Mr Maurice Page (Bridgwater Booklets, No. 4), who by minute searching of parish registers and local inquiries has corrected in numerous minor particulars the hitherto accepted version; and who for the first time quotes the evidence of the Rector of Chedzoy and Mr Paschall.'[2] Although the Rector and Mr Paschall were one and the same, who could wish a better tribute?

Maurice Page also wrote a short 2d pamphlet, part of which is reproduced below. Although obviously a simplified account, it catches the full flavour of his prose style, and represents the local historian at work on the actual ground.

I. BISHOP BURNET

EXTRACTS FROM *A HISTORY OF HIS OWN TIME*, Vol. III
(Edinburgh, 1753 ed.)

But while all these things were in action,[3] the Duke of Monmouth's landing brought the session to a conclusion. As soon as Lord Argyll sailed for Scotland, the Duke set about his design with as much haste as was possible: arms were bought, and a ship was freighted for Bilbao in Spain. The Duke pawned all his jewels: but these could not raise much: and no money was sent him out of England. So he was hurried into an ill-designed invasion. The whole company consisted but of eighty-two persons. They were all faithful to one another. But some spies, whom Shelton[4] the new envoy set to work, sent him the notice of a

[1] I am greatly obliged to my uncle, Mr F. P. Coles of Bridgwater, and to Mr J. F. Lawrence, the well-known local author, for this information.
[2] W. S. Churchill, *Marlborough: his Life and Times*, Vol. 1, p. 187, f/n 11. In fact Paschell *was* the Rector of Chedzoy in question.
[3] Burnet had been describing events in Scotland, and in the Scottish Parliament, including the failure of Argyle's revolt and his subsequent execution.
[4] In fact Bevil Skelton (fl. 1661–92), British Ambassador to the United Provinces of Holland at the Hague; his agents were probably tipped off about Argyle's and Monmouth's expeditions by Stadtholder William of Orange's spies, for William hoped to see England plunged into renewed Civil War to keep it out of French control; at the same time he wished to play a double-game.

suspected ship sailing out of Amsterdam with arms . . . But those on board, hearing what he was come for, made all possible haste. And, the wind favouring them, they got out of the Texel, before the order[-of-search] desired could be brought from the Hague.

After a prosperous course, the Duke landed at Lime [sic] in Dorsetshire: and he with his small company came ashore with some order, but with too much daylight which discovered how few they were.

The alarm was brought hot to London: where, upon the general report and belied of the thing, an act of attainder[1] past both houses in one day: some small opposition being made by the Earl of Anglesey, because the evidence did not seem clear enough for so severe a sentence, which was grounded on the notoriety of the thing. The sum of £5,000 was set on his head. And with that the session of Parliament ended; which was no small happiness to the nation, such a body of men being dismissed with doing so little hurt. The Duke of Monmouth's manifesto was long, and ill-penned: full of much black and dull malice. It was plainly Fergusson's style, which was both tedious and fulsone. It charged the King with the burning of London,[2] the Popish Plot, Godfrey's murder, and the Earl of Essex's death: and to crown all, it was pretended, that the late King was poisoned by his orders: it was set forth, that the King's religion made him incapable of the crown; that three subsequent houses of Commons had voted his exclusion: the taking away the old charters,[3] and all the hard things done in the last reign, were laid to his charge: the elections to the present Parliament were also set forth very odiously, with great indecency of style: the nation was also appealed to, when met in a free Parliament, to judge the Duke's own pretensions:[4] and all sort of liberty, both in temporals and spirituals, was promised to persons of all (religious) persuasions.

Upon the Duke of Monmouth's landing, many of the country people came in to join him, but very few of the Gentry. He had quickly men enough about him to use all his arms. The Duke of Albemarle, as Lord Lieutenant of Devonshire, was sent down to raise the militia, and with them to make head against him. But their ill affection appeared very evidently: many deserted, and all were cold in the service. The Duke of Monmouth had the whole country open to him for almost a fortnight, during which time he was very diligent in training and animating his men. His own behaviour was so gentle and obliging,

[1] Effectively outlawry.
[2] The Great Fire of 1666.
[3] Of ancient boroughs.
[4] Monmouth's strongest arguments were, first that he would be a Protestant King and second that the 'Black Box' allegedly contained proof of his legitimacy.

that he was master of all their hearts, as much as was possible. But he quickly found, what it was to be at the head of undisciplined men, that knew nothing of war, and that were not to be used with rigour. Soon after their landing, Lord Grey was sent out with a small party. He saw a few of the militia, and he ran for it: but his men stood, and the militia ran from them.[1] Lord Grey brought a false alarm, that was soon found to be so: for the men whom their leader had abandoned, came back in good order. The Duke of Monmouth was struck with this, when he found that the person on whom he depended most, and for whom he designed the command of the horse, had already made himself infamous by his cowardice. He intended to join Fletcher with him in that command. But an unhappy accident made it not convenient to keep him longer about him[2] . . . without disgusting and losing the country people, who were coming in a body to demand justice. So he advised him to go aboard the ship, and to sail on to Spain, whither she was bound. By this means he was preserved for that time.

Ferguson ran among the people with all the fury of an enraged man, that affected to pass for an enthusiast, tho' all his performances that way were forced and dry. The Duke of Monmouth's great error was, that he did not in the first heat venture on some hardy action, and then march either to Exeter or Bristol; where, as he would have found much wealth, so he would have gained some reputation by it. But he lingered in exercising his men, and staid [sic] too long in the neighbourhood of Lime.

By this means the King had time both to bring troops out of Scotland, after Argyll was taken, and to send to Holland for the English and Scots regiments that were in the service of the States; which the Prince[3] sent over very readily, and offered his own person, and a greater force, if it was necessary. The King received this with great expressions of acknowledgment and kindness. It was very visible that he was much distracted in his thoughts, and that what appearance of courage soever he might put on, he was inwardly full of apprehensions and fears. He durst not accept the offer of assistance that the French made him; for by that he would have lost the hearts of the English nation. And he had no mind to be much obliged to the Prince of Orange, or to let him into his counsels or affairs. Prince George[4]

[1] The skirmish of Bridport, 15 June, 1685.

[2] See above p. 21 for Fletcher's killing of a local man over possession of a horse.

[3] i.e. William of Orange

[4] Prince George of Denmark, husband of the Princess Anne (later Queen Anne), the Protestant daughter of James II by his first wife, Anne Hyde. Anne was already much influenced by Sarah Churchill, the Whiggish wife of Brig. Gen. John Churchill (later 1st Duke of Marlborough) – hence the reference to her weak husband being 'bound to the counsels of others'. Charles II 'had tried him drunk and tried him sober and found nothing in him'.

committed a great error in not asking the command of the army; for the command, how much soever he might have been bound to the counsels of others, would have given him some lustre; whereas his staying at home in such time of danger, brought him under much neglect.

The King could not choose worse than he did, when he gave the command to the Earl of Feversham, who was a Frenchman by birth, and nephew to Mr de Turenne. Both his brothers changing religion,[1] tho' he continued still a Protestant, made that his religion was not much trusted to. He was an honest, brave and good natured man, but weak to a degree not easy to be conceived.[2] And he conducted matters so ill, that every step he made, was like to prove fatal to the King's service. He had no parties abroad. He got no intelligence: and was almost surprised, and like to be defeated, when he seemed to be under no apprehension (of danger), but was a-bed without any care or order. So that, if the Duke of Monmouth had got but a very small number of good soldiers about him, the King's affairs would have fallen into great disorder.

The Duke of Monmouth had almost surprised Lord Feversham, and all about him, while they were a-bed: he got in between two bodies, into which the army lay divided.[3] He now saw his error in lingering so long. He began to want bread, and to be so straitned, that there was a necessity of pushing for a speedy decision. He was so misled in his march, that he lost an hour's time. And when he came near the army there was an inconsiderable ditch, in the passing of which he lost so much more time, that the [royal] officers had leisure[4] to rise and be dressed, now they had the alarm. And they put themselves in order. Yet the Duke of Monmouth's foot stood longer, and fought better, than could have been expected; especially when the small body of horses that had ran upon the first charge, the blame of which was cast on the Lord Grey: the foot being thus forsaken, and galled by the cannon, did run at last. About a thousand of them were killed on the spot; and fifteen hundred were taken prisoners. Their numbers when fullest were between five and six thousand. The Duke of Monmouth left the field too soon for a man of courage, who had such high pretensions: for a few days before he had suffered himself to

---

[1] To Roman Catholicism, under the pressures following Louis XIV's Revocation of the Edict of Nantes (1685) which, since the reign of Henri IV, had protected the French Protestants in the practice of their religion.

[2] Burnet, a personal friend of the Churchills, is rather unfair to Feversham. He could not forgive Feversham for staying loyal to James II in 1688.

[3] Cf. Macaulay's three (p. 150). In fact Burnet is the more accurate.

[4] This is exaggerated. See p. 60 and Paschall, p. 109.

be called King,[1] which did him no service, even among those who followed him. He rode towards Dorsetshire: and when his horse could carry him no farther, he changed his cloathes with a shepherd, and went as far as his legs could carry him, being accompanied only with a German,[2] whom he had brought over with him. At last, when he could go no farther, he lay down in a field where there was hay and straw, with which they covered themselves; so that they hoped to lie there unseen till night. Parties went out on all hands to take prisoners. The shepherd was found by the Lord Lumley[3] in the Duke of Monmouth's cloaths. So this put them on his track, and having some dogs with them they followed the scent, and came to the place where the German was first discovered: and he immediately pointed to the place where the Duke of Monmouth lay. So he was taken in a very indecent dress and posture.

II. THOMAS BABINGTON MACAULAY

EXTRACTS FROM *THE HISTORY OF ENGLAND FROM THE ACCESSION OF JAMES II*, Vol. II (London, 1848).

The steeple of the parish church of Bridgwater[4] is said to be the loftiest in Somersetshire, and commands a wide view over the surrounding country. Monmouth, accompanied by some of his officers, went up to the top of the square tower from which the spire ascends, and observed through a telescope the position of the enemy. Beneath him lay a flat expanse, now rich with cornfields and apple trees, but then, as its name imports, for the most part a dreary morass. When the rains were heavy, and the Parrett and its tributary streams rose above their banks, this tract was often flooded . . . In . . . remote times this region could be traversed only in boats. It was a vast pool, wherein were scattered many islets of shifting and treacherous soil . . . When Monmouth looked upon Sedgemoor, it had been partially reclaimed by art, and was intersected by many deep and wide trenches which, in that country, are called rhines. In the midst of the moor rose, clustering round the towers of churches, a few villages, of which the names seem to indicate that they once were surrounded by waves. In one of these villages, called Weston Zoyland, the royal cavalry lay; and Feversham had fixed his headquarters there. Many persons still living[5]

---

[1] At Taunton (19 June) and Bridgwater (21 June). As many of his men and several of his senior officers were republicans – this Royal Proclamation was unwise.
[2] Col. Buyse. In fact Buyse tried to distract the hue and cry from his chief.
[3] Lord Lumley was Lord Lieutenant of Sussex at the head of his County's militia.
[4] St Mary's, St Mary Street, Bridgwater.
[5] Lord Macaulay was writing almost 140 years ago.

have seen the daughter of the servant girl who waited on him that day at table; and a large dish of Persian ware, which was set before him, is still safely preserved in the neighbourhood. It is to be observed that the population of Somersetshire does not, like that of the manufacturing districts, consist of emigrants from distant places. It is by no means unusual to find farmers who cultivate the same land which their ancestors cultivated when the Plantagenets reigned in England.[1] The Somersetshire traditions are, therefore, of no small value to a historian.

At a greater distance from Bridgwater lies the village of Middlezoy. In that village and its neighbourhood, the Wiltshire militia[2] were quartered, under the command of Pembroke.

On the open moor, not far from Chedzoy, were encamped several battalions of regular infantry. Monmouth looked gloomily on them . . . He could distinguish among the hostile ranks the gallant band which was then called, from the name of its Colonel, Dumbarton's regiment, but which has long been known as the first of the line and which, in all the four quarters of the world, has nobly supported its reputation.[3] 'I know those men,' said Monmouth; 'they will fight. If I had but them, all would go well.'[4]

Yet the aspect of the enemy was not altogether discouraging. The three divisions of the royal army[5] lay apart from one another. There was an appearance of negligence and relaxed discipline in all their movements. It was reported that they were drinking themselves drunk with the Zoyland cider. The incapacity of Feversham, who commanded in chief, was notorious. Even at this momentous crisis he thought only of eating and sleeping.[6] Churchill was indeed a captain equal to tasks far more arduous than that of scattering a crowd of ill-armed and ill-trained peasants. But the genius, which, at a later period, humbled six Marshals of France, was not now in its proper place. Feversham told Churchill little, and gave him no encourage-

---

[1] Times have changed. A few old families – including the Fishers – remain in the mid-1980s, but improved communications and the car have caused far greater social mobility during the past sixty or so years.
[2] Including Adam Wheeler, private drum. See his account, p. 130–7.
[3] Today the Royal Scots (the Royal Regiment); the First of Foot, nicknamed from its claim to be the most ancient regiment in the British Army 'Pontius Pilate's Body-guard', celebrated its 350th Anniversary in 1983. It has 49 Battle Honours.
[4] John Oldmixon, *History of England during the Reigns of the Royal House of Stuart 1730*, p. 703. He had personal recollections of the Revolt as a boy of twelve.
[5] i.e. the Royal Foot on the moor, the Horse and guns in Weston Zoyland and the militia at Middlezoy. In fact the horse, foot and guns were reasonably concentrated; as discussed elsewhere, the militia was deliberately left at a safe distance.
[6] Macaulay is unfair to Feversham. See p. 153.

ment to offer any suggestion. The lieutenant, conscious of superior abilities and science, impatient of the control of a chief whom he despised, and trembling for the fate of the army, nevertheless preserved his characteristic self-command, and dissembled his feelings so well that Feversham praised his submissive alacrity, and promised to report it to the King.[1]

Monmouth, having observed the disposition of the royal forces, and having been apprised of the state in which they were, conceived that a night attack might be attended with success. He resolved to run the hazard; and preparations were instantly made.

It was Sunday; and his followers, who had, for the most part, been brought up after the Puritan fashion, passed a great deal of the day in religious exercises. The Castle Field, in which the army was encamped, presented a spectacle such as, since the disbanding of Cromwell's soldiers, England had never seen. The dissenting preachers who had taken up arms against Popery, and some of whom had probably fought in the great civil war, prayed and preached in red coats and huge jackboots, with swords by their sides. Ferguson was one of those who harangued . . .

That an attack was to be made under cover of the night was no secret in Bridgwater. The town was full of women, who had repaired thither by hundreds from the surrounding region, to see their husbands, sons, lovers, and brothers once more. There were many sad partings that day; and many parted never to meet again. The report of the intended attack came to the ears of a young girl who was zealous for the King. Though of modest character, she had the courage to resolve that she would herself bear the intelligence to Feversham. She stole out of Bridgwater, and made her way to the royal camp. But that camp was not a place where female innocence could be safe. Even the officers, despising alike the irregular force to which they were opposed, and the negligent general who commanded them, had indulged largely in wine, and were ready for any excess of licentiousness and cruelty. One of them seized the unhappy maiden, refused to listen to her errand, and brutally outraged her. She fled in agonies of rage and shame, leaving the wicked army to its doom.[2]

And now the time for the great hazard drew near. The night was not ill-suited for such an enterprise. The moon was indeed at the full, and the northern streamers[3] were shining brilliantly. But the marsh fog lay

[1] Churchill was more incensed by the fact that Feversham had been appointed over him by James II; in any case it is the duty of a second-in-command to obey his chief.
[2] Macaulay cites Bishop Kennet, who had this tale from an officer of the Blues in 1718 'who had himself seen the poor girl depart in an agony of distress'. Macaulay does not mention the mission of Godfrey from Chedzoy to Monmouth.
[3] The Northern Lights.

so thick on Sedgemoor that no object could be discerned there at the distance of fifty paces.

The clock struck eleven; and the Duke with his bodyguard rode out of the Castle. He was not in the frame of mind which befits one who is about to strike a decisive blow. The very children who pressed to see him pass observed, and long remembered, that his look was sad and full of evil augury. His army marched by a circuitous path, near six miles in length, towards the royal encampment on Sedgemoor. Part of the route is to this day called War Lane.[1] The foot were led by Monmouth himself. The horse were confided to Grey, in spite of the remonstrances of some who remembered the mishap at Bridport. Orders were given that strict silence should be preserved, that no drum should be beaten, and no shot fired. The word by which the insurgents were to recognise one another in the darkness was Soho. It had doubtless been selected in allusion to Soho Fields in London, where their leader's palace stood.

At about one in the morning of Monday the sixth of July, the rebels were on the open moor. But between them and the enemy lay three broad rhines filled with water and soft mud. Two of these, called the Black Ditch and the Langmoor Rhine,[2] Monmouth knew that he must pass. But, strange to say, the existence of a trench, called the Bussex Rhine, which immediately covered the royal encampment, had not been mentioned to him by any of his scouts.

The wains which carried the ammunition remained at the entrance of the moor.[3] The horse and foot, in a long narrow column, passed the Black Ditch by a causeway. There was a similar causeway across the Langmoor Rhine: but the guide, in the fog, missed his way. There was some delay and some tumult before the error could be rectified. At length the passage was effected: but, in the confusion, a pistol went off.[4] Some men of the Horse Guards, who were on watch, heard the report, and perceived that a great multitude was advancing through the mist. They fired their carbines, and galloped off in different directions to give the alarm. One trooper spurred to the encampment of the infantry, and cried out vehemently that the enemy was at hand. The drums of Dumbarton's regiment beat to arms; and the men got fast into their ranks. It was time; for Monmouth was already drawing up his army for action. He ordered Grey to lead the way with the cavalry, and followed himself at the head of the infantry. Grey pushed

[1] Not today; it is probably Marsh Lane.
[2] Today the Black Ditch has been swallowed into the King's Sedgemoor Drain; the Langmoor Rhine has totally disappeared – and also its marker stone.
[3] Near Peasey Farm. The baggage and one gun remained on the Bristol road.
[4] Since Macaulay's time, it has become established that this shot was fired by the unknown trooper of the Blues (or Horse Guards) under Capt. Compton.

on till his progress was unexpectedly arrested by the Bussex Rhine. On the opposite side of the ditch the King's foot were hastily forming in order of battle.

'For whom are you?' called out an officer of the Foot Guards. 'For the King,' replied a voice from the ranks of the rebel cavalry. 'For which King?' was then demanded. The answer was a shout of 'King Monmouth,' mingled with the war-cry, which forty years before had been inscribed on the colours of the parliamentary regiments, 'God with us.' The royal troops instantly fired such a volley of musketry as sent the rebel horse flying in all directions. The world agreed to ascribe this ignominious rout to Grey's pusillanimity. Yet it is by no means clear that Churchill would have succeeded better at the head of men who had never before handled arms on horseback, and whose horses were unused to, not only to stand fire, but to obey the rein.

A few minutes after the Duke's horse had dispersed themselves over the moor,[1] his infantry came up running fast, and guided through the gloom by the lighted matches of Dumbarton's regiment.

Monmouth was startled by finding that a broad and profound ditch lay between him and the camp which he had hoped to surprise. The insurgents halted on the edge of the rhine, and fired. Part of the royal infantry on the further bank returned the fire. During three quarters of an hour the roar of musketry was incessant. The Somersetshire peasants behaved themselves as if they had been veteran soldiers, save only that they levelled their pieces too high.

But now the other divisions of the royal army were in motion. The Life Guards and Blues came pricking fast from Weston Zoyland,[2] and scattered in an instant some of Grey's horse, who had attempted to rally. The fugitives spread a panic amongst their comrades in the rear, who had charge of the ammunition. The waggoners drove off at full speed, and never stopped till they were many miles from the field of battle. Monmouth had hitherto done his part like a stout and able warrior. He had been seen on foot, pike in hand, encouraging his infantry by voice and by example. But he was too well acquainted with military affairs not to know that all was over. His men had lost the advantage which surprise and darkness had given them. They were deserted by the horse and by the ammunition waggons. The King's forces were now united and in good order. Feversham had been awakened by the firing, had got out of bed, had adjusted his cravat, had looked at himself well in the glass, and had come to see what his men were doing. Meanwhile, what was of much more importance,

[1] Macaulay does not mention the rebel horse breaking through their own foot.
[2] The author misses the roles played by Capt. Compton and Col. Oglethorpe's patrols.

Churchill had rapidly made an entirely new disposition of the royal infantry.[1] The day was about to break. The event of a conflict on an open plain by broad sunlight, could not be doubtful. Yet Monmouth should have felt that it was not for him to fly, while thousands whom affection for him had hurried to destruction were still fighting manfully in his cause. But vain hopes and the intense love of life prevailed. He saw that if he tarried the royal cavalry would soon intercept his retreat. He mounted and rode from the field.

Yet his foot, though deserted, made a gallant stand. The Life Guards attacked them on the right, the Blues on the left: but the Somersetshire clowns, with their scythes and the butt ends of their muskets, faced the royal horse like old soldiers. Oglethorpe made a vigorous attempt to break them and was manfully repulsed. Sarsfield, a brave Irish officer, whose name afterwards obtained a melancholy celebrity,[2] charged on the other flank.[3] His men were beaten back. He was himself struck to the ground, and lay for a time as one dead. But the struggle of the hardy rustics could not last. Their powder and ball were spent. Cries were heard of 'Ammunition! For God's sake ammunition!' But no ammunition was at hand. And now the King's artillery came up. It had been posted half a mile off, on the high road from Weston Zoyland to Bridgwater. So defective then were the appointments of an English army that there would have been much difficulty in dragging the great guns to the place where the battle was raging, had not the Bishop of Winchester offered his coach horses and traces for the purpose. This interference of a Christian prelate in a matter of blood has, with strange inconsistency, been condemned by some Whig writers who can see nothing criminal in the conduct of the numerous Puritan ministers then in arms against the government. Even when the guns had arrived, there was such a want of gunners that a sergeant of Dumbarton's regiment was forced to take on himself the management of several pieces. The cannon, however, though ill served, brought the engagement to a speedy close.[4] The pikes of the rebel battalions began to shake: the ranks broke; the King's cavalry charged again, and bore down everything before them; the King's infantry came pouring across the ditch. Even in that extremity the Mendip miners stood bravely to their arms, and sold their lives dearly. But the rout was in a

[1] For details of these moves, see p. 64 above. Also for the rebel and royal artillery.
[2] Patrick Sarsfield (d. 1693), titular Earl of Lucan, was Lt. Col. of Dover's Horse in 1685, and became its colonel next year. He received command of the Irish troops brought into England, and earned an evil reputation at their head – hence Macaulay's inference. He followed James II into exile, fought with him in Ireland (1689–91), and after service at the Boyne and at Aughrim eventually escaped to France. He fought on the French side at Steenkirk (1692) and died of wounds after Landen.
[3] Churchill is now credited with this role.
[4] The royal guns in fact were of greater importance earlier (see p. 65).

few minutes complete. Three hundred of the soldiers had been killed or wounded. Of the rebels more than a thousand lay dead on the moor.

So ended the last fight, deserving the name of battle, that has been fought on English ground.

III. MAURICE PAGE, F.R.Hist.S.

HOW IT [THE BATTLE] CAME ABOUT

When King Charles II died in 1685, his brother James, a Roman Catholic and personally unpopular came to the throne.

He was at once challenged by his nephew, Charles II's illegitimate son, the Duke of Monmouth, who came from Holland and landed at Lyme Regis.

Thence he led the Western Rebellion (which numbered 7,000 men at its peak) through Taunton, Bridgwater, Greinton, Glastonbury and Shepton Mallett towards Bristol.

He intended to march through Bristol to London, but was headed back to Bridgwater by a Royal Army, commanded by Lord Feversham, with Lord Churchill as second in command.

On Sunday, 5th July, Monmouth found himself cornered in Bridgwater in a hopeless position, with about 3,500 men. His army was composed principally of peasants, brave but ill-armed. The adventure was badly prepared and never had a chance of success.

Feversham reached Weston Zoyland that day, with about 2,500 regular troops, and 1,500 distrusted Militia in the rear, at Othery and Middlezoy. All ready to pounce the next day, and wipe out the Rebellion.

THE BATTLE

That morning a villager from Chedzoy came to Bridgwater and offered to guide the Rebels across the Moor, in order to surprise the King's Army that night.

Monmouth, being at his wit's end, jumped at the chance.

This was a difficult task however. The rebels had to find their way in the dark, across two deep Rines, and then attack regular troops behind the dry ditch called the Bussex Rine.

And they had to pierce through Feversham's well-placed patrols.

They marched out of Bridgwater at 10.30 p.m. 3,500 strong, in deep silence, along the Causeway (now the Bath road) till they reached Bradney, where they turned to the right, and reached the Moor by devious muddy lanes.

THE HITCH

All went well until they reached the swampy ditch called Langmoor Rine, where their guide missed his way in the darkness.[1]

After delay he found the crossing, but here a pistol was fired[2], which upset everything and gave the alarm.

THE ATTACK

At this point the bravery and resource of Sir Francis Compton and his handful of Horse Guards Blue saved the day for King James. Although badly wounded he attacked and delayed the advance of the 800 rebel horse, and so gained time until the Royal foot were able to line up behind the Bussex Rine for the fray.

To make things worse, the Duke of Monmouth lost his head and muddled the rebel advance. His so-called Cavalry reached the Rine, but were dispersed by the musketry fire of the Grenadier Guards.[3]

THE HALT

The rebel foot were stampeded up in column, eager to attack Bussex Rine, but arrived in disorder. It was necessary to halt, in order to form some sort of line before charging. This proved fatal. Instead of storming the trench they began to fire across it. Their ill-aimed volleys did little damage, although the fire of their three small guns annoyed the Royal foot.[4]

By this time Lord Feversham had brought up his Cavalry from the village, Life Guards, Horse Guards and Dragoons. These were sent over the Rine to hold the flanks of the rebels until day broke.

Meanwhile his artillery was dragged up, with the help of the Bishop of Winchester's carriage horses, and the fire of the guns began to break the ranks of the desperate peasants.

They still fought with great bravery, driving back the royal horse and keeping up a fire on the foot battalions across the Rine.

---

[1] Page makes no reference to the mist that still further complicated Godfrey's task. In the Bridgwater booklet he writes, however: 'The fog has blotted out everything . . .' (p. 29).

[2] No mention of the Blues' trooper, but in his *Booklet*, after weighing various possibilities, he concludes '. . . it seems probable that the pistol was fired by one of Compton's troopers when he heard the rebels approach' (p. 69).

[3] At that time known as the First Regiment of Foot Guards.

[4] Especially the Royal Scots.

THE DAWN

At last when the sun arose however, Lord Feversham ordered a combined attack from all sides, and the hard pressed rebels broke and fled.

The Militia had by this time reached the Battlefield from Middlezoy and Othery in the rear, and took part in the chase.

The Royal troops disgraced themselves by indiscriminate slaughter of the beaten rebels, many of whom were shot or hanged in cold blood without mercy.

About 500 prisoners were herded into Weston Zoyland Church, where they were kept until the Bloody Assize. Five of them died in the Church.

An entry in the Register says that the battle 'began between one and two of the clock in the morninge. It contineued near one hour and halfe'.

THE DUKE'S FLIGHT

Some time before the final collapse the Duke of Monmouth and Lord Grey, seeing that all was hopeless, threw off their armour, and, with a small band of horsemen, rode from the field, leaving their faithful followers to die fighting. Turning east along the Polden Ridge, which can be seen from the battlefield, they rode hard to reach the south coast in order to get a ship for France. Monmouth got nearly as far as Ringwood in Hampshire, but finding himself pursued and hard pressed was obliged to hide in a coppice. There he was captured and sent to London. He besought James II to grant him an interview and pleaded on his knees for mercy. James never intended to pardon him and ordered his execution next day.

SOME MISTAKEN NOTIONS

It has been often said, even by historians, that the rebels were beaten because when they attacked the Royalists they found a deep impassable ditch in front of them which they had not expected.

This is a mistake. They knew that it was there and could have crossed it, but the surprise failed and they found it thoroughly guarded by the Royal Foot in line.[1]

Another is that Lord Feversham was slack and inefficient. There is little evidence of this. He himself took all precautions against a surprise but was let down by some of his officers.[2]

---

[1] Compton's Blues had also occupied the Upper Plungeon (or cattle crossing).
[2] Most notably by Oglethorpe, although extenuating circumstances exist.

THE BLOODY ASSIZE

Some months after the Battle, Lord Chief Justice Jeffreys set out on the Western Assize, to deal with rebel prisoners. There is no doubt that he had been ordered by James II to make an example in the West of England, particularly in Somerset.

The Assize was held at Winchester, Salisbury, Dorchester, Exeter, Taunton and Wells. The rank and file of the rebels were dealt with very harshly. About 330 were executed, 849 were transported to Barbados[1] and 34 were whipped.

These deliberately cruel measures did much to undermine James II's position, and to dethrone him three years later.[2]

POSTSCRIPT: *A MYSTERY OF THE BATTLE*
(Appendix F of Bridgwater Booklet No. 4)

Although Feversham's story of the battle hangs together fairly well it is a little difficult.

He tells us that at 'a quarter before one' a.m. he rode back from the moor to Weston Zoyland. He had waited late for a message from Oglethorpe, who was supposed to be watching on Knowle Hill. As no message came he returned to his quarters in the village.

But at 'a quarter after one' (please note the hour) 'came Sir Hugh Mydlleton with one of Collonell Oglethorpe's party' bearing the belated message that he 'could not perceive the least motion of the enemy!'

If we give the trooper half an hour for his ride from Knowle he started about a quarter to one.

But Lieutenant Dummer, an exact man, says that the rebels reached the fighting line by 2 o'clock. They must have been swarming, therefore, in the tracks *between* Knowle hill and the moor by 1 o'clock or earlier.

How, then could the trooper ride right along their path via Langmoor stone without seeing or hearing anything of them?

It seems almost an impossibility . . .

All very mysterious. We are almost driven to a suspicion that 'Zummerzet Zider' was more potent than they had imagined, which would account for anything.[3]

[1] See Appendix C below.
[2] The Glorious Revolution which brought William III and Mary II to the throne.
[3] Bridgwater Booklet, p. 75. Once again Page discounts the effects of the thick mist on the moor in both disguising the rebel march and in delaying Oglethorpe's messenger bearing his report. Moreover the messenger might have moved through 'friendly' Chedzoy and reached the moor via the lane through East Field Corn.

7

The Fictional View

The place of the historical novel in the researching and writing of serious military history is not universally recognised. It may be that the average novelist sets out to entertain his reader, but in the case of the writer of good historical fiction there is no doubt that great care is taken to research the background to the story and thus to place the imaginary characters in a credible setting. Of course much care must be taken to avoid according too much historical reliance of an absolute sort on novelists, however distinguished, but there is no doubt that the well-informed and carefully researched work of fiction can add a great deal to the 'feel' of a period, and the reader's interest, appreciation and understanding of a past time can benefit enormously. What Tolstoy's *War and Peace* may be able to contribute to an understanding of the great Franco-Russian confrontations of 1805 and 1812 is assuredly, albeit in smaller measure, reflected in the way authors have chosen to treat the Rising in the West and the Sedgemoor episode.

The grim yet romantic events of 1685 have inevitably attracted the attention of numerous writers. It has been calculated that over fifty novels have been devoted to the subject over the past 120 years. Almost all have championed the oppressed under-dog – the solid craftsman and yeoman soldiery of Monmouth's army, rather than the point of view of King James II and his redcoated soldiery. This is inevitable. The horrors of the post-Sedgemoor repression have left a livid scar. Historically, the failure of 1685 proved but a prelude to the Glorious Revolution three years later – and the evolution of the Whig interpretation of History which enjoyed such a vogue from Burnet to Butterfield ensured that the Revolt in the West became interpreted as one of the final challenges to Stuart absolutism preceding the dawning of constitutional light and inspiration in 1688. Furthermore, England – as well as Oxford – has been known as 'the home of lost causes', and with the healing passage of time (which obscures much of the true horror surrounding great events of a martial nature) the events in the West Country have taken on something of a legendary appearance. This romanticism – however repugnant to a certain genre of serious historian – has much to offer the layman or open-minded student, providing it is not mistaken for the exact and precise truth to every last detail.

The two passages have been placed in their order of writing, and a word must be devoted to both their writers and the books from which they are drawn. Richard Doddridge Blackmore (1825–1900) achieved celebrity – somewhat to his own surprise – in 1869 when he published his famous novel, *Lorna Doone*. Blackmore was brought up in the West Country and was educated at Blundell's School, Tiverton, before going on to Exeter College, Oxford. He was a poet as well as a novelist, and most of his work appeared between 1864 and 1887. He published at least eight historical novels, but, although *Alice Lorraine* (1875) and *Springhaven* (1887) are occasionally referred to, *Lorna Doone* is by far his most celebrated work. The tale is set in the reigns of Charles II and James II, and is basically a romantic tale, but the historical background includes Monmouth's Rebellion and the Bloody Assize, and both the hero John Ridd and the highwayman Tom Faggus have historical antecedents.

John Ridd is a gigantic yeoman farmer from Exmoor, who enjoys fame as a wrestler throughout the West Country. His father had been murdered by a band of outlaws inhabiting a nearby valley, and the main gist of the story is the steps that John Ridd and some friends take to avenge the crime and rid the area of the menace represented by the ferocious, unprincipled and totally unscrupulous Doone family. This vendetta is hopelessly complicated by his falling in love with Lorna, the daughter of the bandit chieftain. Eventually John Ridd rescues the maiden from her associates, only to discover that she is in fact the kidnapped daughter of a Scottish nobleman. The problems placed in the path of true love thus take a new turn, but the combination of Lorna's faithfulness and the services John Ridd renders to both a kinsman of his loved one and also to the Stuart monarchy leads to a satisfactory conclusion.

Thirty years after the publication of *Lorna Doone* came the appearance of possibly the most famous fictional treatment of 1685 – *Micah Clarke*, by Sir Arthur Conan Doyle, creator of the legendary Sherlock Holmes stories. Arthur Ignatius Conan Doyle (1859–1930) came from a Catholic Irish family of artistic bent. The future historical novelist and detective story writer was born in Scotland, educated at Stonyhurst and then at Edinburgh University, and after becoming a doctor he practised medicine at Southsea from 1882 to 1890; after that date he became a professional writer of great distinction. His first book, *A Study in Scarlet* (1887), was followed by a series of historical novels heralded by *Micah Clarke* (1889), and then came *The White Company* (1891) and *Sir Nigel* (1906) set in the Hundred Years War, four romances set in the Napoleonic period – *Rodney Stone*, *Uncle Bernac*, *The Adventures of Gerard* and *The Exploits of Brigadier Gerard* (the last two owing a good deal to the *Memoirs of Baron Marbot*) and a study of

Huguenots in the France of Louis XIV and the Canada of 'New France', *The Refugees*. At the same time and interleaved with these historical romances he was writing the great Sherlock Holmes stories – most especially *The Adventures* (1891) and *The Memoirs* (1894). He wrote a volume of history – a short account of *The Great Boer War* (1900), in fact before the full conflict was over – and the same year a one-act play, *The Story of Waterloo*, which proved a triumph for the actor Sir Henry Irving. In his later years he became increasingly interested in the occult, and in 1926 wrote *A History of Spiritualism*: by then he was a relapsed Catholic.

Micah Clarke is certainly his most important historical novel, and many regard Sir Arthur Conan Doyle as this country's greatest historical novelist after Sir Walter Scott. 'If there had been no *Micah Clarke*, there would have been no *Sherlock Holmes*' avows a recent biographer.[1] The preceding *Study in Scarlet* (certainly a Holmes story) is structurally a weak book; it was the discipline and careful research that underlay his story of the Sedgemoor Rebellion that greatly improved his technique as a writer. His hero, Micah, is the son of a former Cromwellian officer of the Civil War, who brings his son up in the principles of republicanism as a God-fearing Independent. His mother, however, was a Whig loyalist to the throne and an Anglican. He becomes involved in the intrigues preparing the way for Monmouth's landing at Lyme, and befriends one of the Duke's emissaries, Decimus Saxon. As the revolt develops, Micah takes up his aging ironside father's sword, and on his behalf joins the rebels. Many adventures follow, and the pair are joined by Sir Gervase Jerome, a gallant coxcomb. The story follows the main events of the subsequent campaign with remarkable accuracy, and the climacteric engagement is grippingly described. However, in the opinion of Maurice Page, although a great admirer of the book as a whole the 'account of the actual battle is so imaginative that it misleads'.[2] In terms of detail, this is correct, but the extract included below will give a flavour of the author's narrative and descriptive skills. The battle lost, the hero inevitably has a brush with 'the Devil in wig and gown', and is sentenced to transportation to Barbados. His friend Saxon purchases his release, but he is banned from England and he travels to the Netherlands, whence he returns with Dutch William in 1688. It is a spirited and grippingly-written romance, epitomising Conan Doyle's thoroughness in working up his historical periods. His ability is well summarised in the following passage: 'While Sir Arthur read wisely, widely and well such books of authority as helped his literary pur-

[1] Owen Edwards, *The Quest for Sherlock Holmes* (London, 1984), p. 347.
[2] Maurice Page, *The Battle of Sedgemoor* (pamphlet No. 4), p. 4.

poses, he had, also, such vivid imagination and so full and accurate a mind that it was instinctive with him to see truly the persons, facts and conditions of the past in all their colour and circumstance. His mental vision was clear and exact – especially when a period appealed to him.'[1]

I.   R. D. BLACKMORE

EXTRACTS FROM *LORNA DOONE* (London, 1869),
chapters LXIV and LXV

I was by this time wide awake, though much aggrieved at feeling so, and through the open window heard the distant roll of musketry, and the beating of drums, with a quick rub-a-dub, and the 'come round the corner' of trumpet call. And perhaps Tom Faggus might be there, and shot at any moment, and my dear Annie left a poor widow, and my godson Jack an orphan, without a tooth to help him.

[John Ridd quickly dresses, induces the inn's ostler to harness his horse, Kickums, and sets out from the hostelry in Bridgwater for Westonzoyland.]

All this was done by lanthorn light, although the moon was high and bold; and in the northern heaven, flags and ribbons of a jostling pattern; such as we often have in autumn, but in July very rarely. Of these Master Dryden has spoken somewhere[2], in his courtly manner; but of him I think so little – because by fashion preferred to Shakespeare – that I cannot remember the passage; neither is it a credit to him.

Therefore I was guided mainly by the sound of guns and trumpets, in riding out of the narrow ways, and into the open marshes. And thus I might have found my road, in spite of all the spread of water, and the glaze of moonshine; but that, as I followed sound (far from hedge or causeway), fog (like a chestnut tree in blossom, touched with moon-light) met me . . .

What chance then had I and Kickums, both unused to marsh and mere? Each time when we thought that we must be right, now at last, by track or passage, and approaching the conflict, with the sounds of it waxing nearer, suddenly a break of water would be laid before us, with the moon looking mildly over it, and the northern lights behind us, dancing down the lines of fog.

It was an awful thing, I say (and to this day I remember it) to hear the

---

[1] Publisher's Note to *The Conan Doyle Historical Romances* (London, 1946), p. v.
[2] *See* p. 91–2.

sounds of raging fight, and the yells of raving slayers, and the howls of poor men stricken hard, and shattered from wrath to wailing; then suddenly the dead low hush, as of a soul departing, and spirits kneeling over it. Through the vapour of the earth, and white breath of the water, and beneath the pale round moon (bowing as the drift went by), all this rush and pause of fear passed, or lingered, on my path.

At last, when I almost despaired of escaping from this tangle of spongy banks, and of hazy creeks, and reed-fringe, my horse heard the neigh of a fellow-horse, and was only too glad to answer it; upon which the other, having lost his rider, came up, and pricked his ears at us, and gazed through the fog very steadfastly . . . he capered away with his tail set on high, and the stirrup-irons clashing under him . . . We followed him very carefully; and he led us to a little hamlet, called (as I found afterwards) West Zuyland, or Zealand, so named perhaps from its situation amid this inland sea.

Here the King's troops had been quite lately, and their fires were still burning; but the men themselves had been summoned away by the night attack of the rebels. Hence I procured for my guide a young man who knew the district thoroughly, and who led me by many intricate ways to the rear of the rebel army. We came upon a broad, open moor, striped with sullen watercourses, shagged with sedge, and yellow iris, and in the drier part with bilberries. For by this time it was four o'clock, and the summer sun arising wanly, showed us all the ghastly scene.

Would that I had never been there! Often in the lonely hours, even now it haunts me: would, far more, that the piteous thing had never been done in England! Flying men, flung back from dreams of victory and honour, only glad to have the luck of life and limbs to fly with, mud-bedraggled, foul with slime, reeking both with sweat and blood, which they could not stop to wipe, cursing, with their pumped-out lungs, every stick that hindered them, or gory puddle that slipped the step, scarcely able to leap over the corses that had dragged to die. And to see how the corses lay; some, as fair as death in sleep; with the smile of placid valour, and of noble manhood, hovering yet on the silent lips. These had bloodless hands put upwards, white as wax, and firm as death, clasped (as on a monument) in prayer for dear ones left behind, or in high thanksgiving. And of these men there was nothing in their broad blue eyes to fear. But others were of different sort; simple fellows unused to pain, accustomed to the billhook, perhaps, or rasp of the knuckles in a quick-set hedge, or making some to-do, at breakfast, over a thumb cut in sharpening a scythe, and expecting their wives to make more to-do. Yet here lay these poor chaps, dead; dead, after a deal of pain, with little mind to bear it, and a soul they had never thought of; gone, their God alone knows whither; but to mercy we may trust. Upon these things I cannot dwell; and none, I trow, would ask me; only if a plain man saw what I saw that morning, he (if God had blessed him with the heart that is in most of us) must have sickened of all desire to be great amongst mankind.

Seeing me riding to the front (where the work of death went on, among the men of true English pluck; which, when moved, no further moves) the fugitives called out to me, in half-a-dozen dialects, to make no utter fool of myself; for the great guns were come[1], and the fight was over; all the rest was slaughter.

'Arl oop wi Moonmo',' shouted one big fellow, a miner of the Mendip hills, whose weapon was a pickaxe: 'na oose to vaight na moor. Wend thee hame, young mon, agin.'

Upon this I stopped my horse, desiring not to be shot for nothing; and eager to aid some poor sick people, who tried to lift their arms to me . . . While I was giving a drop of cordial from my flask to one poor fellow . . . I felt warm lips laid against my cheek quite softly, and then a little push; and behold it was a horse leaning over me! I arose in haste, and there stood Winnie[2], looking at me with beseeching eyes, enough to melt a heart of stone . . .

[John Ridd sets off to follow Winnie, hoping to find her master.]

A cannon-bullet fired low, and ploughing the marsh slowly, met poor Winnie front to front; and she, being as quick as thought, lowered her nose to sniff at it. It might be a message from her master; for it made a mournful noise. But luckily for Winnie's life, a rise of wet ground took the ball, even under her very nose; and there it cut a splashy groove, missing her off hind-foot by an inch, and scattering black mud over her. It frightened me much more than Winnie . . .

Nearly all were scattered now. Of the noble countrymen (armed with scythe, or pick-axe, blacksmith's hammer or fold-pitcher[3]), who had stood their ground for hours against blazing musketry, from men they could not get at, by reason of the water-dyke, and then against the deadly cannon, dragged by the Bishop's horses to slaughter his own sheep; of these sturdy Englishmen, noble in their want of sense, scarce one out of four remained for the cowards to shoot down, 'Cross the rhaine,' they shouted out, 'cross the rhainem and coom within rache:' but the other mongrel Britons, with a mongrel at their head, found it pleasanter to shoot men, who could not shoot in answer, than to meet the chances of mischief, from strong arms and stronger hearts.[4]

The last scene of this piteous play was acting, just as I rode up.

---

[1] These were the royal guns, brought up by the Bishop of Winchester.
[2] John Ridd's purpose in visiting the area was to find his sister, Annie's, husband Tom Faggus.
[3] A flail, used for threshing corn.
[4] In fact the royal troops were obeying their commander's orders. Ridd is pro-Rebel.

Broad daylight, and upstanding sun, winnowing fog from the eastern hills, and spreading the moors with freshness; all along the dykes they shone, glistened on the willow-trunks, and touched the banks with a hoary grey. But alas! those banks were touched more deeply with a gory red, and strewn with fallen trunks, more woeful than the wreck of trees; while howling, cursing, yelling, and the loathsome reek of carnage, drowned the scent of new-mown hay, and the carol of the lark.

Then the cavalry of the King, with their horses at full speed, dashed from either side upon the helpless mob of countrymen. A few pikes feebly levelled met them; but they shot the pikemen, drew swords, and helter-skelter leaped into the shattered and shattering mass. Right and left, they hacked and hewed; I could hear the snapping of scythes beneath them, and see the flash of their sweeping swords. How it must end was plain enough, even to one like myself, who had never beheld such a battle before. But Winnie led me away to the left; and as I could not help the people, nor stop the slaughter, but found the cannon-bullets coming very rudely nigh me, I was only too glad to follow her.

[They find Tom Faggus, gravely wounded but alive; John Ridd ties him on to Winnie's back, and the mare sets off 'as easy and swift as a swallow' to bear her master to safety. A little later John Ridd falls in with some red-coated 'Kirke's Lambs'.[1] They, surprisingly, give him a breakfast of grilled eggs and cider, ask him to demonstrate his prowess at wrestling, and then begin to row and fight amongst themselves.]

Even while I was hesitating, and the men were breaking each other's heads, a superior officer rode up, with his sword drawn, and his face on fire.

'What, my lambs, my lambs!' he cried, smiting with the flat of his sword; 'is this how you waste my time, and my purse, when you ought to be catching a hundred prisoners, worth ten pounds apiece to me? Who is this young fellow we have here? Speak up, sirrah, what are thou, and how much will thy good mother pay for thee?'[2]

'My mother will pay naught for me,' I answered; while the lambs fell back and glowered at one another: 'so please your worship, I am no rebel; but an honest farmer, and well-proved of loyalty.'

'Ha, Ha! a farmer art thou? Those fellows always pay the best. Good farmer, come to yon barren tree; thou shalt make it fruitful.'

Colonel Kirke made a sign to his men, and before I could think of resistance, stout new ropes were flung around me; and with three men on either side, I was led along very painfully. And now I saw, and

[1] The Queen's Regiment, whose emblem was the Paschal Lamb.
[2] Colonel Piercy Kirke had an evil reputation for 'selling' justice in 1685.

repented deeply of my careless folly, in stopping with these boon companions, instead of being far away . . . I beheld myself in a grievous case, and likely to get the worst of it. For the face of the Colonel was as hard and stern as a block of bogwood oak; and though the men might pity me, and think me unjustly executed, yet must they obey their orders, or themselves be put to death.

It is not in my power to tell half the thoughts that moved me, when we came to the fatal tree, and saw two men hanging there already . . . Though ordered by the Colonel to look steadfastly upon them I could not bear to do so: upon which he called me a paltry coward, and promised my breeches to any man who would spit on my counten-ance. This vile thing Bob, being angered perhaps by the smarting wound to his knuckles, bravely stepped forward to do for me, trusting no doubt to the rope I was led with. But unluckily as it proved for him, my right arm was free for a moment; and therewith I dealt him such a blow, that he never spake again . . . At the sound and sight of that bitter stroke, the other men drew back; and Colonel Kirke, now black in the face with fury and vexation, gave orders for to shoot me, and cast me into the ditch hard by. The men raised their pieces, and pointed at me, waiting for the word to fire; and I, being quite overcome by the hurry of these events, and quite unprepared to die yet, could only think all upside down about Lorna, and my mother, and wonder what each would say to it . . . A cold sweat broke all over me, as the Colonel, prolonging his enjoyment, began slowly to say, 'Fire.'

But while he was yet dwelling on the 'F', the hoofs of a horse dashed out on the road, and horse and horseman flung themselves betwixt me and the gun-muzzles . . .

'How now, Captain Stickles?' cried Kirke, the more angry because he had shown his cowardice; 'dare you, sir, to come betwixt me and my lawful prisoner?'

'Nay, hearken one moment, Colonel,' replied my old friend Jeremy; . . . 'for your own sake hearkem.' He looked so full of momentous tidings, that Colonel Kirke made a sign to his men, not to shoot me till further orders; and then he went aside with Stickles, so that in spite of all my anxiety I could not catch what passed between them. But I fancied that the name of Lord Chief-Justice Jeffreys was spoken more than once, and with emphasis, and deference.

'Then I leave him in your hands, Captain Stickles,' said Kirke at last, so that all might hear him, '. . . and I shall hold you answerable for the custody of this prisoner.'

'Colonel Kirke, I will answer for him,' Master Stickles replied, with a grave bow, and one hand to his breast: 'John Ridd, you are my prisoner. Follow me, John Ridd.'

. . . I wrung the hand of Jeremy Stickles, for his truth and goodness
. . . 'Turn for turn, John. You saved my life from the Doones; and by
the mercy of God, I have saved you from a far worse company. Let
your sister Annie know it.'

II. SIR ARTHUR CONAN DOYLE

EXTRACTS FROM *MICAH CLARKE* (London, 1889), chapter XXXII

Behind the horse, in a long line which stretched from the Eastover
gate, across the bridge, along the High Street, up the Cornhill,[1] and so
past the church to the Pig Cross, stood our foot, silent and grim, save
when some woman's voice from the windows called forth a deep,
short answer from the ranks. The fitful light gleamed on scythe-blade
or gun-barrel, and showed up the lines of rugged, hard set faces, some
of mere children with never a hair upon their cheeks, others of old men
whose grey beards swept down to their cross-belts, but all bearing the
same stamp of a dogged courage and a fierce self-contained resolution.
Here were still the fisher folk of the south. Here, too, were the fierce
men from the Mendips, the wild hunters from Porlock Quay and
Minehead, the poachers of Exmoor, the shaggy marshmen of
Axbridge, the mountain men from the Quantocks, the serge- and
wool-workers of Devonshire, the graziers of Bampton, the red-coats
from the militia, the stout burghers of Taunton, and then, as the very
bone and sinew of all, the brave smockfrocked peasants of the plains,[2]
who had turned up their jackets to the elbow, and exposed their brown
and corded arms, as was their wont when good work had to be done.
As I speak to you, dear children, fifty years roll by like a mist in the
morning, and I am riding once more down the winding street, and see
again the serried ranks of my gallant companions. Brave hearts! They
showed to all time how little training it takes to turn an Englishman
into a soldier, and what manner of men are bred in those quiet,
peaceful hamlets which dot the sunny slopes of the Somerset and
Devon downs. If ever it should be that England should be struck upon
her knees, if those who fight her battles should have deserted her, and
she should find herself unarmed in the presence of her enemy, let
her take heart and remember that every village in the realm is a
barrack, and that her real standing army is the hardy courage and
simple virtue which stand ever in the breast of the humblest of her
peasants.

[1] These locations are in Bridgwater.
[2] Modern research has established that in fact only a minority of the Rebels were
peasants.

As we rode down the long line a buzz of greeting and welcome rose now and again from the ranks as they recognised through the gloom Saxon's tall, gaunt figure. The clock was on the stroke of eleven as we returned to our own men, and at that very moment King Monmouth rode out from the inn where he was quartered, and trotted with his staff down the High Street. All cheering had been forbidden, but waving caps and brandished arms spoke the ardour of his devoted followers. No bugle was to sound the march, but as each received the word the one in its rear followed its movements. The clatter and shuffle of hundreds of moving feet came nearer and nearer, until the Frome men in front of us began to march, and we found ourselves fairly started upon the last journey which many of us were ever to take in this world.

Our road lay across the Parret, through Eastover, and so along the winding track past the spot where Derrick met his fate, and the lonely cottage of the little maid. At the other side of this the road becomes a mere pathway over the plain. A dense haze lay over the moor, gathering thickly in the hollow and veiling both the town which we had left and the villages which we were approaching.[1] Now and again it would lift for a few moments, and then I could see in the moonlight the long, black writhing line of the army, with the shimmer of steel playing over it, and the rude white standards[2] flapping in the night breeze. Far on the right a great fire was blazing – some farmhouse, doubtless, which the Tangiers' devils[3] had made spoil of. Very slow our march was, and very careful, for the plain was, as Sir Stephen Timewell had told us, cut across by great ditches or rhines, which could not be passed save at some few places. These ditches were cut for the purpose of draining the marshes, and were many feet deep of water and of mud, so that even the horse could not cross them. The bridges were narrow, and some time passed before the army could get over. At last, however, the two main ones, the Black Ditch and the Langmoor Rhine, were safely traversed, and a halt was called while the foot was formed in line, for we had reason to believe that no other force lay between the Royal camp and ourselves. So far our enterprise had succeeded admirably. We were within half a mile of the camp without mistake or accident, and none of the enemy's scouts had shown sign of their presence. Clearly they held us in such contempt that it had never occurred to them that we might open the attack. If ever a general deserved a beating it was Feversham that night. As we drew upon the moor the clock of Chedzoy struck one . . .

[1] Including Bawdrip and Chedzoy.
[2] Most of the rebel colours were white – but Monmouth's was green and gold, and each regiment had one standard of the colour of its name.
[3] Kirke's Lambs, the 2nd of Foot.

Very slowly and silently we crept on through the dense fog, our feet splashing and slipping in the sodden soil. With all the care which we could take the advance of so great a number of men could not be conducted without a deep sonorous sound from the thousands of marching feet. Ahead of us were splotches of ruddy light twinkling through the fog which marked the Royal watch-fires. Immediately in front in a dense column our own horse moved forwards. Of a sudden out of the darkness there came a sharp challenge and a shout, with the discharge of a carbine and the sound of galloping hoofs. Away down the line we heard a ripple of shots. The first line of outposts had been reached. At the alarm our horse charged forward with a huzza, and we followed them as fast as our men could run. We had crossed two or three hundred yards of moor, and could hear the blowing of the Royal bugles quite close to us, when our horse came to a sudden halt, and our whole advance was at a standstill.

'Sancta Maria!' cried Saxon, dashing forward with the rest of us to find out the cause of the delay. 'We must on at any cost! A halt now will ruin our camisado.'[1] . . .

To this day I have never been able to make up my mind whether it was by chance or by treachery on the part of our guides that this fosse was overlooked until we stumbled upon it in the dark. There are some who say that the Bussex Rhine, as it is called, is not either deep or broad, and was, therefore, unmentioned by the moorsmen, but that the recent constant rains had swollen it to an extent never before known. Others say that the guides had been deceived by the fog, and taken a wrong course, whereas, had we followed another track, we might have been able to come upon the camp without crossing the ditch. However that may be, it is certain that we found it stretching in front of us, broad, black, and forbidding, full twenty feet from bank to bank, with the cap of the ill-fated sergeant just visible in the centre as a mute warning to all who might attempt to ford it . . .[2]

'If a few of us could make a lodgement upon the other side we might make it good until help came,' said Sir Gervas, as the horseman galloped off upon his mission.

All down the rebel line a fierce low roar of disappointment and rage showed that the whole army had met the same obstacle which hindered our attack. On the other side of the ditch the drums beat, the bugles screamed, and the shouts and oaths of the officers could be heard as they marshalled their men. Glancing lights in Chedzoy,

[1] i.e. 'enterprise'.
[2] An example of the adoption of James II's idea that the rebels had no idea of the existence of the Bussex Rhine.

Westonzoyland, and the other hamlets to left and right, showed how fast the alarm was extending. Decimus Saxon rode up and down the edge of the fosse, pattering forth foreign oaths, grinding his teeth in his fury, and rising now and again in his stirrups to shake his gauntleted hands at the enemy.

'For whom are ye?' shouted a hoarse voice out of the haze.

'For the King!' roared the peasants in answer.

'For which King?' cried the voice.

'For King Monmouth!'

'Let them have it, lads!'[1] and instantly a storm of musket bullets whistled and sung about our ears. As the sheet of flame sprang out of the darkness the maddened, half-broken horses dashed wildly away across the plain resisting the efforts of the riders to pull them up. There are some, indeed, who say that those efforts were not very strong, and that our troopers, disheartened at the check at the ditch, were not sorry to show their heels to the enemy. As to my Lord Grey, I can say truly that I saw him in the dim light among the flying squadrons, doing all that a brave cavalier would do to bring them to a stand. Away they went, however, thundering through the ranks of the foot and out over the moor, leaving their companions to bear the whole brunt of the battle.

'On to your faces, men!' shouted Saxon, in a voice which rose high above the crash of the musketry and the cries of the wounded. The pikemen and scythes-men threw themselves down loading and firing,[2] with nothing to aim at save the burning matches of the enemy's pieces,[3] which could be seen twinkling through the darkness. All along, both to the right and the left, a rolling fire had broken out, coming in short, quick volleys from the soldiers, and in a continuous confused rattle from the peasants. On the further wing our four guns had been brought into play, and we could hear their dull growling in the distance.[4]

'Sing, brothers, sing!' cried our stout-hearted chaplain, Master Joshua Pettigrue, bustling backwards and forwards among the prostrate ranks. 'Let us call upon the Lord in our day of trial!' The men raised a loud hymn of praise, which swelled into a great chorus as it was taken up by the Taunton burghers upon our right and the miners upon our left. At the sound the soldiers on the other side raised a fierce huzza, and the whole air was full of clamour.

Our musqueteers had been brought to the very edge of the Bussex

---

[1] This exchange took place opposite the position held by the First Guards.

[2] A slip – these troops had no firearms.

[3] The matchlocks of the Royal Scots.

[4] In fact in the centre of the overall rebel line, and only *three* guns.

Rhine, and the Royal troops had also advanced as far as they were able, so that there were not five pikes'-lengths[1] between the lines. Yet that short distance was so impassable, save for the more deadly fire, that a quarter of a mile might have divided us. So near were we that the burning wads[2] from the enemy's muskets flew in flakes of fire over our heads, and we felt upon our faces the hot, quick flush of their discharges. Yet though the air was alive with bullets, the aim of the soldiers was too high for our kneeling ranks, and very few of the men were struck. For our part, we did what we could to keep the barrels of our muskets from inclining upwards. Saxon, Sir Gervas and I walked our horses up and down without ceasing, pushing them level with our sword-blades, and calling on the men to aim steadily and slowly. The groans and cries from the other side of the ditch showed that some, at least, of our bullets had not been fired in vain . . .

The men broke out a'cheering and the fire on both sides became hotter than ever. It was a marvel to me, and to many more, to see these brave peasants with their mouths full of bullets[3], loading, priming, and firing as steadily as though they had been at it all their lives, and holding their own against a veteran regiment which had proved itself in other fields to be second to none[4] in the army of England.

The grey light of morning was stealing over the moor, and still the fight was undecided. The fog hung about us in feathery coloured clouds, through which the long lines of red coats upon the other side of the rhine loomed up like a battalion of giants. My eyes ached and my lips pringled with the smack of the powder. On every side of me men were falling fast, for the increased light had improved the aim of the soldiers. Our good chaplain, in the very midst of a psalm had uttered a great shout of praise and thanksgiving, and so passed on to join those of his parishioners who were scattered round him upon the moor. Hope-Above Williams and Keeper Milson, under-officers, and among the stoutest men in the company, were both down, the one dead and the other sorely wounded, but still ramming down charges, and spitting bullets into his gun-barrel. The two Stukeleys of Somerton, twins and lads of great promise, lay silently with grey faces turned to the grey sky, united in death as they had been in birth. Everywhere the dead lay thick amid the living. Yet no man flinched from his place, and Saxon still walked his horse among them with

[1] i.e. 80 feet.

[2] A wad was rammed down on top of the charge of powder and shot to keep the latter firm in the barrel and to improve compression of the charge.

[3] When loading a musket with a cartridge it was the practice to bite off the paper top, holding the ball, and retain it in the mouth until it was time to spit it down the muzzle on top of the powder.

[4] *Nullus Secundus* is the motto of the 2nd, or Coldstream, Guards.

words of hope and praise, while his stern, deep-lined face and tall sinewy figure were a very beacon of hope to the simple rustics. Such of my scythesmen as could handle a musket were thrown forward into the fighting line, and furnished with the arms and pouches of those who had fallen.

Ever and anon as the light waxed I could note through the rifts in the smoke and the fog how the fight was progressing in other parts of the field. On the right the heath was brown with the Taunton and Frome men, who, like ourselves, were lying down to avoid the fire. Along the borders of the Bussex Rhine a deep fringe of their musqueteers were exchanging murderous volleys, almost muzzle to muzzle, with the left wing of the same regiment with which we were engaged, which was supported by a second regiment in broad white facings, which I believe to have belonged to the Wiltshire militia.[1] On either bank of the black trench a thick line of dead, brown on the one side, and scarlet on the other, served as a screen to their companions, who sheltered themselves behind them and rested their musket-barrels upon their prostrate bodies. To the left amongst the withies lay five hundred Mendip and Bagworthy miners, singing lustily, but so ill-armed that they had scarce one gun among ten wherewith to reply to the fire which was poured into them. They could not advance, and they would not retreat, so they sheltered themselves as best they might, and waited patiently until their leaders might decide what was to be done. Further down for half a mile or more the long rolling cloud of smoke, with petulant flushes of flame spurting out through it, showed that every one of our raw regiments was bearing its part manfully. The cannon on the left had ceased firing. The Dutch gunners had left the islanders to settle their own quarrels, and were scampering back to Bridgwater, leaving their silent pieces to the Royal horse.

The battle was in this state when there rose a cry of 'The King, the King!' and Monmouth rode through our ranks, bare-headed and wild-eyed, with Buyse, Wade, and a dozen more beside him. They pulled up within a spear's-length of me, and Saxon, spurring forward to meet them, raised his sword to the salute. I could not but mark the contrast between the calm, grave face of the veteran, composed yet alert, and the half-frantic bearing of the man whom we were compelled to look upon as our leader.

'How think ye, Colonel Saxon?' he cried wildly. 'How goes the fight? Is all well with ye? What an error, alas! what an error! Shall we draw off, eh? How say you?'

[1] The Wiltshire Militia was part of the Royal Army (*see* Adam Wheeler's account above) – but it was almost certainly in the area to the east of Westonzoyland at this time in the battle.

'We hold our own here, your Majesty,' Saxon answered. 'Methinks had we something after the nature of palisados or stockados,[1] after the Swedish fashion, we might even make it good against the horse.'

'Ah, the horse!' cried the unhappy Monmouth. 'If we get over this, my Lord Grey shall answer for it. They ran like a flock of sheep. What leader could do anything with such troops? Oh, lack-a-day, lack-a-day! Shall we not advance?'

'There is no reason to advance, your Majesty, now that the surprise has failed,' said Saxon. 'I had sent for carts to bridge over the trench according to the plan which is commended in the treatise, De Valis et Fossis, but they are useless now. We can but fight on as we are.'

'To throw troops across would be to sacrifice them,' said Wade. 'We have lost heavily, Colonel Saxon, but I think from the look of yonder bank that ye have given a good account of the red-coats.'

'Stand firm! For God's sake, stand firm!' cried Monmouth distractedly. 'The horse have fled, and the canoniers also. Oh! what can I do with such men? What shall I do? Alas, Alas!' He set spurs to his horse and galloped off down the line, still wringing his hands and uttering his dismal wailings. How small, how very small a thing is death when weighed in the balance with dishonour! Had this man but borne his fate silently, as did the meanest footman who followed his banners, how proud and glad would we have been to have discoursed of him, our princely leader. But let him rest. The fears and agitations and petty fond emotions, which showed upon him as the breeze shows upon the water, are all stilled now for many a long year. Let us think of the kind heart and forget the feeble spirit . . .

Out of the haze which still lay thick upon our right there twinkled here and there a bright gleam of silvery light, while a dull, thundering noise broke upon our ears like that of the surf upon a rocky shore. More and more frequent came the fitful flashes of steel, louder and yet louder grew the hoarse gathering tumult, until of a sudden the fog was rent, and the long lines of the Royal cavalry broke out from it, wave after wave, rich in scarlet and blue and gold, as grand a sight as ever the eye rested upon. There was something in the smooth steady sweep of so great a body of horsemen which gave the feeling of irresistible power. Rank after rank, and line after line, with waving standards, tossing manes, and gleaming steel, they poured onwards, an army in themselves, with either flank still shrouded in the mist. As they thundered along, knee to knee and bridle to bridle, there came from them such a gust of deep-chested oaths, with the jangle of harness, the clash of steel, and the measured beat of multitudinous hoofs, that no

[1] Since the days of Gustavus Adolphus, Swedish infantry were accompanied into the field by carts carrying *chevaux de frise* – wooden barricades set with sword blades – which were used to form a barricade around their regiments.

man who hath not stood up against such a whirlwind, with nothing but a seven-foot pike in his hand, can know how hard it is to face it with a steady lip and a firm grip.

But wonderful as was the sight, there was, as ye may guess, my dears, little time for us to gaze upon it. Saxon and the German flung themselves among the pikemen and did all that men could do to thicken the array. Sir Gervas and I did the same with the scythesmen[1], who had been trained to form a triple front after the German fashion, one rank kneeling, one stooping, and one standing erect, with weapons advanced. Close to us the Taunton men had hardened into a dark sullen ring, bristling with steel, in the centre of which might be seen and heard their venerable Mayor, his long beard fluttering in the breeze, and his strident voice clanging over the field. Louder and louder grew the roar of the horse. 'Steady, my brave lads,' cried Saxon in trumpet tones. 'Dig the pike-butt into the earth! Rest it on the right foot! Give not an inch! Steady!' A great shout went up from either side, and then the living wave broke over us.

What hope is there to describe such a scene as that – the crashing of wood, the sharp gasping cries, the snorting of horses, the jar when the push of pike met with the sweep of sword! Who can hope to make another see that of which he himself carries away so vague and dim an impression? One who has acted in such a scene gathers no general sense of the whole combat, such as might be gained by a mere onlooker, but he has stamped for ever upon his mind just the few incidents which may chance to occur before his own eyes. Thus my memories are confined to a swirl of smoke with steel caps and fierce, eager faces breaking through it, with the red gaping nostrils of horses and their pawing fore-feet as they recoiled from the hedge of steel. I see, too, a young beardless lad, an officer of dragoons, crawling on hands and knees under the scythes, and I hear his groan as one of the peasants pinned him to the ground. I see a bearded, broad-faced trooper riding a grey horse just outside the fringe of the scythes, seeking for some entrance, and screaming the while with rage. Small things imprint themselves upon a man's notice at such a time. I even marked the man's strong white teeth and pink gums. At the same time, I see a white-faced, thin-lipped man leaning far forward over his horse's neck and driving at me with his sword-point, cursing the while as only a dragoon can curse. All these images start up as I think of that fierce rally, during which I hacked and cut and thrust at man and horse without a thought of parry or of guard. All round rose a fierce babel of shouts and cries, godly ejaculations from the peasants and oaths from the horsemen, with Saxon's voice above all imploring his pikemen to

---

[1] Each of Monmouth's five infantry regiments had one company of scythemen apiece.

stand firm. Then the cloud of horsemen recoiled, circling off over the plain, and the shout of triumph from my comrades, and an open snuff-box thrust out in front of me, proclaimed that we had seen the back of as stout squadrons as ever followed a kettledrum.[1]

But if we could claim it as a victory, the army in general could scarce say as much. None but the very pick of the troops could stand against the flood of heavy horses and steel-clad men. The Frome peasants were gone, swept utterly from the field. Many had been driven by pure weight and pressure into the fatal mud which had checked our advance. Many others, sorely cut and slashed, lay in ghastly heaps all over the ground which they had held. A few by joining our ranks had saved themselves from the fate of their companions. Further off the men of Taunton still stood fast, though in sadly diminished numbers. A long ridge of horses and cavaliers in front of them showed how stern had been the attack and how fierce the resistance. On our left the wild miners had been broken at the first rush, but had fought so savagely, throwing themselves upon the ground and stabbing upwards at the stomachs of the horses, that they had at last beaten off the dragoons. The Devonshire militiamen,[2] however, had been scattered, and shared the fate of the men of Frome. During the whole of the struggle the foot upon the further bank of the Bussex Rhine were pouring in a hail of bullets, which our musqueteers, having to defend themselves against the horse, were unable to reply to.

It needed no great amount of soldierly experience to see that the battle was lost, and that Monmouth's cause was doomed. It was broad daylight now, though the sun had not yet risen. Our cavalry was gone, our ordnance was silent, our line was pierced in many places, and more than one of our regiments had been destroyed. On the right flank the Horse Guards Blue, the Tangiers Horse, and two dragoon regiments were forming up for a fresh attack. On the left the foot guards had bridged the ditch and were fighting hand to hand with the men from North Somerset. In front a steady fire was being poured into us, to which our reply was feeble and uncertain, for the powder carts had gone astray in the dark, and many were calling hoarsely for ammunition, while others were loading with pebbles instead of ball. Add to this that the regiments which still held their ground had all been badly shaken by the charge, and had lost a third of their number. Yet the brave clowns sent up cheer after cheer, and shouted words of encouragement and homely jests to each other, as though a battle were

[1] The rebel Blue Regiment did repulse one attack by the Royal Cavalry attacking from the Upper Plungeon.

[2] The Rebel Army did include a number of militiamen who had deserted at Bridport to join the cause of Monmouth.

but some rough game which must as a matter of course be played out while there was a player left to join in it.

Again the cannon roared, and again our men were mowed down as though Death himself with his scythe were amongst us. At last our ranks were breaking. In the very centre of the pikemen steel caps were gleaming, and broadswords rising and falling. The whole body was swept back two hundred paces or more, struggling furiously the while, and was there mixed with other like bodies which had been dashed out of all semblance of military order, and yet refused to fly. Men of Devon, of Dorset, of Wiltshire, and of Somerset, trodden down by horse, slashed by dragoons, dropping by scores under the rain of bullets, still fought on with a dogged, desperate courage for a ruined cause and a man who had deserted them. Everywhere as I glanced around me were set faces, clenched teeth, yells of rage and defiance, but never a sound of fear or of submission. Some clambered up upon the cruppers of the riders and dragged them backwards from their saddles. Others lay upon their faces and hamstrung the chargers with their scythe-blades, stabbing the horsemen before they could disengage themselves. Again and again the guards crashed through them from side to side, and yet the shattered ranks closed up behind them and continued the long-drawn struggle. So hopeless was it and so pitiable that I could have found it in my heart to wish that they would break and fly, were it not that on the broad moor there was no refuge which they could make for. And all this time, while they struggled and fought, blackened with powder and parched with thirst, spilling their blood as though it were water, the man who called himself their King was spurring over the countryside with a loose rein and a quaking heart, his thoughts centred upon saving his own neck, come what might to his gallant followers.

Large numbers of the foot fought to the death, neither giving nor receiving quarter; but at last, scattered, broken, and without ammunition, the main body of the peasants dispersed and fled across the moor, closely followed by the horse. Saxon, Buyse, and I had done all that we could to rally them once more, and had cut down some of the foremost of the pursuers, when my eye fell suddenly upon Sir Gervas, standing hatless with a few of his musqueteers in the midst of a swarm of dragoons. Spurring our horses we cut a way to his rescue, and laid our swords about us until we had cleared off his assailants for the moment.

'Jump up behind me!' I cried. 'We can make good our escape.'

He looked up smiling and shook his head. 'I stay with my company,' he said.

'Your company!' Saxon cried. 'Why, man, you are mad! Your company is cut off to the last man.' . . .

And now it was every man to himself. In no part of the field did the insurgents continue to resist. The first rays of sun shining slantwise across the great dreary plain lit up the long line of the scarlet battalions, and glittered upon the cruel swords which rose and fell among the struggling drove of resistless fugitives.

Appendix A

CHRONOLOGICAL TABLE

All dates are Old Style. To convert to New Style, add ten days. Thus the first entry could read '16 February (NS) or 6 February (OS)'.

6 Feb. 1685	– Death of King Charles II at London.
2 May	– Earl of Argyle sails from the Netherlands to start the Scottish revolt.
1 June	– Monmouth sets sail belatedly from the River Texel for the West Country.
11 June (Thurs.)	– Monmouth lands at Lyme Regis, preceded by small party landing at Chideock to collect supporters and horses. Red Regiment is recruited.
13 June (Sat.)	– NEWS OF MONMOUTH'S LANDING REACHES JAMES II IN LONDON.
14 June (Sun.)	– Rebels brush with the Dorset Militia at Bridport.
	– JOHN LORD CHURCHILL APPOINTED TO COMMAND FIRST ROYAL FORCES SENT WEST.
15 June (Mon.)	– Monmouth marches to Axminster, narrowly forestalling Albemarle's Devon militia.
16 June (Tues.)	– Rebels occupy Chard.
17 June (Wed.)	– Rebels camp at Ilminster. ALBEMARLE REACHES WELLINGTON WITH DEVON AND SOMERSET MILITIA.
18 June (Thurs.)	– Monmouth enters Taunton to rapturous welcome. Churchill's horse make contact with the rebels near Chard; final defeat of Argyle in Scotland.
19 June (Fri.)	– Maids of Tauntom present colours to Monmouth; first proclamation of Monmouth.
	– JAMES II APPOINTS LORD FEVERSHAM TO OVERALL COMMAND IN THE WEST.
	– Cavalry skirmish at Ashill; ROYAL HORSE FALL BACK ON CHARD.
20 June (Sat.)	– Second proclamation of Monmouth (as King) at Taunton. Blue Regiment raised.
21 June (Sun.)	– Rebel army marches to Bridgwater; receives warm welcome.
	– COL. KIRKE JOINS CHURCHILL WITH HIS INFANTRY AT CHARD.
	– MAIN ROYAL FORCE EN ROUTE FROM LONDON.
22 June (Mon.)	– Monmouth marches to Glastonbury through rain; minor cavalry encounter at Langport.

23 June (Tues.) – Monmouth reaches Shepton Mallet. FEVERSHAM REACHES BRISTOL.

24 June (Wed.) – Rebel army marches to Pensford, harassed by Churchill's cavalry.
– FEVERSHAM VISITS BATH; MAIN FORCE APPROACHING BRISTOL.

25 June (Thurs.) – Monmouth's rebels repair bridge at Keynsham and cross; skirmish with royal cavalry and militia and bad weather cause rebels to retire; Monmouth holds council-of-war; abandons Bristol project in favour of advance into Wiltshire. Rebels march to Bath overnight.

26 June (Fri.) – Monmouth camps at Norton St Philip. CHURCHILL JOINS FEVERSHAM AT BATH.

27 June (Sat.) – Royalist attack on Norton St Philip repulsed; FEVERSHAM FALLS BACK TO BRADFORD-ON-AVON. Rebels set off after dark for Frome through rain.

28 June (Sun.) – Rebels reach Frome.

29 June (Mon.) – News reaches Monmouth of Argyle's fate. Council-of-war. FEVERSHAM AND ROYAL ARMY MARCH TO WESTBURY AND RECEIVE REINFORCEMENTS INCLUDING THE ARTILLERY TRAIN. Rebels prepare to march on Warminster.

30 June (Tues.) – Thwarted by Royal Army, Monmouth abandons plan to march on London through Wiltshire, and marches to Shepton Mallet. FEVERSHAM OCCUPIES FROME.

1 July (Wed.) – Monmouth reaches Wells, capturing some royal waggons. Desertions mount. FEVERSHAM RESTS ROYAL ARMY AT FROME.

2 July (Thurs.) – Rebels march towards Bridgwater, camp on the moor; joined by Clubmen. FEVERSHAM ENTERS SHEPTON MALLET.

3 July (Fri.) – Monmouth enters Bridgwater to lukewarm welcome; orders its fortification. FEVERSHAM MARCHES THROUGH GLASTONBURY TO SOMERTON.

4 July (Sat.) – Monmouth considers break-away towards Bristol. News of siege preparations reach Feversham. HE RECONNOITRES CAMP-SITES NEAR WESTONZOYLAND.

5 July (Sun.) – ROYAL ARMY CAMPS AT WESTONZOYLAND. Monmouth decides on night-attack.

6 July (Mon.) – Night battle of Sedgemoor. Monmouth flees to Downside. Rebels routed and pursued. Churchill enters Bridgwater. Rebels rounded up.

7 July (Tues.) – COL. KIRKE MARCHES INTO TAUNTON. Monmouth reaches Cranborne Chase.

8 July (Wed.) – Monmouth captured near Woodlands in Dorset.

15 July (Wed.) – Monmouth executed at the Tower.

Note: items in capitals distinguish events involving the Royal Army when not in immediate contact with the Rebel Army.

Appendix B

ORDERS OF BATTLE, SEDGEMOOR FIGHT – NIGHT OF 5/6 JULY 1685 (OS)

A. THE ROYAL ARMY OF KING JAMES II

Lt.Gen. LOUIS DURAS, Earl of Feversham
(commander-in-chief, 19 June)
Maj.Gen. JOHN, LORD CHURCHILL
(second-in-command)
Col. John Ramsay, (Quartermaster-General)

The Royal Horse

First Horse Guards
(today The Life Guards)
Col. Edward Villiers

Oglethorpe's Blues
(today the Royal
Horse Guards)
Col. Lord Oglethorpe

King's Own Royal
Dragoons
(today The Royal
Dragoons)
Col. John, Lord
Churchill

The Royal Foot

The Royal Regiment of
Guards – two battalions
(today the First or Grenadier
Guards)
Col. the Duke of Grafton

The King's Footguards
(today the Second or
Coldstream Guards)
Col. Sackville

Dumbarton's Regiment
of Foot
(today the 1st of Foot or
Royal Scots)
Lt. Col. Lord Douglas

Kirke's Regiment of Foot
(or 'Queen Dowager's')
(today the Queen's
Regiment)
Col. Piercy Kirke

Trelawney's Regiment of
Foot
(today The King's Own
Royal Border Regiment)
Lt. Col. Charles Churchill

The Royal Train

The Tower
Train

The Portsmouth
Bye-Train
Controller
Henry
Sheres (overall
commander of
the cannon)
26 guns in all

Total estimated strength: 750 Horse and Dragoons, 1,900 Foot, 200 Board of Ordnance personnel (26 cannon). NB: no account of the three regiments of Wiltshire Militia taken here, who were kept back at Middlezoy and Othery under Lord Pembroke (est. 3,000).

B. THE REBEL ARMY OF 'KING MONMOUTH'

Capt. Gen. JAMES SCOTT, Duke of Monmouth
(commander-in-chief)
LORD GREY of Warke
(second in command)

The Rebel Horse	*The Rebel Foot*	*The Rebel Train*
Life Guard of Horse (est. 40) Three assorted Troops (plus two detached to Minehead)★	The Red Regiment (est. 800) Major Nathaniel Wade (acting Colonel)	3 small cannon (and one defective) Anton Buyse, and 'the Dutch Gunner'
Lord Grey of Warke Capts. Jones and Hucker (est. 600 horsemen)	The White Regiment (est. 400) Col. John Ffoulkes (or Fowke)	
	The Yellow Regiment (est. 500) Col. Edward Matthews	
	The Green Regiment (est. 600) Col. Abraham Holmes	
	The Blue Regiment (est. 600) Col. Richard Bovet (or Basset)	
	The Lyme Independent Company (est. 80)	

Total estimated strength: 600 horse (mostly untrained), 2,980 Foot, 30 gunners (4 cannon) NB: The figures are based on Wade's Confession – 'never 4,000 when they fought'.

★ under Capts. Hewling and Cary

SPECIAL NOTE:

THE STANDING (OR ROYAL) ARMY OF 1685

It has been customary for reasons touched upon earlier in this book for the lion's share of attention to be paid to the format and composition of the rebel army; this predeliction, whilst understandable, does reveal a degree of unfair bias, and as a result the Royal Army of King James II tends to be classified amongst the 'villains' and accordingly receives relatively short and generally unfavourable attention. And yet there is no doubt whatsoever that it was the loyalty and professional competence of the royal troops in that late summer of crisis, subversion and rumour in 1685 that proved the decisive factor in procuring the defeat of Monmouth's Rebellion. The purpose of this Special Note is fractionally to redress the imbalance by providing the reader with a minimum of information on the Royal Army, its composition, weapons and equipment. Further information on the subject can be found by sampling the books by Fortescue, Walton, Dalton and Childs, or, for the militia Western, cited in the Select Bibliography.

Antecedents and Composition

The reasons why James II's army receives relatively scant attention from historians and writers are not hard to seek. Not only is the emotional appeal of the rebel underdogs stronger, but the period 1660–88 forms something of a watershed for the forces of law and order (and, that, in the last analysis, is what the royal troops represented on home service duties, however unpopular they might be in carrying them out). The armies of Charles II and his brother James were small by comparison with what had gone before and what was to come after. On the one hand, Charles' Guards and Garrisons[1] barely numbered 8,870 regular troops (one fifth of them being assigned to fortress duty) in England at the time of his death, with possibly 2,200 on the establishment of Scotland, a further 7,500 in Ireland, and two ad hoc brigades, one of English and one of Scottish troops,[2] serving overseas in the United Provinces on loan to William of Orange. Troops within England in December 1685 had risen to 19,800. Even at the height of the crisis of 1688, following James II's massive enlargement of the standing army which began during the Rebellion of 1685 and was continued thereafter for reasons that do not lie within the scope of this present work, the troops totalled only some 35,000 men. But when we compare these figures with the estimated 65,000 of the Commonwealth's New Model Army[3], disbanded at the Restoration in 1660[4], or the 93,635 'troops in pay'[5] that William III deployed by 1697, or the 97,897[6] that owed allegiance to Queen Anne at the height of Marlborough's campaigns in the first decade of the eighteenth century – it will be appreciated that the regular army of 1685 was small even by English standards. It is true that the county militias of 'that ancient constitutional force' totalled on paper another 90,000 part-time soldiers (including 6,000 horse), but in military terms their value was slight at any level above supporting Lords Lieutenant in dealing with local minor disturbances or in enforcing royal edicts. The small professional army in March 1685 comprised on the English establishment three troops of Life Guards with attached Horse Grenadiers (effectively three

[1] So-called in the 1660s when the very word 'army' was anathema owing to the misuse of military power to cowe the country during the 'Rule of the Major-Generals' during the 1650s.
[2] Perhaps six battalions or some 3,600 men in all.
[3] According to Fortescue, History of the British Army, Vol. 1, p. 290.
[4] All but two regiments which were re-engaged on the spot to deal with a local crisis.
[5] Including 23,000 mercenaries and subsidy-troops.
[6] Including 30,000 mercenaries.

small regiments of élite cavalry), the King's Regiment of Horse (also known as the Earl of Oxford's 'Blues', later the Royal Horse Guards), the Royal Dragoons (formerly the Tangier Horse), two regiments of Foot Guards (the First and the Coldstream), and five more 'marching regiments of foot' – namely the Royal Scots (or Dumbarton's), the Queen Dowager's Regiment (or Kirke's), Prince George of Denmark's Foot (or Littleton's), the Holland Regiment of Foot (or Mulgrave's) and the Queen Consort's Foot (or Trelawney's). Gunners and engineers came under a separate department of state, the Board of Ordnance.

Officers and Men

The social composition of the standing army reflected the triple stream of officers and men that had enlisted after the Restoration. First there were the troops that had been raised during Charles II's exile in Europe; second, there were the remaining members of the two New Model formations who were re-engaged, (General Monck) Lord Albemarle's Coldstream Guards, and his regiment of horse, (which became the Third Troop of the Life Guards); and third the old royalists who had survived the Interregnum in England and from 1660 sought martial employment. Only a number of the soldiers serving in 1660 would have still been in the ranks twenty-five years later, but it was a leavening, particularly amongst the senior officers. All officers were appointed by commissions issued by the monarch, and tended to reflect the lesser aristocracy and the not-too-well-off young men about Court such as John Churchill. In mid-1685 almost all were Anglican Protestants because of the penal laws which denied employment in offices of profit under the Crown to Roman Catholics and Presbyterians alike. The system of purchase was developing, whereby an officer had not only to be recommended for promotion but also to pay a substantial sum for his next step, and royal patronage and favoritism were also important factors in a military career's development. Officers received no formal training, but were expected to learn their profession 'at the cannon's mouth'. Standards varied enormously; there was much absenteeism, duelling, drunkenness and other social misbehaviour laid at the door of the officers of the army, but a number had served on secondment to French, Dutch and Spanish forces, and still more – especially in the Tangier regiments – had some practical campaigning in North-West Africa against the Moors. So there were some officers with recent military experience. Pay was variable at best, and most officers needed some recourse to private means to get by.

The rank and file – as in every army of this period – consisted mainly of the dregs of society, the wastrels, misfits and unfortunates, fleeing poverty, the law or unemployment, but with a number of dedicated professionals and genuine volunteers who made the formations viable. Some men were pressed into service, but most were volunteers. Pay was poor (8d. a day for a private sentinel before stoppages and 12s. a day for his colonel), discipline strict, and rations and living conditions rudimentary. Few of the NCOs could read or write, and they and the rank and file, and not a few of their officers, like Piercy Kirke, were pretty rough diamonds, unloved by society as a whole but imbued, as a result, with a sense of military freemasonry. A proportion of the troops were Irishmen or Scots, and a further number of foreign mercenaries were also attracted to don the russet-red coat of the English Army.

Weaponry, Uniforms and Organisation

An infantry regiment at full strength comprised some 780 rank and file and forty officers, divided between thirteen companies, one being the Grenadier company, another that of the colonel. The foot were armed with 16-ft pikes or matchlock muskets in the proportion of roughly one to five by 1685. The unwieldy pike was still regarded as the nobler weapon, and was required to form a defensive nucleus or 'hedgehog' when the infantry was under cavalry attack (the predecessor of the famous square of later generations), but it could also be used offensively for 'push of pike'. The matchlock musket was a cumbersome weapon, taking at least a minute to reload (requiring forty separate 'motions' to do so), weighing between 13 and 15 lb. (thus needing a rest to support the barrel), and firing a 1-oz. lead musket ball. The weapon had a calibre of .8 in., was muzzle-loaded with the aid of a wooden ramrod and fired by application of a nitre-soaked length of burning slow-match. Much prone to misfires and other problems, it was frequently used as a club in the heat of close action. Its range was 250 yards, but the weapon was rarely employed at much over sixty. Each musketeer carried twelve rounds in containers hanging from a bandolier (the 'twelve Apostles'). A few troops were equipped with the much better flintlock musket, fired by a spark caused by a hammer-held flint striking the steel 'frisson', which doubled the rate of fire, but this was not on general issue by the time of Sedgemoor – as the incident of the Royal Scots at the battle indicates. Infantrymen were all equipped with a short sword, and many with the plug-bayonet which was placed in the muzzle and thus precluded firing when fixed. The rank and file ('hatmen') wore black felt hats with circular brims pinned up in various ways according to regimental custom. Each man was issued with a russet coat, with facings and cuffs of various colours according to regiment (white for the Royal Scots, sea-green for Kirke's etc), a waistcoat, baggy breeches, shoes and stockings, and a sash around the waist. Officers wore superior-quality clothing with lace at neck and cuff, sported a gorgette around the neck to indicate their rank and gold lace and plumes on the hat, and carried a spontoon (or half-pike) and sword. Sergeants wore bunches of ribbons on the right shoulder and carried a halberd. Grenadiers carried four hand-lit gre-nades in a pouch in addition to their muskets (usually fusils or flintlocks) and, as élite troops, wore more elaborate clothes than the hatmen, including a grenadier cap. This was not yet the famous mitre-shape of later years, but more often a fur cap with, attached to the crown, a cloth-bag ending in a tassel hanging down behind. All troops also carried a rolled blanket on the march, and were provided with a breadbag and a knapsack.

A cavalry regiment was organised into a number of troops, six being a common number, each of fifty troopers at full establishment. The 300-or-so troopers were commanded by a dozen officers. Each man was equipped with a sword and pistols, and in most cases a musketoon or carbine firearm in addition (a short version of the musket, usually of the flintlock variety). A dragoon regiment had companies rather than troops, and lieutenants instead of ensigns, and was paid rather less than one of horse as dragoons were regarded as mounted infantry and were expected to fight on foot when occasion demanded. Each mounted soldier had two horses, the one he rode and the *bât*-horse which carried his kit and a quantity of fodder. Uniform details varied by regiment – but most wore the red-coat (apart from the Blues), waistcoat, breeches and thigh-boots. The Life Guards were mostly gentlemen, and wore splendid uniforms, as befitted their role as royal escorts, and their troops were far larger than those of cavalry of the line – possibly comprising as many as 300 Life-Guardsmen apiece.

Gunners and sappers came under the Master-General of the Ordnance, a high functionary of state operating from a headquarters in the Tower of London. The cannon came in a variety of sizes, the heaviest for field use being 12-pdrs, including 8-pdr 'demi-culverins', 6-pdr 'sakers', 3-pdr 'minions' and 1-pdr 'falconets'. The practice of attaching a pair of 'minions' or 'falconets' to each infantry regiment (served by infantrymen) was just coming in, but most guns were organised into trains or bye-trains under Ordnance officers. Siege trains of heavier guns were employed when needed. Guns fired solid shot of the specified weight or canister, 'partridge-shot' (hessian bags of musket-ball and metal fragments) for close-range work. The larger field-guns had a range of some 450 yards at point-blank, the smaller of about 250 yards. Loose powder measured out from kegs by ladle was still the most customary in 1685, although pre-packaged rounds in serge bags were being used experimentally. Board of Ordnance personnel wore blue coats with red facings and cuffs and red breeches. In action, guns were normally organised in fours or pairs. For movement, they were drawn by varying numbers of horses harnessed in tandem, and were entrusted to civilian drivers and boys – a potential drawback, as we have seen. Many waggons of munitions, tools and general army supplies also accompanied the trains, these being further responsibilities of the Board of Ordnance.

Supply

Although the Board of Ordnance had responsibility for providing much of the powder and shot required by the army and other martial stores, the bulk of the food and forage was supplied by civilian contractors when a campaign was in progress. In time of peace or 'winter quarters', the troops were usually left to fend for themselves out of the 6d. subsistence money included in their daily pay, and live by their wits. There were no barracks, the troops being billeted on ale-houses or unwilling citizens. The standard of the contractors varied immensely – and peculation and downright fraud were often practised. Supply convoys – like the cannon – were drawn by horse-teams hired locally with civilian drivers, and the same was true of the waggons required. All in all, this side of the Royal Army's organisation was the least satisfactory and the most open to abuse and shortfalls in performance.

Effects of 1685 upon the Army

The Campaign in Scotland and the West led to an immense increase in the size of the standing army. Whilst the troubles were taking place, the King through his two Secretaries of State and the Secretary-at-War issued numerous warrants appointing colonels and authorising them to raise new formations – but none of these actually served in the campaign as it was so rapidly conducted and concluded. However, James II did not see fit to disband these new formations – nine regiments of horse (a further troop of Life Guards was added in 1686) and two of dragoons, and nine regiments of foot in all. The three English and three Scottish regiments forming the two brigades in Dutch pay – recalled at the height of the emergency in June 1685 – were returned to the United Provinces in early August without having seen any active service, and in that month the total forces at the King's disposal in England totalled three troops of Life Guards, ten regiments of horse and three of dragoons, fourteen regiments of foot and thirty independent companies – or 15,710 officers and men. By the end of December – when the newly raised formations were more or less effectively in existence – the total had risen to 19,788. A portent of future trouble was the fact that many of the new officers were Roman Catholics, who all received new commissions from the King on 28 November 1685; at once there was much talk about Protestant officers being disadvantaged or even dismissed.

Of course James would use the Army for questionable practices as his brief reign ran on towards its climax – including employing it to overawe London from its large camp at Hounslow, and billeting rowdies on Whig political or religious critics and opponents after the fashion of Louis XIV's *dragonnades* inflicted on the Huguenots in France. When the great crisis came in the autumn of 1688, the full paper strength of James's forces would stand at 34,320 – furnishing him with a field army of about 25,000 men when garrison troops had been deducted. At the same date there were a further 3,300 men in Scotland on its separate establishment. The Irish Army had been increased to a total of almost 8,250 in 1685 and by November 1688 a single new regiment had been added to raise its strength to 8,940 officers and men.

Part of James's justification for these increases in the military establishments – besides the political and military problems they were called upon to meet – was his disillusion with the county militias, particularly those in the West, whose performance was *post facto* much criticised. They had not proved capable of being committed to battle, although in other roles they had in fact proved very useful, helping to contain the contagion of the revolt by arresting known supporters and other disaffected persons, and controlling the movement of people towards the West Country, relieving the standing army of such tedious but important duties. However, they could only be embodied for one month in any particular year, and in 1685 many county militias had not been willing to serve beyond their own county boundaries, whilst their officers – local landowners for the most part under the Lords Lieutenant – were not regarded as the strongest supporters of the Court Party. John Dryden's lines give a pretty fair description of the militia's level of efficiency:

> The Country rings around with loud alarms,
> And raw in fields the rude militia swarms;

Mouths without hands; maintained at vast expense,
In peace a charge, in war a weak defence;
Stout once a month they march, a blustering band,
And ever, but in times of need, at hand.
This was the morn when, issuing on the guard,
Drawn up in rank and file they stood prepared
Of seeming arms to make a short essay,
Then hasten to be drunk, the business of the day.
(*Cymon and Iphigenia*, lines 399–408)

In terms of size it is hard to estimate, but the Wiltshire Militia present (but not engaged) at Sedgemoor alone numbered over 3,000 men. Perhaps 90,000 was the nominal overall strength, but it had little to offer as a serious military force in time of emergency. Hence King James's determination to build a powerful army (by English standards), but compared to continental forces the standing army remained small.

Appendix C

AN ANALYSIS OF THE BLOODY ASSIZE

Note: the information given opposite is taken from what Judge Jeffreys recommended should happen in the disposal of those sentenced to death or to transportation. The numbers are probably inaccurate in many details. They do illustrate, however, the deliberate spreading of the scenes of execution to achieve the maximum impact of the royal vengeance. Many rebels had their heads struck off and their bodies quartered: these grisly remnants were publicly displayed throughout the South-West after being boiled in brine at many locations such as crossroads 'or other convenient places', and were only taken down and buried on James II's express order in August 1686 following his personal visit to the West Country.

SITES OF EXECUTION AND NUMBERS OF VICTIMS		DISPOSAL OF TRANSPORTEES (numbers and main destinations)

1. *Winchester Assize* (total 1)
   Winchester Market
   Square – 1

   Nil

2. *Dorchester Assize* (total 74)

   (total 175)

Sherborne – 12	Poole – 11	Sir Jerome Nipho[1] – 59 (Barbados)
Lyme Regis – 12	Bridport – 9	Sir Wm. Booth – 100 (Barbados)
Dorchester – 13	Wareham – 5	Sir Chr. Musgrave – 16 (Jamaica)
Weymouth and		
Melcombe Regis – 12		

3. *Exeter Assize* (total 12)

   (total 7)

Exeter – 1	Ottery St Mary – 2	Sir Jerome Nipho – 7 (Barbados)
Crediton – 1	Colyton – 2	
Honiton – 4	Axminster – 2	

4. *Taunton Assize* (total 136)

   (total 284)

Taunton – 12	Langport – 3	Sir Chr. Musgrave – 84 (Jamaica, 27 & Barbados, 57)
Chard – 12	Nether Stowey – 3	The Queen, Mary of Modena – 100 (Barbados, 67)
Ilminster – 12	Stogumber – 3	Sir Wm. Booth – 100 (Barbados)
Ilchester – 12	Dunster – 3	
Keynsham – 11	Dulverton – 3	
Crewkerne – 10	Wiveliscombe – 3	
Bridgwater – 9	Wellington – 3	
Yeovil – 8	Chewton Mendip – 2	
Somerton – 7	Milborne Port – 2	
Minehead – 6	Stogursey – 2	
South Petherton – 3	Porlock – 2	
Castle Cary – 3	Cothelstone – 2	

5. *Wells Assize* (total 98)

   (total 383)

Wells – 9	Axbridge – 6	Sir Wm. Stapleton – 100 (Sts Nevis & Kitts)
Philips Norton – 12	Wincanton – 6	Sir Philip Howard – 200[2] (Jamaica)
Frome – 12	Glastonbury – 5	Sir Jerome Nipho – 33 (Barbados)
Pensford – 12	Bruton – 3	Wm Bridgeman (per
Shepton Mallet – 12	Wrington – 3	Sir Richard White) – 50 (Jamaica)
Bath – 6	Ilminster – 1[3]	others[4] – 140 (various)
Bristol – 6	elsewhere – 5	

6. *London* – (total at least 3)
   London – 3[5]

   Maids of Honour – 40 (Maids of Taunton – redeemed)

[1] Names of individuals to whom convicted prisoners were assigned for profitable disposal.
[2] Sir Philip Howard lost 33 through escapes in England en route for the port etc.
[3] Includes Charles Speke, executed before the arrival of the royal reprieve.
[4] Bound over to subsequent assizes but eventually transported in the main.
[5] Includes Elizabeth Gaunt, who was burnt at the stake.

Appendix D

THE MYSTERY OF THE 'BLACK BOX'

The question of Monmouth's legitimacy or illegitimacy remains to this day a matter for debate. There is some circumstantial evidence that Charles II did in fact marry Lucy Walters (alias Barlow) at Liège in 1648. The lady was related on the maternal side to the Percys of Northumberland and the Sidneys – and thus was hardly a 'hedge-wife' or a 'light-of-love' as was later imputed. There is no doubt that Monmouth was the son of Charles and Lucy, being born on 6 April 1649. The only question is whether or not – and Lucy Walters was adamant that it was so to her death in 1659 – a formal and binding ceremony of marriage was conducted with the handsome young Prince (who became King on the day his father was executed in Whitehall on 31 January 1649).

Such a marriage was later denied by King Charles II on several occasions, but then it was a matter of high politics that it should be so after the Restoration, for a dynastic marriage to Catherine of Braganza, a princess of the Portuguese royal house, was deemed essential. However, there is ample evidence that Charles's mother, Queen Henrietta Maria, recognised young James as her grandson, and even adopted him – steps she would never have taken if he had been the fruit of a casual affair. Mary, Princess of Orange, in several letters to her brother Charles, uses the specific word 'wife' when referring to Lucy Walters. It is also known that a certain royal document was confiscated by Cromwellian officials when Lucy Walters visited England in 1656, taking her two children with her (a second child, a girl baptised Mary, had been born to the 'royal' couple in 1651); however, it is incredible that she would have been allowed to take the Prince of Wales – as the young future Monmouth might accurately be called – to the land ruled by his father's sworn enemies, or that they would not have seized the child forthwith if the document was, as some have inferred, her 'wedding lines' or marriage certificate. She and her children were held in the Tower of London for a number of days and then released on, of all days, 16 July 1656. Twenty-nine years later, to the day, James Scott, Duke of Monmouth, would secure another release from the Tower – but of a wholly different and more final nature. Unfortunately for Lucy and her children, 'Black Boy' (the young Charles's nickname at this time) soon thereafter tired of her, and the King unscrupulously had the young boy virtually kidnapped from his mother's care and also had a number of papers seized from her baggage. Thereafter royal policy dictated that the marriage was to be denied.

However, rumours continued to circulate and receive wide credence that James was Charles's legitimate son. The names of the witnesses at the marriage ceremony were known to Bishop Patersen. About 1680, at the height of the Exclusion Crisis, stories of the existence of a Black Box –

containing proof of the King's marriage – were widely circulated, and the Country Party (or Whigs) seized upon them with glee. Indeed, at the insistence of the Duke of York, an official enquiry was held, and the King was noticed at this time to be very untypically out-of-sorts and glumly pre-occupied. The Black Box was not produced, and many witnesses appear to have 'adjusted' their evidence to what was well known both the King and the Duke of York desired – and the story was dismissed. But the story would just not die, and in 1681 Robert Ferguson – 'the Plotter' – whose sinister role in later events we have referred to earlier in the book, wrote two pamphlets on the subject, inferring that the King-in-exile had married Lucy Walters with his mother's permission when his life was despaired of through the combi-nation of an attack of smallpox and his frustration at being denied marriage to Lucy. Once again official denials were issued – and Charles apparently affirmed to Monmouth's face in 1684 that he was only his natural son – but many continued to believe the veracity of the popular story.

A tantalising postscript dates from 1905, when evidence – admittedly second-hand – was put down on paper to the effect that the third Duke of Buccleuch (1746–1812) – Henry Scott, direct descendant of Monmouth's wife whose name he adopted after marriage – one day found a marriage certificate between Charles II and Lucy Walters in the muniment room at Dalkeith, and, in the presence of the Duke of Abercorn, proceeded to burn it.

Therefore, unless a careful search of all registers at Liège should produce the original document, the matter will rest unproven for all time. The implications for the House of Windsor might be indirectly embarrassing, were such a certificate to be found – but 'stone dead hath no fellow' as the seventeenth century adage runs, and there is no doubt whatsoever (despite certain legends in the West Country in the eighteenth century as mentioned in the Introduction to this book) that the handsome head of James Scott, Duke of Monmouth, was struck from his shoulders by Jack Ketch on Tower Hill, 16 July 1685. The reader, therefore, must make up his or her own mind on this matter.

Appendix E

TOURING THE CAMPAIGN AND BATTLEFIELD AREAS

What follows is the author's personal suggestion on how such a tour by car (and on foot) might be planned and executed. He has carried it out – with variants – a number of times at different times of year, and found it satisfyingly varied and interesting, as did his companions from *The Daily Telegraph*, the *Daily Express* and the *Standard* and *Illustrated London News* on a recent occasion. Naturally, there are many other tours that could be suggested – both longer and shorter. What follows is essentially a three-day (two nights away) tour, which is reasonably comprehensive. Naturally, it can be adapted to suit individual requirements. The only basic requirements are enthusiasm, a little thought and study beforehand, good maps and a grasp of the subject. The ideal base for the West Country section of the tour is the Taunton or Bridgwater area. Good hotels are available in both towns – including the luxurious Castle Hotel and the very comfortable County Hotel at Taunton, and Old Vicarage Hotel at Bridgwater, but every level of accommodation is available in the locality, and lists of hotel, guest house and bed-and-breakfast addresses may be obtained by application to the Taunton Borough or Sedgemoor District Leisure and Recreation Offices[1]. Bristol, Bath, Wells, Frome and Lyme, not to forget Exeter, are other possible starting points within easy reach of the main centres of activity. One preliminary point: at a number of staging-points below it is suggested that certain church-towers be visited; it is advisable as a matter of courtesy to check with the Vicar or Rector in advance that it will be convenient for you to visit his church. Some towers involve slightly tricky climbs, and insurance considerations as well as ecclesiastical convenience have to be borne in mind. Other churches are kept locked, and it can be a lengthy and time-consuming business seeking the key-holders. Two further hints: be careful about 'rights of access' to historic sites – trespass is clearly to be avoided; and always close gates, forebear from dropping litter, and in general follow the Countryside Code. In the pages that follow, letters or roman numerals in parentheses relate to locations on the maps provided.

DAY ONE   THE APPROACH MARCH FROM LONDON

The visitor starting from London, time permitting, may choose to visit the following as a preliminary to setting out for the West. The National Portrait Gallery in Trafalgar Square contains portraits of Monmouth, James II, John

[1] Somerset Tourist Officer, County Hall, Taunton, TA1 4DY and the Information Officer, Berrow Road, Burnham-on-Sea, Somerset respectively.

Churchill and other prominent persons associated with our story. The Tower of London is, of course, intimately connected: from its grey walls the ponderous Tower Train set out for the West to provide Feversham's army with real bite and fire-power, whilst the tragic end of James Scott at the bungling hands of Jack Ketch occurred on a scaffold on neighbouring Tower Hill. The chapel of St Peter-ad-Vincula in the Tower with its somewhat chilling associations is also worth a visit as the last resting-place of many a high-born prisoner-of-state who paid the ultimate penalty for aspiring to take the crown. St James's Palace, then as now, was intimately concerned with the Royal Family, although Whitehall Palace – apart from its famous Banqueting Hall – has completely disappeared. Lawrence Street, in Chelsea, contained a house where Monmouth's widow, Anna, Countess of Buc-cleuch, lived after her second husband's execution. The original house was pulled down in 1834, but the unusual double door hood was incorporated in a later building further down the street, and adjoining houses are called 'Duke's House' and 'Monmouth's House' to the present day to recall the association. James Scott, however, *pace* many a Chelsea guide, never lived in Lawrence Street. Two more visits might be to the Tate Gallery, Millbank, which contains Edgar Bundy's evocative 1905 painting, 'The Morning of Sedge-moor', showing Monmouth's soldiery sleeping in a barn, and to the National Army Museum, Chelsea, where period relics are on display.

The Royal Army headed for the West along the Great West Road (A4) before diverging. Lord Churchill, with the advance guard, at some unspeci-fied point (probably Newbury (A)), headed South-west for Salisbury (B) (the A343 via Andover may have been his route), and thence to Blandford Forum (C) (still A343) and Dorchester (D) (visit the upper room of the Antelope, scene of the Boody Assize trials), where his cavalry headed for Bridport (E) and Charmouth (use the A35) before moving up to Axminster (F) and then on to Chard (G). Axminster is linked to both Chard and Taunton (H) by the A358, the distance being 23 miles. This route takes the visitor through some fine countryside and past many notable sights – including Salisbury Cathed-ral, under whose tall spire, and near the market-place, Adam Wheeler and the Wiltshire Militia mustered before marching for Wilton (with its historic house). If using this route a brief stop at Woodyates (11 miles from Salisbury on the A354) where the fleeing Monmouth exchanged clothing with a puzzled shepherd at the inn, before moving on to Cranborne – doubtless through the woodland skirting Pentridge Hill although the driver should use the B3081 off the A354 two miles beyond Woodyates, and then the B3078 – before making for Woodlands (follow the country road from Cranborne through Edmonsham). From Woodlands make for Horton, and there inquire for 'Monmouth's Ash', the stump of which, in a ditch at a neighbouring farm (in 1960 belonging to a Mr Higgs) long bore a small brass plate recounting Monmouth's discovery by Militiaman Parkin at this point.

The second route used by Lord Feversham and the main body of King James II's Army was as follows: using the Great West Road (A4) past Chiswick, Kew and Brentford (a detour south to visit Hampton Court Palace in East Molesey is recommended if time allows), this famous old road leads past Heathrow Airport to Slough (I) (adjacent to Royal Windsor, to whose famous castle Maj. Wade was brought to write his *Further Account*) and then on through Maidenhead (J) and Reading (K) to Newbury (do not miss the old Cloth Hall, or the remains of Donnington Castle two miles North of the town). Proceeding to Hungerford, still on the A4, try to include a visit to neighbouring Littlecote House, with its fine displays of mid-seventeenth century furniture and military equipment, and Roman mosaic. The Great West Road breaks away from the lush meadows of the River Kennet and enters Savernake Forest before descending to Marlborough (L), with its broad High Street and famous public school, Marlborough College, inside which is the famous Castle Inn (where the Elder Pitt, Earl of Chatham, died) and the *motte* of its ancient castle, which has associations with the legendary wizard Merlin. In later years, John Churchill would become first Earl (1689), and later (1702) Duke of Marlborough – selecting the title because of his maternal grandmother's association with the town through her sister's marriage to the first Earl of Marlborough – a title that had become extinct in 1680. From Marlborough the A4 sweeps on along the fine Kennet valley along the southern edge of the chalk-based Marlborough Downs with its distinctive countryside, skirting Avebury (M) with its Stone Age 'Woodhenge', strange Silbury Hill, whole series of barrows and tumuli, prehistoric Oldbury Castle with its White Horse, to Calne (N) and Chippenham (O) (notice the fifteenth century Yelde Hall in St Mary's Street). From Chippenham, Lord Feversham rode ahead with his cavalry through Kingswood (P) and its ancient mining district to ensure that Bristol was secure (probably following what is now the A420), before riding along the banks of the River Avon (Q) to ensure that all the bridges were closed to Monmouth's approaching army, and thence to Bath (R), where the various parts of the Royal Army were at last re-united on Kingsdown Hill (S) beyond the city between Bathford and Box to the south of Bath. Bath with its Abbey Church, Roman Baths and Georgian terraces requires a holiday stay to itself; but our purpose being to follow the events of 1685 it is only suggested that the visitor moves on as soon as possible for Taunton (H) and (T), the base of operations, travelling thither (if from Bristol) along the M5 – joining at entrance 17 (T) or 18, and leaving at Exit 25 (U).

Clearly, if it is decided to take in some of the additional attractions en route from London, at least an extra day will be required. On the other hand, the traveller wishing to get to Taunton from the capital by the fastest route should take the M4 as far as Exit 20, (V) and there join the M5 (Entrance 15) for the South-West. Such a journey from London should not take more than four hours.

The Approach March – Summary:
    London to Taunton
        Motorway M4/M5 – 170 miles
        A4/M5 – 205 miles
                via Salisbury, Dorchester and Chard – 183 miles
N.B. Only the direct route in each case is reflected in these mileages.

DAY TWO   THE MARCH OF MONMOUTH'S ARMY

Leaving Taunton along the A358 for Ilminster and Chard, it is suggested that a direct route to Lyme Regis is followed (taking about one hour). If a break is required, visit Chard to see the sixteenth century courthouse (used for the *second* Assize in early 1686), and the fifteenth-century church (where Lord Churchill and his officers and men attended a long sermon by the Rev. Rich on 21 June 1685). Having arrived at Lyme Regis (1), park at Ozone Terrace off the Cobb (a fourteenth-century breakwater), and walk through boat marinas and holiday chalets to the beach west of the harbour. This is where Monmouth landed in the early evening of 11 June 1685. It was in Broad Street that he was first acclaimed, and his proclamation took place near St Michael's Church. Other points of interest in Lyme Regis include Umbrella Cottage which has a remarkable roof, and the Philpot Museum.

Driving east along the A35 through Charmouth and Morcombelake, the town of Bridport (2) is reached. At the west bridge took place the first skirmish of the Revolt. The town has long been famous for its rope and fishing-net manufactories – the original rope-walks accounting for the width of the streets. Returning to Lyme Regis, take the A3070 out of the town through Uplyme, and thence to Axminster (3) after joining the A35. Here took place a brush with the coverging militias on 15 June 1685. The town is famous for its carpets and King John's Hunting Lodge, now a museum. Driving on to Chard (4) along the A358, you are hard on the tracks of both Monmouth's rebels and the shadowing royal cavalry of Lord Churchill. Turning off the A358 along the A3037 for Ilminster (5), a brief visit to this town (it was in the square that Charles Speke shook hands with Monmouth, for which he was later hanged by Jeffreys), is followed by driving along the A303 past Winterhay Green to your right (where Monmouth camped on 16 June 1685) to Horton. Take the right fork unnumbered road for Bickenhall for two miles. There, in a dip of the road where it crosses Venner's water (there is no apparent direct association with Col. Venner), took place on 19 June 1685 the so-called action of Ashill (6), between patrols of royal and rebel horsemen, on a spot still called 'Fight Ground' locally (GR. ST 300165, 1 in. O.S. Map Sheet 193, Series M726). Returning to the A358 over Barrington Hill, turn left and drive to Hatch Beauchamp. If it is wished to follow an exact section of Monmouth's march into Taunton (7) (the lanes concerned have probably changed but little in the past 300 years, so all due caution needs to be observed as many concealed corners in sunken cuttings are involved), turn left to West Hatch and make your way through Stoke St Mary and thence through Shoreditch to join the B3170, which takes you down into Taunton after crossing above the M5. Monmouth probably camped west of the town in Bishop's Hull (Without) near the River Tone, and an area near the Technical College is named 'Tangier' – no doubt after 'Kirke's Lambs'.

Taunton contains many fine sights. The Great Hall of the Norman Castle, 120 feet long, is where Judge Jeffreys held the Taunton part of the Bloody Assize. The Lord Chief Justice's living quarters were reputedly in the gabled and half-timbered house in Fore Street near the pedestrian precinct, which is now a Berni Steak House. The main square may have been the scene of the hangings to music of some twenty rebels by the enthusiastic Col. Kirke. The Museum holds interesting relics of both the battle of Sedgemoor and of the Assize that followed it. Exactly where Monmouth stayed 'in Captain Hucker's house', was proclaimed King, or received the petticoat colours from the Maids of Taunton, is uncertain, but the latter events probably took place in the Market Place surrounded by Fore Street on its three sides – a very busy traffic thoroughfare today. For those seeking a little relief from the seventeenth century, the town also contains a famous cider company and a Telecommunications Museum with a collection of instruments going back over one hundred years. There is also the Museum of the Somerset Light Infantry in part of the Castle, and a well-known County Cricket Ground. The church of St Mary Magdalene was almost wholly rebuilt in 1863, but to its original late fifteenth century design. Nearby Hammet Street contains some fine Georgian houses.

From Taunton take the A361 through North Petherton to Bridgwater (8) (whose main sights will be described later). Turning on the A372 after going round the roundabout to the north of the town and doubling back, pass the railway station and drive through Westonzoyland to Othery (9). There turn left on to the A361 and head for Monmouth's next port of call, Glastonbury (10), hopefully not through torrential rain such as the rebels encountered on 22 June 1685. The rebels camped in the Abbey Grounds and in two other churches. The Abbey ruins date from 1180, and stand on the site of an earlier building of c. AD 700. The nearby abbot's kitchen contains a small museum. The Tor has many important associations of a miraculous or legendary nature. There is also a fine Lake Village Museum in a house dating from the 1400s, reflecting the Iron Age antecedents of an important trading centre which flourished from 200 BC until the Roman conquest and on Bere Lane off the A361 Shepton Mallet road is the Abbey Barn Somerset Rural Life Museum. All in all, Glastonbury has seen its share of history.

Leaving Glastonbury, take the A361, through West Pennard and Pilton, to Shepton Mallet (11), site of regional agricultural shows each June and August and a carnival in November. Its church of St Peter and St Paul has a fine barrel ceiling and a sixteenth-century stone pulpit. In 1685 the town was famous for its cloth-weaving industry and strong Nonconformity, and Monmouth was duly welcomed there.

Moving north along the A37 we come to Downside (12), today the site of the Roman Catholic public school, and in 1685 the home of a fervent Monmouth supporter, Edward Strode, who provided the fugitive Monmouth with food and shelter and fresh horses on the night after the fatal battle of Sedgemoor. Two weeks earlier, the rebel army had passed the same way heading for Pensford, under harrassing attacks from Lord Churchill's cavalry. Passing through Midsomer Norton, we follow Monmouth's route by way of Temple Cloud and Clutton to Pensford (13). There turn right towards Publow, Woollard and Compton Dando along the valley of the River Chew. It was near the first-named village that Lord Churchill, in hot pursuit, paused on 25 June 1685 to hang 'one Jarvis, the felt-maker', who had been a prisoner in his hands for two days – and who died bravely and unrepentantly – before riding on to join Lord Feversham near Bath that same evening.

Climbing steep Fairy Hill, drive on through Chewton Keynsham into Keynsham (14) itself. Here it is important not to get diverted on to the A4, but rather drive to the centre of the town to pass the main church to join the A4175 (turn right) and then to cross over the A4 by an overpass. Drive over a modern bridge crossing the River Avon and immediately beyond it turn down a short road past a marina and boat-building works to park (after passing over an ancient bridge) near to a restaurant in a tall grey-stone building, a sometime mill. You are now at the scene of the skirmish of Keynsham bridge on 25 June. Walking back to the main road you can see on the further (northern) side of the road a large field adjoining the river with a chocolate factory beyond. This is Sydenham Meads, where Monmouth reviewed his entire army, the high-water mark of his rebellion. Bad weather drove him back into Keynsham there to be attacked from two sides by royal cavalry. Returning into Keynsham, by ascending the church-tower already referred to it is possible to take the view down the High Street that Col. Venner scanned on Monmouth's order to determine, if he could, the scale of the attack.

Small and transient though the attack proved, it badly shook Monmouth's confidence, and abandoning all idea of attacking Bristol (15), he headed south-east through the rain towards Bath. The turning-point in the revolt had now been reached. We follow Monmouth's approximate route by rejoining the A4 at a large roundabout east of Keynsham, and then driving through Saltford to Bath (16). The treasures of Bath have already been indicated, but the road system is complex to the south and west of the city, and drivers are advised to leave the A4 at its junction with the A39 and drive straight over onto an unnumbered road leading through Newton St Loe up hill and down dale, skirting modern suburbs to cross the A367 at a large roundabout to briefly follow the A3062, before turning right on to the B3110 towards Midford and Hinton Charterhouse to reach Norton St Philip (17). Park behind the magnificent George Inn, a building dating back to the thirteenth century, where Monmouth spent an uneasy night on 26 June whilst his army slept even worse in the rain on the fields below and around the main village. The George Inn – besides Monmouth's chamber (now the landlord's private sitting-room) from the window of which he is reputed to have narrowly avoided assassination – an old beam with a bullet in it is shown which may, or may not, have been the shot concerned – also has the Dungeon Bar, from which nine men of the village were taken to suffer execution for high treason about a year after Sedgemoor. This is certainly one of the finest Elizabethan buildings in the land, and with its far older monastic associations (it was a mediaeval guest house) deserves close inspection. Samuel Pepys, the famous diarist, stayed there with his wife in 1668. Our main purpose in this hill-top village is to visit the scene of Monmouth's only – and transient – military success, the skirmish of 26 June 1685. Crossing the major road outside The George, follow North Street at the same elevation away to the half-left from the Inn, past houses of various dates, until your way is blocked by a line of garages. The road running to left and right is Chevers Lane (known as 'Bloody Lane' locally), and just short of the narrow road is almost certainly the site of the barricade Monmouth set up to block any approach from the direction of Bath towards his headquarters – which became the scene of the first stage of the action when Feversham's advance guard blundered into Monmouth's rearguard early on the 26th. The royal line of approach has now disappeared completely in the field beyond, but by turning right to reach the modern road B3110 and walking or driving some little way along it to the north, the general area below the road to your left and through the fields to your right are the scenes of Monmouth's outflanking moves. The hedgerows are mainly very different today to those of 1685, but by driving about half a mile towards Bath a low ridge will come into sight which was almost certainly the position that Feversham took up whilst his guns came up, and from which he decided to retreat to Bradford-on-Avon to the north-east so as to reorganise his shaken army and at the same time to block a possible line of advance for the victorious Monmouth towards Warminster and distant London.

Monmouth, however, decided otherwise, and retreated south along the line of the modern B3110 and A361 through Woolverton, Beckington and Oldford to Frome (18) (although the rebel column may have moved slightly to the west through Lullington for the first part of this sodden night-march). This interesting town contains many mediaeval and Tudor buildings, whilst flagstoned Cheap Street has a medieval watercourse running down its centre. The town contains a museum, and in 1985 celebrates the 1300th anniversary of its charter. Where Monmouth lodged on the two nights of 28th and 29th June we do not know, but crucial discussions were held against the background of the bad news of the failure of the Scottish rebellion. Hoping to meet the promised 'Clubman Army', on the 30th the rebels moved off towards Shepton Mallet. The presence of Longleat House, four miles away to the south-east, with its Lion Park and other attractions should be mentioned in case any children accompanying the 1685 tour become a trifle fractious.

To follow Monmouth's retreat, take the A361 towards Shepton Mallet. Three miles out from Frome, turn right to visit Nunney (19) and its moated fourteenth-century castle, which definitely was on the rebel route. Indeed, the line of march was probably along the unclassified road from Frome over Gibbet Hill, which doubtless had grim associations with the post-campaign repression, which runs parallel to the north-west with the A361, before merging with it beyond Nunney near Holwell Farm. At Shepton Mallet (11) and (20), Monmouth held a review of his army on a hillside – probably Windsor Hill – before moving to Wells through Croscombe. In Wells (21), his men ran amok in the beautiful cathedral and its close, damaging the thirteenth-century west front and stripping lead from the roof (the Canons and clergy reputedly had to pull up many floor brasses in the cathedral to sell for the value of the metal in order to fund the necessary overhead repairs). It is hard to imagine such dire happenings today, in the cathedral with its fine astronomical clock, or in the peaceful close, where the swans ring the bell for their meal in the moat around the bishop's palace, one of the oldest still-inhabited houses in the country, whose walls date back to the early thirteenth-century. The superb line of mediaeval houses near Vicars Hall and the beautiful Chapter House with its steps worn away by countless thousands of visitors through the ages, are also a compulsory sight to visit. By tradition, the famous Quaker William Penn preached in the yard behind the Crown Hotel before being arrested. Wells also has a theatre and a museum, besides almshouses, and the church of St Cuthbert is also well worth a visit. The town must have been glad to see the last of Monmouth's men.

From Wells our route lies back along the A39 to Glastonbury (10) and (22), and through Street towards Westonzoyland, along the A361 to Othery (9) and (23) and then north-west along the A372, where the army passed the night 'in the moor'. Finally, on 3 July, Monmouth and his men limped back into Bridgwater (8) and (24) to a chilly welcome, and there camped out on Castle Field (now a somewhat derelict area) on the northern side of the town. Bridgwater has vital associations with the climax of the campaign. St Mary's church-tower contains the Monmouth Chamber where the Duke and his officers solemnly debated on the afternoon of the 5th, and also the Monmouth turret from which he reputedly studied the details of the royal camp near Westonzoyland. His quarters were probably in Sydenham Manor, now the guest-house (not open to the public) of a large industrial concern off the A39 on the outskirts of the town. The town also holds the Blake Museum with rooms devoted to Sedgemoor and Monmouth as well as the famous Commonwealth General-at-Sea whose statue overlooks the Cornmarket. The excellent museum in Blake Street [off Dampiet Street] is best approached past the public library and is open most days from 11 a.m. to mid-afternoon. There is also a fine terrace of Georgian houses down Castle Street and in King Square.

At the end of the second day of a comprehensive tour, return to Taunton by the A361.

The March of Monmouth's Army – Summary:
   176 miles (to include the Bridport detour as described).
Naturally, to visit the extra places suggested would require at least a further day.

DAY THREE   THE BATTLE OF SEDGEMOOR

Half a day is sufficient to study and visit on the ground the climax of the Revolt in the West, thus leaving time to return to London by Motorway in the early evening. Of course, longer can be spent – and if it is proposed to walk the route from near Bawdrip to Westonzoyland a whole day should be allocated for this purpose.

First I shall describe the half-day visit. From Taunton return to Bridgwater (I). Then, from St Mary's Church, cross over the Parrett bridge along Fore Street, where Monmouth's wagons and guns were drawn up ready to march. After crossing the river carry on down to the main road, turn left, and at the large roundabout (II) ignore the A38 Bristol road but take the A39 Bath (or 'Old Bristol') road. This follows the line of the seventeenth-century 'long causey' down which Monmouth's army marched silently out in a double column between eleven o'clock and midnight on Sunday, 5 July. After crossing over the motorway look immediately for the sign to Chedzoy, off to the right. Follow this lane to Chedzoy village and park near the church (III).

From the tower – the key having been procured from the captain of bell-ringers' house in the village – the view of Farmer Sparke towards Westonzoyland (whose church-tower is easy to spot to the south-east) can be appreciated. If the key is not available, a similar, albeit more restricted, view over the moor can be obtained from the corner of a field entered by an iron gate about fifty yards beyond the church on the right. The so-called 'sword-sharpening' marks to be seen on the main-door side of the church – often erroneously attributed to Monmouth's rebels (in fact Chedzoy remained a 'loyal' village) – are far older, and are arrow-sharpening marks dating from the Tudor period when by law able-bodied men had to practise archery at the butts in the churchyard after Divine Service on Sundays.

Carrying on down the lane with due caution, stop at Parchey Bridge (IV) (a favourite spot for fishing clubs) over the broad King's Sedgemoor Drain – which here approximates to the course of the smaller Black Ditch of 1685. Looking north one sees Peasey Farm on its small knoll where Monmouth left his ammunition wagons about two-thirds of a mile away. Looking in the other direction one sees the continuation of Monmouth's ill-fated line of advance. Approximately four hedgerows and fences away would have been the fatal Langmoor Rhine, now completely disappeared, where Godfrey missed the way to the vital crossing and thus gave the game away. The Royal Camp lay behind the Bussex Rhine, which has also now disappeared without obvious trace about one mile further away, the lines of tents being pitched some small distance on the nearside of St Mary's, Westonzoyland (V). The hill due north of Parchey Ridge is Penden Hill (VI), and beyond that on the horizon is the long line of the Polden Hills, running north to Knowle Hill (VII) above Bawdrip village. It was on Knowle Hill that Oglethorpe's night patrol eventually posted itself, above the mist, but in total ignorance of what was happening so close-by below.

Returning through Chedzoy, rejoin the A39 at the Motorway bridge, turn right, and after half a mile take the next turning right. This is Bradney Lane (VIII). A quarter mile down it take a turning left into March Lane (IX) – an unmade track running north-east. If it is wet, do not attempt to take any vehicle other than a Landrover down it. If dry, it is perfectly feasible to drive cautiously down to the King's Sedgemoor Drain embankment, although care will have to be taken to turn the vehicle in a suitable field-gateway. This is the exact route Monmouth followed, and just after he had swung south along the Black Ditch took place the near-encounter with Oglethorpe's Blues riding past about 150 yards away, completely blinded by the mist, whilst the frozen rebel army held its breath. Looking north, Knowle Hill with its tree-cap is readily visible. Looking south-east, Peasey Farm (X) is clearly to be seen about half a mile distant. Returning to Bradney Lane, turn left to drive down to the farm. If permission is obtained, a fine view along the King's Sedgemoor Drain towards Westonzoyland (V) some two miles away can be obtained from the 50-foot rise on which the farm stands.

Retracing your steps to the A39, return into Bridgwater, and follow signs beyond the large A38/A39 roundabout (II) for the A372 off to the left after one-quarter of a mile. This road is the route taken by Monmouth (coming the other way, of course) when he arrived at Bridgwater over the moor on 3 July, and was also that followed by an anxious Oglethorpe three days later returning to the Royal Camp after he had found Bridgwater unexplainably bare of rebels in the early hours. Crossing over the Motorway once more, drive by Half-Way Inn, past Penzoy Farm (XI) (near which a sheepfold occupied by an outlying royal picquet once stood, called 'Pitzoy Pound') and thence down a long straight stretch with a fine view over the moor to the approaches to Westonzoyland (V). First drive through the village, noting such names as 'Standards Way', to park outside the Sedgmoor (XII). This hospitable and well-appointed period place of refreshment contains framed prints relevant to the Revolt, and prints of the battle may often be purchased from the landlord. If permission has been obtained at least half-a-week in advance from the Vicar of St Mary's (XIII), it may be possible to ascend the narrow and winding tower stairway at one's own risk to overlook the battlefield area to the north of the village, Chedzoy tower (III) being a helpful point of reference. The Royal Camp lay beyond the last line of red-roofed modern houses in the northerly direction, and after an interval the Bussex Rhine to its front, and with care the position of the monument to the battle can be found.

Returning down the tower, do not fail to appreciate the church's truly magnificent carved tie-beam roof and rood-loft, amongst the finest in the country. Naturally, the cost of its preservation and upkeep is enormous, and any contribution to church funds will be most welcome. A church was on the site from about 1200, but the present church with its splendid Perpendicular west tower with its six bells and fan-vaulted roof dates in the main from the fourteenth century. The late fifteenth-century tower stands some 100 feet from base to pinnacled summit. On the south-west wall of the south transept will be found framed copies of documents, including two of Andrew Paschall's map and narrative of the battle. It was for long believed that a small window set up in the wall on the northern side of the church was the site of the small door through which one rebel prisoner managed to escape, but it turns out that this opening was only made long after the battle. It is hard but salutary to imagine how appalling the conditions must have been within during the imprisonment of 500 untended and largely unfed captives, many of them wounded. Well might one ponder in such an inspiring yet chilling setting on man's inhumanity to man and on the pointless agony of almost all wars and rebellions. Near this place of worship some twenty rebels were executed out of hand within twenty-four hours of the battle.

To the south-east of the village is an abandoned Second World War RAF airfield, Weston Field (XIV), near the eastern side of which is the site for the 1985 re-enactment of the battle by the Sealed Knot Society (part of the tercentenary celebrations). To the south-west is the village of Middlezoy (XV), with its smaller but very fine church which contains on the floor of the nave under the carpet the brass memorial to the French officer in the Royal Army who was killed at the 'Battle of Weston'. This village had quarters for the three regiments of Wiltshire Militia that Feversham and Churchill were careful to leave out of the battle, but which proved of great use in the mopping-up operations afterwards.

Returning through Westonzoyland (V), the line of the long-since filled-in

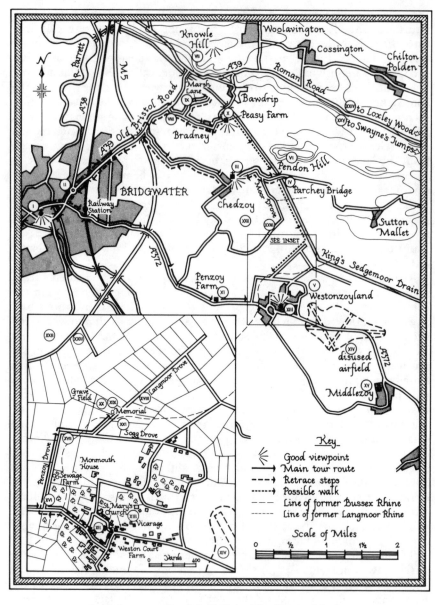

8. Sedgemoor Battlefield Tour: The Scene of Action

Bussex Rhine ran through the western edge of the modern orchard. Take the first track (XVI) running north from the A372 immediately after the trees, and passing a small sewage farm, proceed carefully along Penzoy Drove, part of which is made up. At the top turn right down Sogg Drove (XVII), which is a track, and can be very treacherous after wet weather – so be warned. After 700 yards turn left again down Langmoor Drove (XVIII), and after a similar distance more stop at a small clump of trees on the left. Amongst these will be found the small but moving memorial (XIX) erected in 1927, with its inscription composed by Maj. M. C. Cely-Trevilian and four staddlestones. The Bussex Rhine ran along Langmoor Drove at this point, as recent air weather surveys have revealed, and about fifty yards into the field was the position of Monmouth's three guns (XX) which caused such havoc to Dumbarton's Regiment of Foot (XXI) (or the Royal Scots) some 150 yards to their front, whose position was given away by the glow of their slow-matches in the misty darkness. This field is also the Gravefield, and contains a large pit where the slain were shallowly buried; later a mound of sand was erected on top. Trial excavations in 1927 revealed the sand and, beneath, many human bones. All necessary respect should here be paid to the fallen. A service is held at the memorial on the Sunday nearest to the anniversary each year.

Visitors with time enough may wish to walk over some of these fields, whose hedges, gateways and ditches were not of course there in 1685 when the Lang Moor was far less enclosed than it is today. The local farmers generally tolerate this providing the gates are all left shut, and the crops are not crushed or otherwise disturbed in any way. It is possible to walk a mile towards Chedzoy, where the southern edge of 'Chedzoy Corn' (XXII) – the slightly higher cultivated area of the 1680s – is clearly delineated by Moor Drove (XXIII). The line of the waterfilled Langmoor Rhine, in which many rebels were drowned or cut down in the early stages of the pursuit ran near to this track.

It is also possible for the adventurous, fit and keen to walk all the way from Peasey Farm (X) along the King's Sedgemoor Drain via Parchery (IV) and thence over the Moor to Westonzoyland (V), but this involves crossing many stiles, hedges, fences and ditches and is not recommended for everybody. Three hours at least should be allowed for a one-way trip – and double if a return to the departure point is envisaged.

One postscript: if time permits and inclination encourages, drive up the A39 along the old Roman Road atop the Polden Hills to Loxley Woods (XXIV), about four miles south-east of Bawdrip. Here, at the one decided bend in an otherwise almost straight road, pull in and park. In the under-growth amongst the trees to the south or right of the road a careful search can reveal the three markers known as Swayne's Jumps (XXV), the story behind which has been mentioned earlier.

Here ends this suggested campaign and battlefield tour. Many variants are possible to suit all tastes and periods of available time – but always try to leave a 25% margin of time for unforseen developments. Good maps (the 1 in. to 1 mile, O.S. Series M 726 Sheet 182 or larger scale if much walking is envisaged) are vital, although it is hoped that this book – both text and maps –

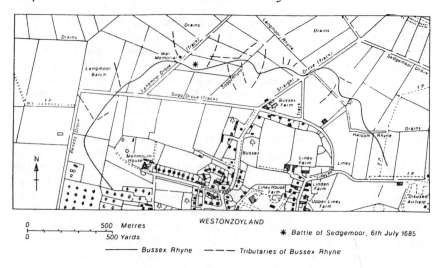

9. The Bussex Rhine's Course: 1980

may prove of some assistance, both intellectual and practical, to the interested visitor. Good strong shoes, a trusty stick, a compass, a waterproof, a developed imagination and above all a stout but sympathetic heart, are all that are otherwise required. Visiting battlefields can be a very rewarding and emotive adventure. It can also be a tiring and occasionally frustrating one. To quote Napoleon, 'Time spent in reconnaissance is seldom wasted' – so careful preparation is obviously desirable if the maximum pleasure and benefit are to be derived from visiting these, the most interesting (for me) 'Haunted Acres' in the fair county of Somerset.

The Battle of Sedgemoor – Summary:
   35 miles by car (along the specified route) plus an additional 3 to 5 miles by foot (if undertaken).

Select Bibliography

Amongst the books and documentary sources I found of particular value during the preparation and writing of this book were the following:

I. MANUSCRIPT SOURCES

Additional Manuscript 31,956 (transcript of E. Dummer's *Brief Journal of the Western Rebellion*). British Library.
    41,812 (Skelton's diplomatic reports from the Hague). British Library.
    41,817 (intelligence reports on exiles and plotters). British Library.
    90,337 (Jeffrey's report on the Bloody Assize etc). British Library.
The Axe Papers, Harleian Manuscripts 6845 (Papers of Rev. Thomas Axe, N. Wade etc). British Library.
The Book of the Axe (Axminster town records)
Harleian Manuscript 7006 (Monmouth's Government Proclamations). British Library.
James II's *Account*, Harleian Manuscript 6845. British Library.
Lansdowne Manuscript 1152 (interrogations of captured rebels etc). British Library.
The Paschall Narratives. Ayscough Manuscripts 4162. British Library.
Sloane Manuscript 4194 (Bramston reminiscences). British Library.
Tanner Manuscripts 129 (agent's reports on West Country etc. Bodleian Library.)
Wade, N., *Narrative* and *Further Information* Harleian Manuscripts 6845. British Library.
Westonzoyland, St Mary's Church Parish Records. Parish Register & Accounts.
Wheeler, A., *Iter Bellicosum*, Camden Miscellany Vol. 12.

2. PRINTED DOCUMENTARY SOURCES

Calendar of State Papers (Domestic). 3 Vols. James II – many legal documents. Public Record Office.
    ibid (Colonial). Transportation of convicted felons etc. Public Record Office.
English Historical Documents, Vol. VIII (1660–1714). Ed. A. Browning (Oxford 1956).

3. PUBLISHED WORKS (CONTEMPORARY)

Aylesbury, Lord, *Memoirs of Thomas Bruce, 3rd Earl* . . . (Edinburgh, 1840)
Akerman, J. Y., (ed.) *Moneys received and paid for Secret Service of Charles II and James II* (the Camden Society, London, 1851).
Burnet, Bishop, *A History of His Own Time* Vol. III (Edinburgh, 1753).
Defoe, D., *Tour through England and Wales in 1724* (London n.d.).
Dryden, J., *Absalom and Achitophel* and *Hind and Panther* in *Dryden's Poetical Works*. Ed. W. D. Christie (London, 1874).
Hansard's State Trials, Vol. II (London, n.d.).
Heywood, S., *A Vindication of Mr. Fox's History of the Early Part of the Reign of James II* (London, 1811).
Historical Manuscripts Commission, Vol. 1 – the Dartmouth Papers.
    5th Report, 1876.
    12th Report, 1891.
Muddiman, W., *The Western Martyrology* (London, 1689).
Oldmixen, J., *The History of England during the Reigns of the Royal House of Stuart* (London, 1730).
The Oxford Book of English Talk Ed. J. Sutherland (Oxford, 1956).
Proceedings of the Somerset Archaeological and Natural History Society. 3rd Series, Vol. XVII (Taunton, 1911).
Somerset and Dorset Notes and Queries. Vol. XXVII.
Stopford-Sackville Manuscript Dartmouth Papers, Historical Monuments Commission. Vol. 1.

4. PUBLISHED WORKS (GENERAL)

Churchill, W. S., *A History of the English-speaking Peoples*, Vol. II (London 1956)
Clarendon, Earl of, *Correspondence and Diary* (London, 1827).
Clarke, G. N., *The Later Stuarts* (Oxford, 5th ptg, 1949)
Dalton, C., *English Army Lists and Commission Registers*, 6 vols. (London, 1898–1904).
The Dictionary of National Biography and its *Epitome*.
Fortescue, Sir C., *History of the British Army*, Vol. 1 (London 1899).
Trevelyan, G. M., *England under the Stuarts*, London, 1930, 21st ed., 1951.
Walton, C., *History of the British Standing Army, 1660–1700* (London 1894).

5. PUBLISHED WORKS (SECONDARY)

Ashley, M., *John Wildman, Plotter and Postmaster* (London, 1947).
Bevan, B., *James, Duke of Monmouth* (London, 1973).
Blackmore, R. D., *Lorna Doone* (London, 1869).
Burne, A. H., *The Battlefields of England* (London, 1950).
Chandler, D. G., *The Campaigns of Napoleon* (London, 1967).
    Marlborough as Military Commander (London, 1973).
    The Art of War in the Age of Marlborough (London, 1975).
Childs, J., *The Army of Charles II* (London, 1976).

The Army, James II and the Glorious Revolution (Manchester, 1980)

Clifton, R., *The Last Popular Rebellion: the Western Rising of 1685* (London, 1984).

Davis, J., *The History of the Second Queen's Royal Regiment*, Vol. 2 (London 1895).

Doyle, A. C., *Micah Clarke* (London, 1889).

D'Oyley, E., *James, Duke of Monmouth* (London, 1938).

Earle, P., *Monmouth's Rebels* (London, 1977).

Emerson, W. R., *Monmouth's Rebellion* (London, 1951).

Fea, A., *King Monmouth* (London, 1902).

Gough, J. W., *Mines of Mendip* (London, 1930).

The Harbinger (ed. R. Gouldsworthy), *News from the County of Somerset* (1984–5).

Hardwick, M., *The Verdict of the Court* (London, 1964).

Little, B., *The Monmouth Episode* (London, 1956).

Locke, R., *The Western Rebellion* (1782 edn reprinted London, 1912).

MacDonald Wigfield, W., *The Monmouth Rebellion* (Bradford-on-Avon, 1980).

Masefield, J., *Martin Hyde – the Duke's Messenger* (London, 1910).

Macaulay, Lord, *History of England from the Accession of James II*, Vol. 1 (London, 1856).

Melville, L., *Mr. Crofts, the King's Bastard* (London, 1929).

Morley, I., *A Thousand Lives; an Account of the English Revolutionary Movement 1660–1685* (London, 1954).

Muddiman, I. G., *The Bloody Assize* (London, 1929).

Nepean, E., *On the Left of a Throne* (London, 1914).

Page, M., *The Battle of Sedgemoor* (Bridgwater, 1932).

Price, C., *Cold Caleb* (London, 1956).

Ryall, E., *Second Time Round* (London, 1974).

Roberts, G., *The Life, Progress and Rebellion of James, Duke of Monmouth* (London, 1844).

Shepperd, J., 'Redlegs, Myth and Reality' in *The West Indies Chronicle* (May 1974).

Trench, C. C., *The Western Rising* (London, 1969).

Turner, W., *James II* (London, n.d.).

Watson, J. N. P., *Captain-General and Rebel Chief* (London, 1979).

Western, J., *The English Militia in the 18th Century* (London, 1965).

Young, P., and Adair, J. E., *Hastings to Culloden* (London, 1964).

Index

See following pages for the maps of
The Sedgemoor Battlefield Tour: The Monmouth Route
and The Royal Army's Routes

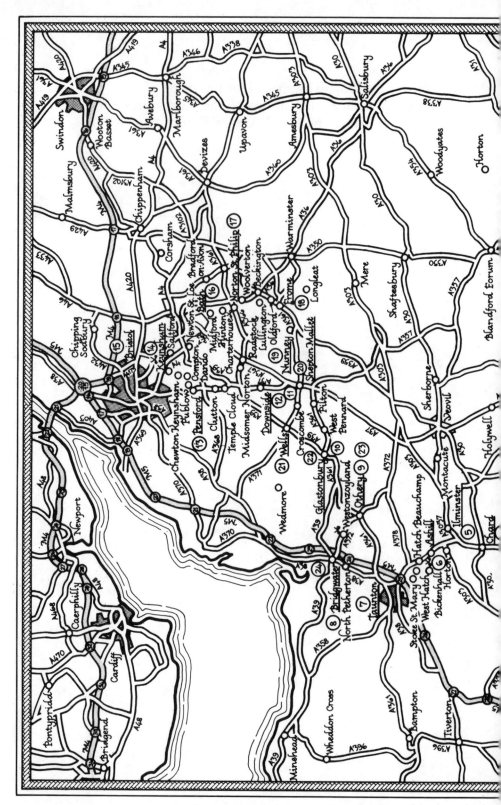

10. Sedgemoor Battlefield Tour: The Monmouth Route
(Inset: The Royal Army's Routes)

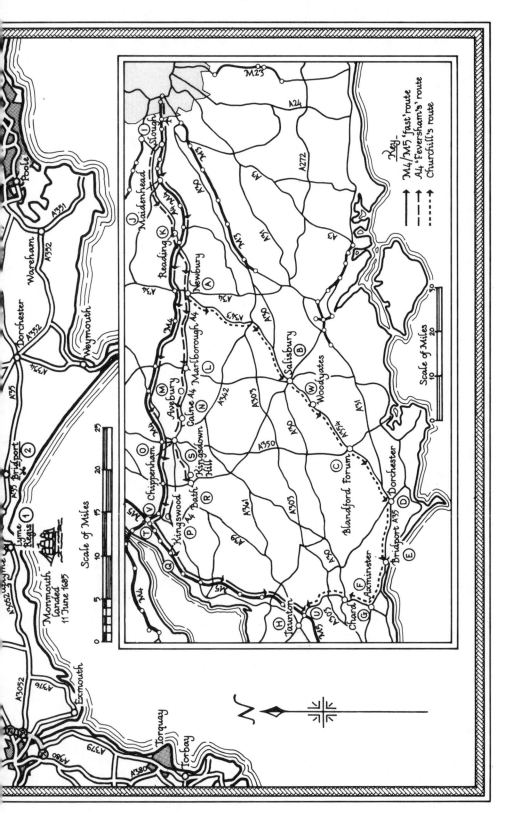

Key:—
M4/M5 'fast' route
A4 'Feversham's' route
Churchill's route

Scale of Miles

Scale of Miles

Monmouth landed
11 June 1685